The New Architectural Pragmatism

HARVARD DESIGN MAGAZINE READERS
William S. Saunders, Editor

The New Architectural Pragmatism

A Harvard Design Magazine Reader

William S. Saunders, Editor

University of Minnesota Press I Minneapolis I London

The essays in this book previously appeared in *Harvard Design Magazine*, Harvard University Graduate School of Design; Peter G. Rowe, Dean, 1992–2004; Alan Altshuler, Dean, 2005– .

Chapter 2 was previously published as Robert Somol and Sarah Whiting, "Notes around the Doppler Effect and Other Moods of Modernism," *Perspecta* 33 (2002): 72–77; copyright 2002 *Perspecta*; reprinted with permission. An abridged version of chapter 5 was published in Anne Hoogewoning et al., *Architecture in the Netherlands Yearbook, 2003–04* (Rotterdam: Nai Publishers, 2004).

Thanks to coordinator Meghan Ryan for her work on this book series and on *Harvard Design Magazine*.

Published by the University of Minnesota Press
111 Third Avenue South, Suite 290
Minneapolis, MN 55401-2520
http://www.upress.umn.edu

Library of Congress Cataloging-in-Publication Data
    The new architectural pragmatism : a Harvard design magazine reader / William S. Saunders, editor.
        p.   cm. — (Harvard design magazine readers ; 5)
    Includes bibliographical references.
    ISBN: 978-0-8166-5263-1 (hc : alk. paper)
    ISBN-10: 0-8166-5263-5 (hc : alk. paper)
    ISBN: 978-0-8166-5264-8 (pb : alk. paper)
    ISBN-10: 0-8166-5264-3 (pb : alk. paper)
        1. Architecture and society.   2. Architecture, Postmodern.
    3. Architectural criticism.   I. Saunders, William S.   II. Harvard design magazine.
    NA2543.S6N49 2007
    724'.7—dc22
                                                    2007028545

Printed in the United States of America on acid-free paper

The University of Minnesota is an equal-opportunity educator and employer.

15 14 13 12 11 10 09 08 07   10 9 8 7 6 5 4 3 2 1

Contents

Introduction
Accept, Resist, or Inflect?
Architecture and Contemporary Capitalism
William S. Saunders

Collected here are the most noteworthy attempts over the past decade to define what architectural practice should now be. This book is a record of an intellectual history that is still in motion and still expressed in strong disagreements. The central question is whether architects who in their work try to resist and criticize the norms of the general contemporary culture/society are engaged in a futile and self-deluding activity. Is accepting and working from within those norms more realistic and effective, without being morally and politically compromised to an unacceptable extent?

As is typical in intellectual history (think of Marx and Freud), the thinkers who come to define the important issues are surprisingly few—an elite, perhaps a self-appointed elite, or perhaps a deserving, naturally emerging elite. There are probably no more than two dozen broadly influential intellectual leaders in the relatively small subculture of American architecture. This is why at theoretically focused academic conferences the same people keep reappearing.[1] Of course there is something absurd in this restriction to a klatch of so few—many more people who think carefully about architecture have comparable intelligence and perceptiveness. And, as usual, the thinkers in the spotlight come from major coastal cities where spotlights are most common and bright.

Yet even as one may bemoan by how few The Issues are being defined, one must admit that the tiny spotlighted group of architectural intellectuals has offered us more stimulating, sophisticated, coherent, and compelling ideas about contemporary architecture than any others that can be found, for reasons good or poor, in the print media.

At least since Modernism of the 1920s, a central if not *the* central concern of thoughtful architects has been architecture's role in the broader culture and society. Most early Modernism was idealistic if not utopian—architects could and should create more affordable, appropriate, and beautiful things, from spoons to cities, and thus significantly advance the well-being of humankind. This dream was shattered by many factors, foremost the ever-increasing sense of powerlessness in the face of the onslaughts of capitalism, war, and barbaric politics. In addition, utopianism in action—particularly in the guises of Communism and Nazism—seemed always to devolve into totalitarianism. Designers with total visions of how societies should be—Le Corbusier, Frank Lloyd Wright, and others—began to seem like monsters of hubristic tyranny.

In some quarters and by the late 1960s, reaction set in: the focus shifted to architecture's aesthetic and intellectual potentials, to the pleasures and illuminations to be derived from single designed objects. Architecture could be free from the mediocrity and conventionality of ordinary society, above all that. At the same time, socially idealistic designers did not give up; they simply became more humble and realistic. And for some, no matter how impotent they believed enlightened minorities to be, there was and is no acceptable alternative to working against the ill-conceived ways of the majority. Formalists and social meliorists shared a position of wanting to work separate from, outside of, social norms and dominant powers. When, during the 1970s, certain rigorous, exciting, and seemingly liberating European cultural criticism (e.g., that of Michel Foucault) and radically skeptical theory (e.g., that of Jacques Derrida) were welcomed in America, this position of detachment from the banality of ordinary life was reinforced.

Fast-forward to the mid-1990s: many highly intelligent young architects and architectural intellectuals were getting fed up with this detachment, theoretical abstraction, and helplessness. They wanted to (and could, with an improved economy) get to work on real projects, real conditions, real places; they wanted to be ambitious without being dreamy, to improve bits of the world without self-aggrandizing delusions. Rather than looking down on ordinary American experience and culture, they more likely participated in it with frequent pleasure. Popular music, movies, and even consumerism were, to them, fun—more energizing than corrupting. They wanted to be in the game. Their intellectual elders struck them as overly serious, overly self-important, overly righteous, and "pure." They singled out Rem Koolhaas as an exception: a brilliant, non-aloof participant-observer of mainstream culture, who, in *Delirious New York,* was able to see more vitality in the architecture of American mainstreamers like Raymond Hood than in that of the European intellectual elite.

By and large, the voices heard in this anthology express or criticize this spirit of engagement with ordinary culture and impatience to get results, even if flawed or minor. At its most raw, we hear this in the "fed-up" tone of Alejandro Zaera-Polo's lament about the default mode of architectural thinking in American architectural schools in the early 1990s: " 'Critical practice' was the thing to do if one wanted to do architecture, and that meant to nag about everything and try to embody architecturally all sorts of psychological and political perversions and subversions. . . . The effects of 'the empowerment of theory' have been translated into the confusing coupling of theoretical practice and detachment from architectural production, with the offspring being legions of bad novels, bad sociology, bad psychology, bad philosophy, and bad movies being presented at juries as advanced architectural 'research.' "

In truth, the "discourse" at leading architectural schools and intellectual publications in this period was amazingly muddled by pseudo-intellectuality, by dazed and confused attempts to import the language and ideas of arcane philosophy and cultural studies. Abstraction of extraordinary vagueness to readers and, one should have known, to its creators was all too often treated as a sign of high intelligence and a key to the kingdom. It took a more honest intelligence and greater self-confidence and independence for people like Zaera-Polo to think, "This is b.s."

The disgusted desire to destroy, expel, and escape from pseudo-intellectual "difficulty" goes a long way toward explaining both the tone and the content of what has emerged as the alternative to "criticality." In a way, this reaction against a hyper-intellectual house of cards *needed* to be irreverent, wiseass, and even slightly anti-intellectual. Someone had to blow a raspberry, since, as Sarah Whiting and Robert Somol wrote in 2002 (see their "Doppler" essay, this volume) "disciplinarity has been absorbed and exhausted by the project of criticality . . . the overly difficult, belabored, worked, complicated." For proudly wiseass art critic Dave Hickey, an inspiration for Somol and other postcritics and a contributor to this book, the guilty party is not so much "criticality" as academization, which turned the radical and rebellious iconoclasm of 1950s structuralism into joyless, conventional identity politics and institutionalism by the 1990s.

Somol is the consummate Bad Boy of this reaction, willing, even eager, to appear less sophisticated (and smart) than he is, so that he can broadcast his iconoclasm with more flair: "Architecture doesn't have to hurt," he writes.[2] It was Somol who had the cheek, on the occasion of a meeting to honor the critical journal *Assemblage* as it closed shop, to try to dispel fake and righteous seriousness with a blast of candor: "I never subscribed to *Assemblage*. . . . Out of the 240-odd items published, I read about 12 all the way through. No shit. *Five percent*. Three of those were mine. . . . The simple fact— one that we should celebrate rather than hide—is that *criticism isn't necessary*." Similarly, in a 2005 issue of *Log* edited by Whiting and Somol, David Solomon, in an essay tellingly titled "Letting Go," writes, "in the current postcritical moment, in which one recognizes that modernism's dual stance of formal autonomy and political earnestness failed to make architecture better or more relevant, a revisiting of [Charles] Jencks's reckless abandon and enjoyment might prove valuable." We should, says Solomon, be "shedding modern architecture's guilty conscience once and for all. . . . [H]umorous or witty approaches are necessary to wrest power away from the still very much alive pairing of modernism with criticality."[3]

The freshness (in both senses) of this rebellion has been liberating for a younger generation, but its anti-intellectual posing does endanger its own achievement, its further progress, and its being taken seriously by those outside its clique. Whiting and Somol's *Log* issue quotes a silly Philip Johnson naughtiness on its back cover: "Architecture is the art of how to waste space." Their invigorating lowbrow anti-pretentiousness slides easily into self-indulgence, *whatever*-ism, and deafness to its own self-importance:

> At most, [this issue is] organized by sensibility and personal affinity. [The contributors] are the people with whom we hang out, play cards, drink until closing, escape conferences, plot futures, compete

with laughter, and fight with conviction. . . . [T]his criminal pack
calls for action more than observation, privileges speculation over
erudition, and aims wildly at getting something going. . . . [L]ike all
great plans, it's so stupid it just might work. . . . [W]e embrace the
possibility that failure may be a new form of success.

A much-needed critique of gratuitous and pompous complexity
sometimes descends into slacker complacency—"Are we having fun
yet?" Somol's brilliant perception, in Koolhaas's *Content*, that one-
off, unprecedented shapes (like that of Koolhaas's concert hall in
Porto) are, in architecturally avant-garde works, replacing labored
and rationalized geometric forms is given a needlessly Alfred E.
Newman twist: "Shape is graphic. . . . It performs precisely because
of its 'defective' condition: crude, explicit, fast, material. . . . Dismis-
sible, shapes are simply cool or boring, and have a more vulgar, or at
least vernacular, provenance. . . . Regulated not by the articulation
of geometry but by the seduction of contour, shape has a requisite
degree of slack."4 When "Cool!" becomes a criterion of judgment,
self-reflective thoughtfulness is being shoved aside as too much of
a drag.

Strikingly similar in attitude were Zaera-Polo's actions and Philippe
Starck's comments seven years earlier: To steer his students away
from theorizing, the former, as a teacher at London's Architectural
Association, removed from his course bibliography everything but
Architects' Data and Architectural Graphic Standards. Meanwhile
Starck, the king of the design elite, in an extraordinary and entertaining performance printed here, played the role of a lazy simpleton,5 a
Shakespearean fool, whose sole purpose in running his business empire is to give all people, especially poor people, just a *leeetle* fun. He
owns his empire (and tropical island retreats) because his design sells
products, but he would have us believe he is against consumerism,
products, and even design itself. In other words, like Somol, Zaera-
Polo, and Whiting, he is a sophisticated promoter of the sophisticat-
edly unsophisticated.

For K. Michael Hays, Starck's leftism and anti-design design are
mainly delusions; Starck, like everyone, is inescapably trapped in capitalism: "The transgressive, the brush against the grain, and above all
the politically correct, are as consumable as anything else. . . . [W]e
have no really substantial choice about what we consume." Although
Hays asserts that thoughtful design offers "a proposition about how

we should live and a critique of how we have failed so far," this remains only in the realm of ideas. He seems not to recognize that many people are indifferent to cool products and trends, and some shop as little as possible.

The "easy" and "relaxed" and the anti-product product—these make their points and establish their important values. But, as George Baird, Hal Foster, Sanford Kwinter, Reinhold Martin, and Jeffrey Kipnis point out, they can only be a starting point: once the golden calves are torn down, some effortful building up must begin.[6] As Martin writes, "we might ask the affirmative, projective practitioners of the 'postcritical' just what sort of world they are projecting and affirming." Kwinter went so far as to publish an essay in a 2003 *Harvard Design Magazine* about the necessity of "difficulty" in all intellectual efforts that are to rise above dilettantism. Dave Hickey, a compatriot in the postcritical embrace of popular and commercial culture, nevertheless worries that the postcritical will become the "postintellectual." In the most passionate and devastating political criticism in print of "postcriticality," Martin here links the December 2003 chest-beating architectural proposals for Ground Zero,[7] especially that in which Zaera-Polo participated (from United Architects), to a surrender to and collaboration with America's corporate imperialism, jingoism, and militarism: "Since by responding obediently to the call for architectural 'vision' while remaining utterly blind to the violence of the package they served up, these architects and others put themselves in a position of docile compliance with the imperatives of a nation at war."

Another cultural guru who is guilty, in the analysis of Robert Levit and Evonne Levy here, of being overly "easy" in a hip kind of way is Bruce Mau. In his contribution to Rem Koolhaas's *S,M,L,XL,* Mau produced bold, wild graphics that were yet disciplined to the service of content. But in his recent *Massive Change* book and exhibition, the seductions of form have left content far behind: "Design," as Levit and Levy say, "becomes a mode of liberation from communicative purpose"; the graphics "revel in a purely visual excess." This excess elides smoothly into Mau's facile politics, his Pollyannaish faith that new technology will solve all the world's major problems. "Such views," write Levy and Levit, "have the effect of suggesting, erroneously, that preeminently political challenges are technical problems susceptible to technical solutions." Mau has, as may Somol and other "postcritical" thinkers, the "fantasy of effortless (i.e., politics free) agency."

So what, then, is this new generation of architects achieving beyond, to our partial satisfaction, blowing raspberries and chilling out? Plenty, I believe. I spoke of this earlier, spoke of their drive to get constructive things done to whatever extent possible. Lucy Bullivant here phrases it perfectly: they do not ask "too much or too little from architecture." They are neither naive utopians nor hopeless dystopians, nor are they disengaged formalists. They are melioristic pragmatists, maybe just as good architects have always been. Thus, after half a century of extremism in the profession, they represent a return to sanity and balance. They display, as Bullivant says, a "pursuit of idealistic goals combined with a realistic modesty of means." What makes them different from good architects of any era is their self-awareness about and emphasis on the design process. They are acutely aware that to maximize their responsiveness to each design challenge, they must work incrementally, adaptively, and openly, without a fixed and dictatorial idea.

James Corner here articulates this best, comparing good designing with the healthy growth of biological organisms, which must be both flexible and robust, both responsive and self-directed. This notion is constantly echoed in phrases and sentences from this collection: "allowing the process of production to transform the initial idea for the project" (Bullivant); "by systematically researching reality as found with the help of diagrams and other analytic measures, all kinds of latent beauties, forces, and possibilities can, projective architects maintain, be brought to the surface" (Roemer van Toorn); "the design process became in itself a process of creating knowledge. The Yokohama project [was] . . . surprising us at every moment with how the technical requirements were organizing themselves into arrangements that we could not predict at the onset of the project" (Zaera-Polo); "a Doppler architecture acknowledges the adaptive synthesis of architecture's many contingencies. . . . The Doppler focuses upon the effects and exchanges of architecture's inherent multiplicities: material, program, writing, atmosphere, form, technologies, economics, etc. . . . [behaving like] an active organism or discursive practice, unplanned and ungovernable" (Somol and Whiting); "a form of practice at once more agile and more effective" (Stan Allen).

Happily, all this does not remain simply abstraction in this volume: van Toorn and Bullivant, in particular, carefully detail the work of emerging firms in the Netherlands and England, respectively. Stan Allen points to the exemplary work of the European UN Studio,

MVRDV, Abalos + Herreros, and Foreign Office Architects, and American SHoP, Open Office, and Lindy Roy firms. And Kenneth Frampton discusses the undeserved relative neglect of recent architecture by Will Bruder, Rick Joy, Wendell Burnette, Carlos Jimenez, Lake/Flato, John and Patricia Patkau, Howard Sutcliffe and Bridget Shim, and Alberto Kalach.[8]

Again and again, three goals of architectural practice are affirmed in this volume: efficacy, innovation, and realism. I applaud the fact that efficacy is premiated: it means architecture is credibly political again. That newness is repeatedly fetishized—cited as the one true goal of architecture ("the eruption of the unexpected," Somol and Whiting in *Log*; "I was so excited to discover external fields that could at last become excuses for new architectural effects," Zaera-Polo; and so on)—concerns me. There is no reason to assume that just because something is new it is therefore life enhancing and to be valued. It seems to me that this obsession with innovation results from tentativeness or uncertainty or embarrassment about the articulation of less sexy goals like durability, energy efficiency, and a meeting of deeper human needs.

The emphasis on realism, on tough-mindedly finding out what is, however much what is disappoints one's wishes, has been inspired by Rem Koolhaas. His investigative attitude—toward New York in the 1920s and 1930s, toward Atlanta and Singapore in the 1980s, toward Lagos, China, and shopping in the 1990s, and toward historic preservation in the 2000s—has spread widely among young architectural thinkers, as well it should have. His "position" is "Let's not be fools. Let's not have delusions of grandeur and potency, as architects usually do." The new realism also represents a rejection of poststructuralist detachment, most extremely embodied in the intellectual cliché of the 1980s that there is no reality, only versions of it. If anything, as we now shall see, submission to reality has been taken to such an extreme in some architectural practices that it results in an abdication of the inescapable need to direct one's design activities lest they become robotic, arbitrary, and conservative.

It is Jorge Silvetti, in his "The Muses Are Not Amused" here, who keenly and devastatingly diagnoses the strange motivation among many younger high designers not only to be aware of but also to be directed by "external," supra-personal forces and things, to go with some flow. Zaera-Polo expresses this when he says of his Yokohama

Terminal project that it was "surprising us at every moment with how the *technical requirements were organizing themselves into arrangements.* . . . Yokohama was an experiment in how to evolve a systematic, rigorous, *alienated,* and *technical* approach to produce the most outrageous architecture" (my emphasis). On the one hand, this reflects the admirable flexibility and openness I discussed earlier—a healthy resistance to predetermining fixed ideas. On the other, it is an abdication of the unavoidable responsibility to direct and shape the project to meet objectives one believes worthy and important, an abdication "turning the architect," in Silvetti's words, "into a dazed observer of seductive wonders."[9] Look! When I feed these algorithms into my computer, it creates all these cool new shapes! All I have to do is pick one! "Nobody," Silvetti laments, "involved in these attempts seems to want to be responsible for the outcome and its authorship insofar as *form* is concerned. . . . They all relegate the architect to the role of the intermediary—the midwife." Technology, materials, data, computer outputs—all these need to be subsumed by the designer's will to achieve humanly worthy goals, whether aesthetic, psychological, or social. "Indifferent inclusiveness," maintains Silvetti, leads to "passive ratification of the status quo." As Foster asks, "What is the difference, politically, between . . . postcritical affirmation [of whatever is] and the dominant neoconservativism?" And as Baird warns, we need "to be able to measure the ambition and the capacity for significant social transformation of such ['projective'] forms. Without such models, architecture could all too easily again find itself conceptually and ethically adrift."

Although Stan Allen is personally close to the thinkers espousing postcriticality, he takes the most balanced and subtle view of the ideas about architectural thinking that this book presents and critiques. He praises "a practice open to innovation and play, capable of confronting the complexities of realization without facile compromise." "Such a practice would find material for experimentation, critique, and theoretical speculation in the methods and procedures of day-to-day architectural practices." But he warns that "architecture, which is nothing if not a social art form, loses effectiveness precisely to the degree that it becomes exclusively a cultural phenomenon." As a social art form, architecture would not be, as it currently is, "absent from the key sites of everyday life: the workplace, the freeway, the mall, houses, and housing."

So even now, when "high" architectural production seems more lively, exciting, diverse, and engaged than ever, a parallel architectural theorizing has yet to grow beyond its adolescence.

Notes

1. People like Jeffrey Kipnis, Sanford Kwinter, Sarah Whiting, Mark Wigley, Peter Eisenman, Robert Somol, Kenneth Frampton, Michael Hays, Stan Allen, and Sylvia Lavin.

2. Robert Somol, "12 Reasons to Get Back in Shape," in *Content*, Rem Koolhaas, editor-in-chief, Brendon McGetrick, ed. (Köln: Taschen, 2004), 86.

3. *Log 5* (Spring/Summer 2005): 144.

4. Somol, "12 Reasons," 86, 87.

5. "I go to bed after working. No cocktail. No reading *Domus, Wallpaper,* Rousseau, or anything else" ("Starck Speaks," chapter 3, this volume).

6. According to Baird, a supporting body of projective theory is needed. "Without it, I predict that this new architecture will devolve to the 'merely' pragmatic, and to the 'merely' decorative, with astonishing speed" ("'Criticality' and Its Discontents," chapter 10, this volume). Hal Foster notes, "Today one often hears that we have too much theory and interdisciplinarity; I think we have never had enough. In my experience at the Princeton School of Architecture, which is known for its emphasis on these kinds of inquiry, the critiques are not often well informed in relevant philosophy or other pertinent fields (including art). We are not sufficiently theoretical, and we have not yet been critical" ("Stocktaking 2004," chapter 9, this volume).

In "Concepts: The Architecture of Hope" (*Harvard Design Magazine* 19 [Fall 2003/Winter 2004]: 37), surely a response, in part, to Somol and Whiting, Sanford Kwinter writes, "It must not be forgotten that the work of [Schoenberg and Picasso] is purposely and necessarily *difficult*—and it is this difficulty that we must find a way to celebrate today. Without constant contact with the culture and ethos of difficulty we are hard pressed to make ourselves better than dilettantes. And it is arguable that dilettantism—whose many modern forms include parochialism, specialism, 'expertise'—represents a deeper and more menacing form of mediocrity in our present culture than the other more noticeable and transient ones (such as the *surfeit* of design) that are plaguing the design world today. Nor should we neglect the cryptic difficulty of a Siza (whose cryptic-ness is itself no virtue) in favor of the more exhibitionist (and sometimes ersatz) forms of difficulty of a late Eisenman or a post-Libeskind pretender."

In Somol and Whiting's issue of *Log*, Jeffrey Kipnis argues, in "Is Resistance Futile?" that Somol and Whiting "have not advanced a convincing metacritical account," and "the argument for 'the easy' and its cognates risks lapsing into a mere bias of tastes or worse, an apologia for the accommodation of mere service practice, however cool its product may be" (107).

7. Hal Foster carries this further: "'Build them higher than before,' one often heard after the fall of the Towers, as if our problem were penile dysfunction—and, perhaps, imperially speaking, it is. If the hole in the ground figures the tragedy for Libeskind, his spire 'will let the world know that the terrorists have failed.' A large part of the great attraction of his scheme is disclosed right there: it gives us both commemorative prop and imperial thrust, both the traumatic and the triumphal. Or, more exactly, it gives us trauma troped as triumph, a site of civilian tragedy turned into a symbol of militaristic defiance" ("Stocktaking 2004," chapter 9, this volume).

8. In the United States, Tim Love, head of the firm Utile, exemplifies this approach. See his "Urban Design after Battery Park City: Opportunities for Variety and Vitality in Large-Scale Urban Real Estate Development" in *Harvard Design Magazine* 25 (Fall 2006/Winter 2007); and "Double-Loaded: Everyday Architecture and Windows for Improvement" in *Harvard Design Magazine* 21 (Fall 2004/Winter 2005).

9. Silvetti's phrase "seductive wonders" prompts an awareness that post-critical, projective architecture has emphasized effects and affects rather than representation, ideas, or formal realization. As a call to efficacy, it is a much needed political wake-up, but as a call to a passive, distracted experiencing of architecture, anti-intellectualism again becomes a concern. In "Is Resistance Futile?" (*Log* 5: 108), Jeff Kipnis, despite his criticality, is seduced by architecture's potential to create feelings: "Such an architecture would behave more like a sound-track in a film than a concert piece in an auditorium. . . . This architecture would be at its most effective when just immersive and most political when it evades both emotions and understanding, that is, when it moves directly to affects." But is this not very close to endorsing an architecture of manipulation, like the manipulation to produce sales embedded in the sequencing of products in supermarkets? Granted, one might manipulate people for good political ends, but isn't politics at its best a celebration of the fullest possible understanding and consciousness?

1

A Scientific Autobiography, 1982–2004: Madrid, Harvard, OMA, the AA, Yokohama, the Globe

Alejandro Zaera-Polo

In recent years, the nature and the relationship of theoretical specula-tion and practical knowledge have become critical subjects in archi-tectural debate. Within a field traditionally focused on practice, theo-retical discourse, especially during the 1990s, expanded enormously while the borders of the discipline dissolved into neighboring fields.

I here want to describe, rather than propose, a relationship in which theory and practice are no longer understood either in opposition or in a complementary, dialectical relationship but rather as a complex con-tinuum in which both forms of knowledge operate as devices capable of effectively transforming reality. Such devices form parts of a com-plex engine operating in different ways depending on circumstances. To say that practical knowledge is devoid of significant theoretical contents is as false as to say that theoretical knowledge lacks prag-matic purpose. I would prefer to describe their assemblage as two epis-temological tendencies within a particular discipline and a particular domain of reality, one toward virtualization (i.e., theory), the other toward actualization (i.e., practice). In this capacity, theory is never generic or universal; it relates very directly to things like currency ex-change, cultural traditions, and geopolitics. It has, just like practice, a site and an age. Virtualization often operates there as reality's vector of change, as an index of tendencies. Practice is not a pure form of local knowledge. On the contrary, pragmatics strongly depend on the repetition and generalization of preexisting ideas. If I can claim some authority on the relationship between theory and practice, it is because my experience as an agent in the building industry, in academia, and as a critic is hinged around it.

I was lucky enough to have been in some of the more stimulating milieus for architecture at the border between centuries—Spain in the 1980s, American academia in the late 1980s and early 1990s, Holland in the mid-1990s, London in the late 1990s, and Japan at the dawn of the twenty-first century.

Spain in the 1980s: *El Croquis* and the Noncritical Virtual

I grew up as an architect in Madrid in the early 1980s. The Spanish economy was thriving in that period of simultaneous political and social development, and architecture in this climate found one of those historical and geographical singularities in which opportunities and expectations grew to unprecedented levels.

The formula was as follows: a powerful, guild-driven, professional structure (inherited from the dictatorship) + a booming economy (generated by the new democracy) + a process of cultural and political revolution (produced by the new regime and by the repressed ambitions created during the old one) = interesting architecture.

Architects had become confident and optimistic to a degree that I have elsewhere experienced only in South Korea—another ex-dictatorship—before the economic slump of the mid-1990s. Most of the knowledge needed to operate in this milieu was practical, and architects just needed to keep pace with external processes and to actualize their potentials to produce innovation: There was no need to establish strategies of "virtualization," since reality was already beyond anybody's wildest dreams.

Within the Technical School of Architecture in Madrid, those who were committed to "virtualizing" (i.e., theorizing) the discipline could be put in two bands:

An older group of great designers, well oiled through years of intense "holistic" practice (the average size of practices was about three members, which meant everybody did everything: structures, detailing, site supervision, environmental systems . . .), designers who drew their inspiration from sports cars, sailboats, poetry, sculpture, holidays in Majorca, and beautiful women (they were obviously all male).

A younger group, more intellectual and influenced by historical and linguistic studies, who focused their experiments on evolving the disciplinary language. For them, sublime practice was to evolve block typologies, design innovative corners, pervert conventional fenestration orders, and so on.

In a typical Oedipal reaction, I became critical of both groups and resorted to extradisciplinary fields—philosophy and literature—as a strategy of virtualization. Since nobody was very interested at that time in virtual activities, at an early age I was given the opportunity to participate in an emerging industry of professional publications, grown in the shadow of the building industry and the ambitious cultural policies of the architects' associations across the country. Writing at that time was considered a bit too intellectual—something for wimps—and some of my tutors, informed of my literary activities, would tell me with a skeptical grin, "What really matters is the site supervision."

One of my early engagements was with *El Croquis,* a magazine that started up as a pamphlet publishing thesis work of students in Madrid so that other students could learn how to organize a graduation thesis (a complicated technical enterprise at the time). *El Croquis* was then shifting toward the professional market, with the same zest and focus in the description of details that they had used for the student market. Then lacking a particular theoretical agenda—as far as I could tell—they had a vague notion that they needed some text to go with the illustrations. In this situation, writing allowed me enormous freedom, as long as I remained within the word limit. Most importantly, I could not be overtly critical (I was never told this explicitly but gathered it pretty fast). Some of my friends who were also interested in a more theoretical approach criticized me for working in that most "pornographic" of architectural magazines. (Now all of them want to be published in it.) Others accused me for not being critical enough, which was entirely true but also the very point of the exercise, and certainly the operative basis of what I have been doing since as a critic. Once the possibility of judgment of somebody's work has been removed, you can use the work only as a raw material to construct your own affirmative statements. Relating it to other dimensions or domains appeared suddenly as a broad field of potential. Once writing abandons the role of the critical—establishing benchmarks, comparisons, judgments, and value systems—it becomes a projective tool in itself, an instrument that processes others' work into one's own.

To some degree this was the secret of *El Croquis*'s phenomenal success: the lack of a critical agenda and an extreme commitment to the detailed portrayal of architectural artifacts, encompassing their innermost secrets. The magazine made an art of describing work in itself, independent from age, trend, or situation. In the same way, the magazine had complete independence from institutions, professional or academic power groups, and individuals. (To the editor's credit, I witnessed some rather important architects begging for a monograph and being consistently ignored way beyond political tactfulness.) One may question whether its choices have been right, but that is beside the point: once the editors chose something, they turned it to gold. *El Croquis*'s case is a paradigm of the power of production versus that of critique.

Not only did these activities provide me with the opportunity to construct a theoretical approach, they also allowed me to mount one of the largest operations of industrial espionage ever carried out in this profession: there is nothing more revealing than meeting architects and visiting their offices to learn about their techniques. It was only after a few years of these activities that I decided to stop writing on others' work, since doing so was hampering my own career as an architect—people tended to associate my name automatically with that writing.

The American Academia in the Early 1990s: Economic Recession and the Empowerment of Theory

In a radical change of milieu, I landed in August 1989 at the Harvard University Graduate School of Design to work toward a post-professional degree. The favorable exchange rate between peseta and dollar after a few years of economic crisis in the United States presented me with a good opportunity to maximize a scholarship and find a more benevolent climate in which to theorize.

In the American academic environment, the smartest guys from the then "around forty" generation had already figured that in the contemporary economic conditions the practice of architecture had become impossible. After the great corporate architecture of the first half of the twentieth century, Americans had invented more profitable forms of creating public "space" than architecture—they had shifted their investment to movies, art, information technology, advertising, marketing, and the like. As a result, this emerging generation of architects shifted to film theory, art criticism, cybernetics, cultural studies, graphic design, and economics to produce the era of "the empowerment of theory."

A shrinking demand for quality architecture in the United States had neatly split American practice between the "stars"—also known among the politically correct newcomers as the "Boys' Club"—and corporate practices. With an economic milieu rapidly deteriorating after the 1980s excess, this new generation was left with little opportunity to grow through familiar modes of architectural practice. Exchanging critique for production as an operative mode, it mounted an assault on both forms of practice—stardom and the corporate— as corrupt and politically incorrect, and devoted itself to enterprises more noble than making buildings.

Theory, critique, and cultural production appeared as the ideal field of potential for this secretly power-hungry generation, whose members grouped very much in the old boys' style, promoting the least threatening and manipulating institutions, publications, and words under the mask of ethical behavior. Bred in the "yuppie" generation, they had learned a couple of lessons from their luckier high school mates who became brokers during the 1980s: the more remote your practice is from the making of the real goods, the less overhead and the more flexibility, money, and power you have. As the stock market became the Mother of All Things, the new generation of American architectural thinkers moved to theoretical speculation and became progressively estranged from anything physical.

"Critical practice" was the thing to do if one wanted to do architecture, and that meant to nag about everything and try to embody architecturally all sorts of psychological and political perversions and subversions.

After an initial shock at the brightness of the ongoing discourse— all the greater due to my then poor command of English—I became suspicious of this brave new world, particularly of the fact that, at juries, projects that in Spain would provoke disdain were able to trigger hour-long debates about Lacanian psychology, poststructuralist semiotics, and the like. For the first time I was facing the symptoms that I would face repeatedly across several educational institutions worldwide: The effects of "the empowerment of theory" have been translated into the confusing coupling of theoretical practice and detachment from architectural production, with the offspring being legions of bad novels, bad sociology, bad psychology, bad philosophy, and bad movies being presented at juries as advanced architectural "research." The fundamental problem was the systematic exile of architectural effects outside the discipline, leaving the architectural capacity of the students in a precarious state. (Some years later, as an antidote, we removed from our Architectural Association studio bibliography everything but the Neufert *Architects' Data* and the *Architectural Graphic Standards*.)

Skeptical about the proliferation of cultural studies and arty-farty seminars on the menu at the Harvard University Graduate School of Design, and moreover unable to understand them due to my language handicaps, I defected—to much contempt from my classmates and some of the faculty—to the uncool options of real estate, construction management, and especially computer-aided design (CAD), which at the time was a subject reserved for nerds with no real interest in architecture.

However, I could not completely escape theory: Within my focused assault on American production technologies, I did come across some potentially useful neo-Marxist urban theory, most notably that of David Harvey and Henri Lefebvre, and most importantly, I bumped into Sanford Kwinter, a lunatic who curiously did not speak about scopophilia, gender, and other issues related to the construction of the subject, but about all sorts of multiplicities—swarms, forests, glaciers, and other unorthodox matters. He gave a seminar on complexity with a reader full of Henri Bergson, Ilya Prigogine, Gilles Deleuze, Manuel De Landa, and the like. I was so excited to discover external fields that could at last become excuses for new architectural effects that I toyed with the idea of enrolling in a PhD program, profiting from the possibility of extending my scholarship. But another encounter at the Harvard University Graduate School of Design with another outsider, Rem Koolhaas, aborted a promising career as a theorist: He offered me a job.

Rotterdam 1991–93: OMA and the SuperDutch: The Engineering of Cultural Production

I landed in Rotterdam in August 1991 loaded with my recently acquired American arsenal: on one hand, CAD proficiency; on the other, a cocktail of Deleuze's materialism and Harvey's neo-Marxist globalization theory.

The first missile, CAD production technology, failed miserably: My computer skills were at odds with OMA's company policy at the time of a radical split between designers and computer operators; since I wanted to be a designer, I had to go back to the parallel bar and the foam cutter for two years.

The second missile, the theory cocktail, was far more successful: Koolhaas was amused at my attempt to wrap in pretentious new words the stuff going on in the office. Previous theoretical encapsulation dated from Foucault and Barthes, extending toward Derrida, so it was time for an update. Paradoxically, production at OMA was remarkably nontheoretical by American standards. The pressure of deadlines did not leave much time for constructing critical arguments before diving into the blue foam. Discussions were only on matter-of-fact stuff. It was like undergoing a shock detox treatment against the critical thought that by the end of my American residence was threatening to paralyze my architectural nerves.

Holland was an artificial paradise. Everything was new and worked—trains, doctors, highways, telecommunications, architects. . . . Certainly the happiest population in Europe and maybe in the world, the Dutch looked like the Americans in the 1950s. Beefed-up Europeans, sporting permanent Caribbean suntans and perfectly gelled hair were drinking in fashionable cafés and shopping their hearts out at reasonable prices. The people themselves were the very best example of Dutch engineering: Everybody was friendly but fast, smart but cool, daring but responsible, liberal but effective. The SuperDutch were there before Bart Lootsma coined that term.

Among the architects, a new generation of busy bees was emerging, excited by the international success of their local star, "Rem," as everybody seemed to call him in a bout of spontaneous collective familiarity later to be exported worldwide. No wonder, because Koolhaas had put together the recipe for international stardom as an ingenious assemblage of theory and practice, speculative vision and ruthless realism. After Rem, the typical path of a Dutch architect was to do a few of those projects growing everywhere in Holland, put together some theory, write a book with a cool name—branding is one of the best skills of the Dutch—and sell it worldwide. As opposed to what happens in the United States, Dutch architects, given the level of opportunity in Holland, write after—or at least during—the fact, and some of them even evolve their own customized publishing programs to construct, through language, a discourse of the actual. Maybe also to undercut the critical, but even that seems to be consistent with a form of virtualization focused on production.

Unlike in Spain, where the potential for virtualization in architecture was primarily developed from the mighty associations of architects and was therefore enslaved to practice, and unlike in America, where virtualization resided within the walls of academia and never got out, in Holland architecture was being taken care of by much higher authorities: the Ministries of Culture and of the Built Environment. As I arrived in Rotterdam, the Netherlands Architecture Institute was under construction and the Berlage Institute was just starting, both generously funded by the government as brand-new infrastructures for architectural speculation and, most importantly, networking and dissemination. All deserving Dutch architects made books subsidized by the ministry, and all architectural start-ups progressed with governmental funding. (See my postscript below for updates on the now-altered Dutch scene.)

This high-level management has devised a system in which cultural production and speculation have become perfectly integrated in the making of the environment, and this arrangement is paying handsome dividends. Dutch architecture is considered—with good reason—one of the most innovative today. A highly industrialized and effective construction sector, mobilizing important resources, produces large benefits, which are severely taxed by the government (I was paying 40 percent of my income on a less than ideal salary). In return, the administration provides generous support for those who decide to speculate further (I was eligible to collect start-up funds, even as a foreign citizen, and was generously compensated by the Berlage as a visiting critic). Advanced speculation is then disseminated worldwide by subsidized magazines, schools, and museums and absorbed back by the construction industry and the public. Architects' cultural production becomes essential as a way to place architecture in the wider cultural context and the politics of space so that in return culture and politics are aware of architecture's potentials. In response, Dutch theory is deeply committed to the actual. (Koolhaas formulated this approach, either theorizing after the fact on cases [New York, Atlanta, Singapore, Lagos] or on method [critical paranoia, bigness . . .].)

Out of Modernist Dutch planning, a new architectural culture of progress and difference has emerged and is being colorfully interpreted by the SuperDutch generation, which is obtaining worldwide success and is acclaimed by the local developers. It is so varied and progressive that one sometimes wonders whether the variations are mere scenography, like the choices at McDonald's. But it is an incredible achievement that such a smooth marriage of theory and practice has been created not by historical coincidence—as in Spain in the 1980s—but by the artificial arrangement and ruthless determination of competent authorities.

London in the Late 1990s: The AA—Eccentrics and Pragmatics

Out of the Dutch artificial paradise and into the British gloom, I landed in London in August 1993 to teach at the Architectural Association (AA), at the rock bottom of the recession. The city was literally falling apart, especially in comparison with the shining Dutch environment. The AA and the other academic institutions in London were filled with 1960s debris of the ideological, methodological, and even personal sorts. Archigram heroes were doing odd jobs in the corners of academia—for a Spanish architect educated in the 1980s, it was like watching Mick Jagger sweeping floors. Generally well preserved in alcohol, these heroes were no longer able to understand what was going on and kept a distant air, like bankrupt aristocrats. What happened to all those wonderful ideas? How could they have vanished like that?

After a year at the AA, I started to understand and, worse still, feel like one of them. The AA, which originated as a club, had become an ivory tower for the English Eccentrics. This typically local figure had developed a unique model of education of enormous success, exported everywhere during the 1980s. Its uniqueness, especially in comparison with the stale Continental polytechnic model, was assembled as a hybrid between a liberal arts school and a gentleman's club. It gave support to the most outrageous experiments and the most unique personalities and produced work of an intensity difficult to match within any other academic infrastructure. The very British system of local allegiances and networks of defensive legitimation had produced in the AA a powerful vehicle for architectural experimentation and a precinct where the Eccentrics and other outsiders—many of them foreign—were given a socially productive role.

The price to pay was the certainty that none of it would ever effectively transform reality. In this most peculiar pact with the Devil, the English Eccentrics knew that their job was to form an alibi for the system to remain as unaltered as possible. In this scenario, the more outrageous and removed from reality, the more effective work becomes as a legitimization of the conservative. The reason why those wonderful ideas never touched down on the earth is because their makers, totally committed to their social role as true Eccentrics, never actually believed in them as potential reality. Or rather, these ideas were actually being developed by the other side of the British mind: the pragmatic. Through the Thatcher era, the high-tech Lords were actually having a ball exploring the most pragmatic aspects of the 1960s and exporting them worldwide.

Partly out of survival instinct and partly out of fear of becoming an Eccentric—a capital sin for a Castilian—the more I heard the continuous dismissal of their work inside the ivory tower, the more interested I became in the Pragmatic Lords. All they actually needed was to grow a virtualizing branch—just as the Eccentrics needed to grow an actualizing one—somebody to read their work as an actualization of potentials of building technology rather than as optimal solutions for technical problems. But this would probably have endangered their public profile, the fiction they sold of technical optimization. Being truly pragmatic, they were not interested in spreading confusing virtualized messages.

After having escaped from the Spanish polytechnic education and having attempted to find solace in the Anglo-American liberal arts tradition, I had found the limits of liberalism and the advantages of a less individualistic, more technically oriented education. Diploma 5, the unit I ran with Farshid Moussavi at the AA for seven years, was precisely an attempt to virtualize pragmatics. Built up on a mix of Jacobin radical faith in the transformation of reality with a Calvinistic commitment to production and rigor, the ethos of Diploma 5 was aimed at exploring and proliferating the potentials of a technical repertoire for contemporary practice. Curiously, Lord Foster was to become the single largest employer of ex–Dip 5 students after our own office, which became an extension of the people and ideas in the unit.

This Continental departure from the local liberalism did not go down very well with the 1960s derivatives, who immediately understood our radicalization of pragmatics and technique as a threatening force to individual self-statement and free thinking. To worsen matters, we met and immediately aligned ourselves with Jeff Kipnis, one of the most volatile explosives concocted by American academia through the empowerment of theory, who encouraged us to abandon our pseudo-multidisciplinary approach to concentrate on the irreducible secrets of the discipline. Echoes of Spanish brutality resonated in his words, as he also blasted the 1960s debris. (I would later introduce Kipnis to *El Croquis*, and he would become a local legend: the first intelligible American theorist after transplant-to-America Kenneth Frampton.)

Diploma 5 was to become a kind of sect for techno-freaks who wandered around the school with bloodshot eyes speaking in a strange jargon. Despite the initial mistrust, at least a few students understood that exercising dexterity in sophisticated techniques and temporary submission to rigorous and alienating regimes might become as powerful a weapon of virtualization as the cult of personality and extravagance had been during the 1980s. The quality and amount of work they were able to produce were legendary. It was the first realization of the power of a culture as an engine of experimental production. So, after all, one has to give some credit to the AA as the best school for the synthesis of architectural cultures.

Yokohama 1999–2002: A Matter of Culture

After more than four years of doubts, the Yokohama municipality decided in January 1999 to proceed with the construction of the Yokohama International Port Terminal building, a project we had won in 1995 in an international competition. After a period of incredulity on the client's part, we finally realized that this time the project was serious and that the only way to do it well was to move our entire project team to Japan. In London we formed a team styled like British military intelligence, a team whose core was constituted mainly of Japanese "Sherpas"—operators with local knowledge— who had either worked in the London office for some time or been our students at the AA or the Berlage Institute, to guide us through the difficult Japanese ground. We also took with us some Spanish "Gurkhas"—a fierce deterritorialized contingent, ignorant of the basic rules of local behavior and capable of the worst atrocities—to crack local boundaries. In August 1999, Foreign Office Architects (FOA) was at last at large in Japan.

Japan is an interesting case for this text, since it is by Western standards a particularly theory-proof environment. The architect as an agent almost completely detached from the construction process is a Western import dating from the age of Metabolism. In Japan, the contractor—responsible for material actualization—is ultimately the architect; there is no split between a theorizing agency and an actualizing practice, for better or worse. Material organization can reach unbelievable levels of excellence in Japan, since the cultural and industrial commitment to material perfection is there unmatched, but it can also produce the most incongruent assemblages, since there are no means in place to provide consistency fast enough to an exponentially growing capacity to build. This produces a particular form of architecture that can best be seen in local architectural magazines, where one can witness hundreds of truly inspired moments of material assemblage—sometimes several in the same project—without any consistency. Western architectural culture could live for a month with the ideas in a single Japanese magazine, using them one by one rather than all at once.

The production of the detail design of the Yokohama project was an exhausting process in which we had to concentrate all our energy for seven months, followed immediately by a no-less-demanding supervision phase. No time for theorizing, and yet the key for success was the theoretical consistency of the team. The Yokohama team's core was built up with very talented, mostly Japanese architects who had gone through further training in the West. We kept a very small team, with whom we had close communication, since its members had been part of the cultures of either our academic or our professional practices in London. Practically trained in Japan and theoretically trained in the West, these people made up the only workforce capable of producing the cultural synthesis that the project needed. Together we could discuss topological grids, intensive tessellation, differentiation of systems, diagrammatic performance, and many other techniques that we had been developing jointly for the practices of material organization. The design process became in itself a process of creating knowledge. The Yokohama project not only gave us the possibility of actualizing a theory we had been developing but also started growing its own lines of virtualization, surprising us at every moment with how the technical requirements were organizing themselves into arrangements that we could not predict at the onset of the project.

Our most important role as project directors was to assemble the team members and defend them from unavoidable attacks from the different professionals involved in the project, who would naturally dismiss them because of their age. Most difficult and yet most crucial in allowing the growth of the project was to resist forming a corporate bureaucracy in which team structure is aimed at maximum efficiency in decision making. The Yokohama team shared an extreme work ethic, and anybody who did not share that had to be dismissed to avoid contaminating others, to keep the energy focused. To have given the power to "experienced" architects, as most of the conservative forces around us were demanding, would have been catastrophic, since it would have destroyed the team's cultural consistency. Our main task was to synthesize and maintain a team culture through an exhausting process. As an architect, one can operate either within a linear structure where decisions are made in a hierarchy of command or within a culture in which a more complex system of relationships between the team members allows a much greater flexibility, innovation, and feedback. It was as important to introduce Jeff Mills, Autechre, Miles Davis, or Boulez to the other members of the team as to design the structural grid or the wood deck pattern on time. Since there was no experience of such a building, the Yokohama project had to be "grown" and could not be "designed." The team had to grow with it: Nothing "grows" without a culture.

The experience of Diploma 5 at the AA was critical for our constructing a culture aimed at the exploration of material organizations that develop simultaneously a project, a series of techniques, and a group of individuals. Building cultures: isn't this what we do whether we work as experimental architects, as critics, or as teachers? The Yokohama project has not only been a great architectural experiment and a producer of virtuality. We hope it has also been a producer of some very fine architects. Japan is, like Britain, a country of pragmatics and eccentrics: You succeed either through maximum compliance or through the most outrageous behavior. Having gone to Europe to maximize their potential of individual eccentricity, our Japanese colleagues had come across some Europeans fascinated by Japanese populational (vide De Landa), intensive, machinelike behavior.

Yokohama was an experiment in how to evolve a systematic, rigorous, alienated, and technical approach to produce the most outrageous architecture.

Recently, I heard from Arata Isozaki—who has been, together with Toyo Ito, our Japanese godfather through the project—that young Japanese architects have lost the appetite for design and beauty. As an improbable link in the chain of architectural lineage in Japan, I would like to think that this generation has perhaps favored realizing the potentials of growing designs rather than making decisions or manifestos—and that the Yokohama project has been not only an experiment in growing buildings but also an unlikely multicultural graft that will open an alternative for Isozaki's skeptical grandchildren. We just hope that the economy will allow them to actualize it. A culture always needs a material substrate.

To be continued. . . .

2004: Post-¥€$ Postscript

The preceding text is a revised version of articles published in the February and March 2002 issues of *A+U* but was actually written in the last half of 2001 and finalized in the aftermath of September 11. In retrospect, this temporal coincidence seems to acquire unexpected relevance. The text was a personal account of the milieus in which my generation grew up and had to practice and theorize, an attempt to index a paradigm of carefree optimistic globalism and opportunism that was being challenged—if not severely questioned—by the events taking place as the text was being written.

Many things have changed in the two years since the text was published, both on a global and on a personal level—in a curiously intertwined manner—that lend themselves to reflection as they become an interesting verification of the ephemerality and temporal and local specificity of any theoretical or practical proposition. This introduces a historical dimension to my argument, beyond its initial focus on the geographical diversity of certain modes of practice and theory.

Rem Koolhaas, who was the first to theorize the processes of global capital and their effects and potentials in architecture, branded these the ¥€$ regime, and started to criticize it as soon as its phenomenology became specific: Architecture had been deprived of any utopian potential and subject to the whimsical reign of global capital and its accelerated processes. With characteristic speed, he created AMO and the *Content* project to escape such enslavement and the onslaught of *junkspace*. The Harvard Project on the City, like *Content* and AMO, shifted from Shopping and the Pearl River Delta to Rome, Lagos, and Communism as new domains of knowledge and operation where there might still be chances for architecture to be utopian and work for collective well-being.

Cover of *Content,* by AMO, OMA, and Rem Koolhaas.

Koolhaas may very well be right about contemporary conditions, although the current delays in the CCTV project suggest that the pace of evolution in those domains is even faster than he calculated, and the new political establishment has already learned about over-heated economies, soft landings, and democratic demagogy, without completing the phase of mad development: Hu Jintao has allegedly stated more interest in "people" than in "big projects."

In light of this, what I would like to do as a follow-up to my slightly cynical argument about the ephemerality and local diversity of theoretical and practical operations is to revisit some of those well-trodden architectural scenarios in which we are directly involved before venturing into those brave new worlds of the wild Far East, post-Communist Eurasia, and darkest Africa.

In Spain, for example, after two decades of architectural prowess and orthodox commitment to the ¥€$ regime, the country had achieved full acceptance as a distinguished member of Mr. Rumsfeld's New Europe and the Azores Summit. Spain has now fallen under the spell of the architects' star system and become easy prey for the international design elite. (As a Spanish architect, I am lucky to stalk from outside.) *Newsweek* has saluted Mr. Aznar's model of public-private partnership as a new model for a European sustainable economic and urban development and pointed to Barcelona's Forum 2004, where we have been directly involved, as the maximum expression of this regime, despite the very public confrontation between local governments and Mr. Aznar's government. But after the March 11 bombings in Madrid, Mr. Aznar was democratically dismissed and replaced by what the critics have already described as "the first democratic European government of Al-Quaeda." Mr. Rodriguez Zapatero, new president-elect, has set the two first important policies for the new government: Pull all Spanish troops out of Iraq and create a new housing ministry—an institution revived from General Franco's technocratic era—aimed at rescuing a housing-handicapped population.

After two decades of dogged commitment to the ¥€$ regime, 17 percent of the country's GNP is produced in the real-estate and construction sectors, and Spain has become Europe's main investment zone for real estate, sending the prices of housing out of control. The municipalities of both Barcelona and Madrid, from different political positions and under the pressure of potential total collapse if the prices of residence are not brought back under control, are developing massive programs of publicly funded urban housing at a scale not seen for decades in Europe, and involving some unusual architects—like us—in the process. Will this revival of socially controlled urbanism also bring back the need for utopian thinking and replace the ¥€$ regime by a kind of new urban fundamentalism? Watch this space for interesting developments. . . .

In the meantime, in New York, the Ground Zero saga has been proceeding wonderfully. At the epicenter of the struggle of the ¥€$ regime and where the potential for architectural fundamentalism should have been maximal, things are looking a bit bland. After popular clamor trashes the proposals from Beyer Blinder Belle, the Lower Manhattan Development Corporation is forced into an international competition to search for proposals for what should become the future embodiment of Western culture. Rem Koolhaas and Frank Gehry are sidelined, allegedly for not being willing to participate without being properly paid. Political fundamentalists hammer them for their shameless commitment to the ¥€$ regime and lack of moral stance. SOM, who had been working for Larry Silverstein almost since the day after, resigns officially to enter the competition. The list is reduced to two corporate behemoths camouflaged in mixed teams, a British lord of impeccable reputation and size, a highbrow intellectual/Old Boy, a group of pre-critical Old Boys, and an international group of postcritical Young Turks (us among them). Each team gets paid a miserable $40,000. Allegedly the communications company in charge of the process gets paid a cool $3,000,000. Architects lose again to the ¥€$ regime.

A few remarks on the short list: Old Boys and Young Turks have to group to be accepted. Critical architects from the intermediate generation are remarkably excluded. The corporate establishment, determined to regain the intellectual legitimacy that it lost in the 1970s to the Old Boys, resorts directly to the very keen Young Turks as camouflage. But the strategy does not work properly the first time around, and Daniel Libeskind, an Old Boy with an inappropriate CV for the job but with an impeccable moral trajectory, wins the contest. David Childs, the retired corporate captain contemporary of the Old Boys, returns from his grave to publicly dismiss the SOM entry—that had been entrusted to a younger generation within the company—and resigns from the competition to work again for Larry Silverstein. A public fight ensues between Libeskind and Childs for control over the project. Libeskind's moral stance is by now very worn out by years of confrontation with the ¥€$ regime and is surprisingly ready for alignment: He abandons his trademark slurry wall and with Childs produces the Freedom Tower, the Phoenix of Western architecture, for an alleged million bucks "genius fee." Childs's real management genius succeeds in returning cultural legitimacy to the corporate establishment in America after thirty years. Both Old Boys and Young Turks have been erased from the scene. Other birds are landing on Ground Zero in what promises to become an interesting architectural spectacle. Whether it will remain an expensive cosmetic operation à la Times Square dictated by the ¥€$ regime or it will actually become an urban manifesto for the emerging fundamentalisms is yet to be seen.

Meanwhile, the Netherlands has become a victim of its own success: The highway system is permanently clogged, trains are systematically delayed after the privatization of the rail network, Schiphol is coming apart at the seams. . . . Even the royal family is plagued by infighting. The Social-Democrats, who reigned for decades over the economy, the welfare state, and the culture, have collapsed. Wim Kok resigned over the failure of Dutch troops to prevent the massacres of Sarajevo. My own official nomination as the new dean of the Berlage Institute is severely delayed by the period of political turmoil that follows the election. In the middle of the process, Pim Fortuyn, the maverick right-wing/gay politician poised to become the prime minister, is shot dead by an animal rights activist in front of MVRDV's VPRO campus in Hilversum. The newly elected Christian-Democrat government of Jan Peter Balkenende has very serious doubts about whether it belongs to the Old or to the New Europe and is posting the worst GNP growth expectations in the Eurozone.

In 2003 a widespread scandal involving many developers and contractors explodes, revealing dubious morals and systematic price rigging in an industry regarded for years as very profitable, well organized, and efficient—one of the pillars of the Dutch economy. The enormous office space pool developed during the past ten years remains 60 percent empty. The current state of the economy and the new liberal government are threatening to cut down severely the expenditure in cultural subsidies that made the Netherlands a mecca for emerging artists in Europe. The Netherlands Architecture Institute and the Berlage Institute, the two institutions set up in the 1980s to reflect on the city and architecture, are on the firing line, despite being potential sources of regeneration for the whole of the real-estate sector after the price-rigging scandals. As the miraculous balance between the welfare state and the ¥€$ regime that became the trademark of the Dutch for a few decades collapses, Dutch architects are selling their expertise in welfare management, becoming especially appreciated in master planning, social housing, and open public grounds and landscaping. These expertises are particularly appreciated in those countries moving forward to a welfare state, like those in Eastern Europe, and those moving back to a welfare state after deregulation, like the U.K. Many Dutch architects are also seen in China, bidding for work.

In the U.K., Urban Renaissance is on a roll. Birmingham, Brighton, Bristol, Leeds, Leicester, Liverpool, Manchester, Newcastle—all are discreetly turning their city centers into massive shopping malls. ¥€$ urbanism has finally come to rescue the dormant British cities. The real power behind Urban Renaissance is not ideological but purely pragmatic: The inner-city land value in midsized cities has dropped so far that land costs of building there have become negligible. Why keep building suburban shopping malls when whole city centers are for sale and come with great transport infrastructure, central locations, and population density? The merit of Richard Rogers and his Urban Task Force is to have identified these commercial potentials and set up a synergy between them and a politically sellable agenda. High-density city centers, brownfield sites reuse, and the like are probably less polluting, more sustainable, and community-oriented policies, but they are also able to produce larger commercial revenues for inner-city landowners. ¥€$ urbanism in Britain has given rise to a new breed of more pragmatic and efficient architecture that does not comply with the categorization of conservatives and eccentrics that became the legacy of years of welfare state and conservative planning policies. ¥€$ density is moving wealth from the Tory-voting, fox-hunting, Barbour-clad, Euroskeptic farmland to the Labour-voting, jet-setting, metrosexual, Europhile urbanites. The Prince's and English Heritage rhetoric has been replaced by the Task Force and the Commission for Architecture and the Built Environment—a body formed by developers, architects, planners, journalists, and academics with a rather pragmatic approach veiling the new ¥€$ urbanism—and actually enticing developers to look for more experimental architects as a source of added value.

Under the advice of Lord Rogers, Ken Livingstone, a colorful politician expelled from Labour for opposing party discipline and then warmly readmitted once he had become mayor of London as an independent candidate, is implementing some advanced—and risky—urban governance policies: He has managed to implement the first congestion charge scheme in Europe, has been fighting in court with the government for a new policy to fund metropolitan transport, has imposed a quota of 40 percent social housing on all housing developments in London, and, with the Thames Gateway scheme, has initiated the most ambitious extension of London since Queen Victoria's time.

Rogers's and Livingstone's achievements of dressing ¥€$ urbanism with lighthearted ideology are mirrored by Blair's commitment to take the ¥€$ regime to an ideological level. His confrontation with the traditional forces of the Old Europe led him to the even more traditional fundamentalism of Bush's evangelical crusade, internalizing the potential contradictions of the regime within his government to catastrophic effects.

Blair's and Livingstone's twin versions of the ¥€$ regime have, however, found a common *grand project:* The London Olympic bid for 2012 and a master plan for the Lea Valley, in which we have become involved. After having discovered our potentials as camouflage through our involvement in the Ground Zero project, we decided to accept the invitation from a team formed between the local chapters of two American corporations, EDAW and HOK Sports, and a British one, Allies & Morrison, to bid for the project. Our camouflage is spread very thin, since every other partner is on average ten times our size, but this mix of 75 percent corporate savoir faire and 25 percent experimental naïf was able to beat not only the naïveté of some important international bidders but also both Pragmatic Lords! A triumph of meritocracy over pedigree whose effectiveness has still to be proven. So far so good. The Lords are cool about it, and we have found that the corporate monsters are made of reasonable people of more or less our generation with a slightly different career path and with whom it is easy to work. The question now is whether this ¥€$ team will be able to deliver the architectural ideology needed to represent Britain in front of the International Olympic Committee and to provide some soul to the fifty thousand housing units that Mr. Livingstone wants to place in the Lea Valley. Is there an architectural future for a post-¥€$ Britain?

No news from Japan except from the *Financial Times:* After amassing a fortune in dollars trying to keep the yen at bay, Heizo Takenaka, Koizumi's finance superminister, is well on his way to clearing up the bad loan mess. There is a record number of IPOs as people move their money out of the banks to become minority shareholders in those emerging companies. Keiji Tachikawa, mobile communications company NTT DoCoMo's CEO, is close to getting W-CDMA mobile phone transmission technology adopted as the third-generation global standard after years of heavy unilateral investment. Carlos Ghosn has turned Nissan around from a liability into the economic engine of the Renault-Nissan group. Koizumi is sending troops to Iraq, rebuilding the Japanese army, and honoring war criminals. Shintaro Ishihara, the charismatic neonationalist governor of Tokyo City, predicates a new national pride and the creation of a super-airport in Tokyo Bay. The economy is rebounding and so is national self-esteem, not as a result of ¥€$-alignment, but on the contrary as the result of charismatic, disciplined ideological and financial commitment to ideas.

A clear architectural output is not yet emerging. Roppongi Hills, Tokyo's fanfare 2003 skyscraper eclectic development, failed catastrophically as a mirror for post-¥€$ Japan when six-year-old Ryo Mizokawa was crushed to death as he tried to slip through one of the automatic revolving doors, and public confidence in architecture dropped to an all-time low after the government declared the end of the big public projects. All well-known Japanese architects are working mostly abroad, and our only commission there after Yokohama is one for a foreign government. But in the same way that savings are moving toward minority stakes in emerging companies, a new generation is starting to produce work of carefully measured effects in small private commissions. I sense that they are on the verge of a secret fundamentalist revolution. . . .

The plot is thickening. . . .

2005

2

Notes around the Doppler Effect and Other Moods of Modernism

Robert Somol and Sarah Whiting

No matter how often I tell myself that chance happenings of this kind occur far more often than we suspect, since we all move, one after the other, along the same roads mapped out for us by our origins and our hopes, my rational mind is nonetheless unable to lay the ghosts of repetition that haunt me with ever greater frequency. Scarcely am I in company but it seems as if I had already heard the same opinions expressed by the same people somewhere or other, in the same way, with the same words, turns of phrase and gestures. . . . Perhaps there is in this as yet unexplained phenomenon of apparent duplication some kind of anticipation of the end, a venture into the void, a sort of disengagement, which, like a gramophone repeatedly playing the same sequence of notes, has less to do with damage to the machine itself than with an irreparable defect in its programme.

    —W. G. Sebald, *The Rings of Saturn*

I would like to show that these unities form a number of autonomous, but not independent domains, governed by rules, but in perpetual transformation, anonymous and without a subject, but imbuing a great many individual works.

    —Michel Foucault, *The Archaeology of Knowledge*

From Critical to Projective

In 1984, the editors of *Perspecta*, Carol Burns and Robert Taylor, set out an ambitious agenda for issue 21: "Architecture is not an isolated or autonomous medium, it is actively engaged by the social, intellectual, and visual culture which is outside the discipline and which encompasses it. . . . It is based on a premise that architecture is inevitably involved with questions more difficult than those of form or style." While this orientation bears a curious connection to the "realist" or "grey" tradition of an earlier Yale generation, it also serves as a sign of the nascent mixture of a critical neo-Marxism with a celebration of the vernacular or everyday with which Yale would soon become synonymous.[1] Published in that same issue, K. Michael Hays's canonic essay "Critical Architecture: Between Culture and Form" offered a useful corrective to the editorial position of the issue by indirectly implying that the editors were insufficiently dialectical in their understanding of engagement and autonomy. Hays's sophistication has always been to recognize that autonomy is a precondition for engagement. Using Mies as a paradigm, Hays argued for the possibility of a "critical architecture" that would operate between the extremes of conciliatory commodity and negative commentary.

Twelve issues and seventeen years later, the editors of issue 33 have returned to the theme of interdisciplinarity. This time, however, the topic is explicitly underwritten by the terms established in Hays's 1984 essay: "*Perspecta* 33 is built around the belief that architecture stands in the critical position between being a cultural product and a discrete autonomous discipline." Yet, while Hays was suggesting that only critical architecture operated in his privileged "between" position, the editors of 33 imply that *all* architecture now automatically occupies a de facto critical status. What for Hays was then an exceptional practice has now been rendered an everyday fact of life. If nothing else, however, this inflation of critical practice by the editors of 33 has perhaps unconsciously identified a fact of the past twenty years: namely, that disciplinarity has been absorbed and exhausted by the project of criticality. As Hays's first articulation of critical architecture was a necessary corrective to the realist position of *Perspecta* 21, it may be necessary (or, at least, useful) to provide an alternative to the now dominant paradigm of criticality, an alternative that will be characterized here as projective.

As evidenced by Hays's insightful polemic, critical architecture, under the regime of textuality, required the condition of being "between" various discursive oppositions. Thus "culture and form" can alternatively be figured as "kitsch and avant-garde" (Clement Greenberg), "literal and phenomenal" (Colin Rowe), "objecthood and art" (Michael Fried), or "capitalist development and design" (Manfredo Tafuri). Within architecture, Rowe's and Tafuri's discourses most fully enable, if never completely realize, the critical project of "betweenness," whether within history/theory, as with Hays, or in terms of design, as with the work of Peter Eisenman.

It is from Rowe's and Tafuri's conceptual genetic material that architecture's critical project has been formulated. For both authors, there is a requisite assumption of contradiction or ambiguity, regardless of whether it is subsumed or sublated (dialectical materialism) or balanced (liberal formalism). Even before examining the various reconfigurations of Rowe and Tafuri, however, it is important to recognize that the opposition between them is never as clear as would be imagined: Rowe's ostensibly formal project has deep connections to a particular liberal politics, and Tafuri's apparently engaged practice of dialectical critique entails a precise series of formal a prioris as well as a pessimistic prognosis with regard to architectural production. Seen in this way, there is no more political writer than Rowe, and none more formalist than Tafuri.

The criticality of Hays and Eisenman maintains the oppositional or dialectical framework in the work of their mentors and predecessors, while simultaneously trying to short-circuit or blur their terms. In their various attempts to hybridize Rowe and Tafuri in order to fashion a critical position,[2] both Hays and Eisenman rely on dialectics—as is immediately evidenced in the titles of the journals each was responsible for founding: *Oppositions* and *Assemblage*. Despite their implicit critiques of Michael Fried's aesthetics,[3] both Eisenman and Hays ultimately fear literalism as much as Fried does; both warn against the isomorphic remapping of life and art. For both, disciplinarity is understood as autonomy (enabling critique, representation, and signification) but not as instrumentality (projection, performativity, and pragmatics). One could say that their definition of disciplinarity is directed against reification rather than toward the possibility of emergence. While reification concerns itself with the negative reduction of qualitative experience to quantification, emergence promises that serial accumulation may itself result in the production of new qualities. As an alternative to the critical project—here linked to the indexical, the dialectical and hot representation—this text develops an alternative genealogy of the projective—linked to the diagrammatic, the atmospheric and cool performance.

From Index to Diagram

In the significant production of both Hays and Eisenman, as parallel realignments of Rowe and Tafuri, the critical project is inevitably mediated; in fact, it is perpetually obsessed by, and inextricably linked to, reproduction.[4] This obsession manifests itself both in Hays's account of Mies van der Rohe's Barcelona Pavilion and Peter Eisenman's rereading of Le Corbusier's Dom-ino, where both authors adopt the technique of the index.[5] The index emerges as the most opportune mediator (or critical instigator of the between) in part because it automatically combines materialism with signification: in other words, it exists as a physically driven sign, one that is not culturally or visually determined, as are the symbol and icon. For Hays, Mies's architecture situates itself "between the efficient representation of preexisting cultural values and the wholly detached autonomy of an abstract formal system."[6] This status of being in the world yet resistant to it is attained by the way the architectural object materially reflects its specific temporal and spatial context, as well as the way it serves as a trace of its productive systems. Hays describes the Barcelona Pavilion as "an event with temporal duration, whose actual existence is continually being produced," or whose meaning is continually being decided. This act of decision is both in fact and etymologically the critical gesture par excellence.

In Eisenman's reading of the Dom-ino, it is the design process itself that is being registered rather than the material productive and technical systems or specific context discussed by Hays. In marking the status of its existence, in its ability to function as a self-referential sign, the Dom-ino is one of the first Modernist and critical gestures in architecture: "Architecture is both substance and act. The sign is a record of an intervention—an event and an act which goes beyond the presence of elements which are merely necessary conditions."[7] For Eisenman and Hays, the Dom-ino and Barcelona Pavilion are at once traces of an event, indices of their procedures of design or construction, and objects that potentially point to a state of continual transformation. In both cases, the critical forms of self-referentiality are demonstrated via serial reproductions: respectively, Eisenman's redrawn axonometrics of the nonexistent Dom-ino perspective, and the historical photographs Hays uses to extract the experience of the defunct, original Barcelona Pavilion. Just as the architectural artifacts are indices of a missing process or practice, the objects themselves are also significantly missing in both cases, so that a series of reproductions must stand in as their traces. This process of infinite regress or deferral is constitutive of the critical architectural project: architecture inevitably and centrally preoccupied by its status as representation, and its simultaneous commentary on that condition.

As an alternative to Eisenman's reflections on the high European frame, which situated the structural grid within the context of the critical-indexical project of the 1970s, one might look to Rem Koolhaas's appropriation of the mass cultural American frame at the same moment. As suggested above, Eisenman understands Le Corbusier's Dom-ino as the trace of a transformative process, and thus deviates from Rowe by animating the grid. Just as the indexical project assumes or invents a particular kind of reading subject for architecture, its imagination of architectural movement relies on a narrative for the grid. Thus, although the indexical program for architecture may proceed through diagrams, it is still tied to a semiotic, representational, and sequential ambition. Koolhaas's invocation of the "cartoon-theorem" from *Life* magazine—as well as the section cut from the Downtown Athletic Club—alternatively enlists a vision of architecture as contributing to the production and projection of new forms of collectivity. These New York frames exist as instruments of metropolitan plasticity and are not primarily architecture for paying attention to; they are not for reading but for seducing, becoming, instigating new events and behaviors. The skyscraper-machine allows the projection infinitely upward of virtual worlds within this world, and in this way extends Michel Foucault's reflections on heterotopias and prisons. Gilles Deleuze argues that Foucault understands Jeremy Bentham's Panopticon not simply as a machine for surveillance but more broadly and productively as a diagram that "imposes a particular form of conduct on a particular multiplicity." Koolhaas's investigation of the frame structure is diagrammatic in the same way.

From these two inventions of the frame structure in mid-1970s architectural discourse, one can discern two orientations toward disciplinarity: that is, disciplinarity as autonomy and process, as in the case of Eisenman's reading of the Dom-ino, and disciplinarity as force and effect, as in Koolhaas's staging of the Downtown Athletic Club. Moreover, these two examples begin to differentiate the critical project in architecture, with its connection to the indexical, from the projective, which proceeds through the diagram. The diagram is a tool of the virtual to the same degree that the index is the trace of the real.[8]

From Dialectics to Doppler

Rather than relying upon the oppositional strategy of critical dialectics, the projective employs something similar to the Doppler effect— the perceived change in the frequency of a wave that occurs when the source and receiver of the wave have a relative velocity. The Doppler effect explains the change in pitch between the sound of a train as it approaches and then moves away from the listener.[9] If critical dialectics established architecture's autonomy as a means of defining architecture's field or discipline, a Doppler architecture acknowledges the adaptive synthesis of architecture's many contingencies. Rather than isolating a singular autonomy, the Doppler focuses upon the effects and exchanges of architecture's inherent multiplicities: material, program, writing, atmosphere, form, technologies, economics, and so on. It is important to underscore that this multiplying of contingencies differs greatly from the more dilute notion of interdisciplinarity, which seeks to legitimize architecture through an external measuring stick, thereby reducing architecture to the entirely amorphous role of absorber of heterogeneous life. A projective architecture does not shy away from reinstating architectural definition, but that definition stems from design and its effects rather than a language of means and materials. The Doppler shifts the understanding of disciplinarity as autonomy to disciplinarity as performance or practice. In the former, knowledge and form are based on shared norms, principles, and traditions. In the latter, a more Foucauldian notion of disciplinarity is advanced in which the discipline is not a fixed datum or entity but rather an active organism or discursive practice, unplanned and ungovernable, like Foucault's "unities form[ing] a number of autonomous, but not independent domains, governed by rules, but in perpetual transformation."[10] Rather than looking back or criticizing the status quo, the Doppler projects forward alternative (not necessarily oppositional) arrangements or scenarios.

A projective architecture does not make a claim for expertise outside the field of architecture, nor does it limit its field of expertise to an absolute definition of architecture. Design is what keeps architecture from slipping into a cloud of heterogeneity. It delineates the fluctuating borders of architecture's disciplinarity and expertise. So when architects engage topics that are seemingly outside of architecture's historically defined scope—questions of economics or civic politics, for example—they do not engage those topics as experts on economics or civic politics but, rather, as experts on design and how design may affect economics or politics. They engage these other fields as experts on design's relationship to those other disciplines, rather than as critics. Design encompasses object qualities (form, proportion, materiality, composition, etc.), but it also includes qualities of sensibility, such as effect, ambience, and atmosphere.

An example of a projective architecture that engages the strategy of the Doppler effect in lieu of that of the dialectic is WW's IntraCenter, a 40,000-square-foot community center located in Lexington, Kentucky. The IntraCenter's client provided WW with a program list of dizzying operational heterogeneity: day care, athletic facilities, social services, café, library, computer center, job training facilities, shops, and so on. Rather than figuring these multiple programs so as to provide each with its own formal identification, or rather than establishing a neutral field so as to allow the programs to define the project, the IntraCenter elides the expected overlap between form and program. Their lack of alignment leads to a perpetual Doppler shift between the two. This strategy of nonconcentricity generates other Doppler effects, including the many reverberations among overlapping constituencies as well as material and structural conditions. The IntraCenter is projective rather than critical in that it very deliberately sets into motion the possibility of multiple engagements rather than a single articulation of program, technology, or form (contemporary architecture's commodity, firmness, and delight).

The Doppler effect shares some attributes with parallax, which, as Yve-Alain Bois notes, comes from the Greek parallaxis, or "change": "the apparent change in the position from which it is viewed."[11] Claiming that Richard Serra consciously responded to the possibilities of parallax, Bois cites as an example Serra's description of his sculpture titled *Sight Point:* "[It seems at first] to fall right to left,

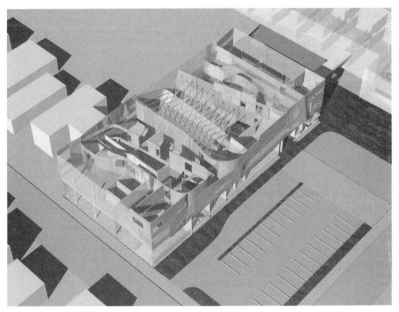

Form-Program Diagram 1, IntraCenter, WW 2001. Courtesy of Sarah Whiting.

make an X, and straighten itself out to a truncated pyramid. That would occur three times as you walked around."[12] In other words, parallax is the theatrical effect of a peripatetic view of an object. It takes into account how the context and the viewer "complete" the work of art.

Where the Doppler differs from parallax is in that it is not purely optical. Predicated on waves that can be auditory or visual, the Doppler suggests that the optical and conceptual are only two of many sensibilities. Additionally, it is not a reading strategy—that is, it is not just an unfolding reading of an artwork—but an atmospheric interaction. It foregrounds the belief that both the subject and the object carry and exchange information and energy. In short, a user might be more attuned to certain aspects of a building than others. He or she might understand how the building responds to a formal history of architecture or deploys a specific technology, or he or she might have particular associations with a building's material palette or site. As the novelist W. G. Sebald explains, each one of us experiences moments of repetition, coincidence, or duplication, where echoes of other experiences, conversations, moods, and encounters affect current ones. Such momentary echoes are like tracks out of alignment, hearing and seeing out of phase that generate momentary déjà vus, an overlap of real and virtual worlds.

From Hot to Cool

Someone should establish an anthropology of hot and cool . . .
—Jean Baudrillard

Overall, one might characterize the shift from critical to projective modes of disciplinarity as a process of cooling down or, in Marshal McLuhan's terms, of moving from a "hot" to a "cool" version of the discipline. Critical architecture is hot in the sense that it is preoccupied with separating itself from normative, background, or anonymous conditions of production, and with articulating difference. For McLuhan, hot media like film are "high-definition," conveying very precise information on one channel or in one mode. By contrast, cool media, such as television, are low-definition, and since the information they convey is compromised, they require the participation of the user. In this regard, the formalist-critical project is hot in its prioritization of definition, delineation, and distinction (or medium specificity). As a historical alternative to that project, minimalism can be understood as a cool art form; it is low-definition and requires the context and viewer to complete it, lacking both self-sufficiency and self-consciousness. Minimalism explicitly requires participation and is related to Robert Smithson's promotion of entropy. While cooling suggests a process of mixing (and thus the Doppler effect would be one form of cool), the hot resists through distinction and connotes the overly difficult, belabored, worked, complicated. Cool is relaxed, easy. This difference between the cool and the hot may be amplified by briefly examining a medium McLuhan does not discuss: performance.

In his obituary on the actor Robert Mitchum, Dave Hickey writes that with Mitchum you get performance,[13] and performance, he says, not expressed (or represented) but delivered. The Mitchum effect relies on knowing something is back there but not being sure exactly what it is. Hickey says that what Mitchum does, then, is always surprising and plausible. And it is exactly this trait of surprising plausibility that might be adapted as a projective effect, one that combines the chance event with an expanded realism. There are two kinds of actors, Hickey argues. First are those who construct a character out of details and make you believe their character by constructing a narrative for them. One could say that this is the school of the "Method," where the actor provides gesture and motivation and supplies a subtext for the text of the script. The second group of actors create plausibility by their bodies; Hickey says they are not really acting but rather "performing with a vengeance." While Robert De Niro is an actor in the first category, Mitchum is in the second.

In the 1980s and 1990s, architecture's relationship to philosophy was like that of De Niro to his character. In other words, it fostered a kind of Method acting, or Method designing, where the architect expressed a text or where architecture represented its procedure of formation. As with the "critical project," Method acting was connected to psychoanalysis, to calling up and reenacting memories and past events. In contrast, Mitchum, Hickey says, is

> Like Coltrane, playing a standard . . . investing the text with his own subversive vision, his own pace and sense of dark contingency. So what we see in a Mitchum performance is less the character portrayed than a propositional alternative: What if someone with Mitchum's sensibility grew up to be a sea captain? A private eye? A school-teacher?[14]

In De Niro's acting, one witnesses the struggle not just within the character but between the actor and the character, such that the trace of the construction of the character is visible. There is no other way to say this except that when watching De Niro, it looks like work (think of the signature mugging and concentrated gestures). The opening scenes in both versions of *Cape Fear* are instructive in this regard. The 1991 remake begins with De Niro working out in prison, exercising or rehearsing, where the sweat rolling off his back is visible. In the original, Mitchum is in no rush: rakish, lascivious, enjoying a cigar and checking out two women as they leave the courthouse, cool as the breeze. He makes it look easy. So "De Niro architecture" is hot, difficult, and indexes the processes of its production: it is clearly labored, narrative, or representational or expresses a relationship of the representation to the real (the provision of a psychic subtext from a real event for a fictional text). In the remake, Mitchum has a cameo role as a detective, and as he is watching De Niro/Cady strip-searched, he sees his body covered with biblical proverbs and comments, with a degree of reproach (as much for the Method-acting

De Niro as the character Cady?): "I don't know whether to *look* at him or to *read* him." In contrast to this narrative mode, "Mitchum architecture" is cool, easy, and never looks like work; it is about mood or the inhabitation of alternative realities (what if? the virtual). Here, mood is the open-ended corollary of the cool, producing effect without high definition, providing room for maneuver, and promoting complicity with subject(s). With Mitchum, there are scenarios, not psychodramas. The unease and anxiety of the unhomely have been replaced with the propositional alternative of the untimely.

Within architecture, a project of delivering performance, or soliciting a surprising plausibility, suggests moving away from a critical architectural practice—one that is reflective, representational, and narrative—to a projective one. Setting out this projective program does not necessarily entail a capitulation to market forces but actually respects or reorganizes multiple economies, ecologies, information systems, and social groups.

2002

Notes

1. See the collection of essays *Architecture of the Everyday*, edited by Deborah Berke and Steven Harris (New York: Princeton Architectural Press, 1997).

2. Formulating their own critical positions, both Hays and Eisenman misread Rowe and Tafuri, according to Harold Bloom's understanding of misreading as poetic influence: "Poetic influence—when it involves two strong, authentic poets—always proceeds by a misreading of the prior poet, an act of creative correction that is actually and necessarily a misinterpretation." Harold Bloom, *The Anxiety of Influence: A Theory of Poetry* (New York: Oxford University Press, 1973; 1997), 30.

3. Significantly, the "between" for Fried was a theatrical anathema that undermined Modernist specificity.

4. *Mediated* here refers both to Fredric Jameson's theorization of mediation as an active between—that is, as an engaged interaction between two subjects or between a subject and an object, rather than a passive between that operates as pure conciliation between two terms—and to Marshall McLuhan's understanding of mediation as mass media's translatable reproducibility.

5. "Repetition thus demonstrates how architecture can resist, rather than reflect, an external cultural reality." K. Michael Hays, "Between Culture and Form," *Perspecta* 21 (Cambridge: MIT Press, 1984), 27. Also see

Peter Eisenman, "Aspects of Modernism: Maison Dom-ino and the Self-Referential Sign," *Oppositions* 15/16 (Winter/Spring 1979).

6. Hays, "Between Culture and Form," 15.

7. Eisenman, "Aspects of Modernism," 128.

8. For more on this distinction, see Gilles Deleuze and Félix Guattari: "Diagrams must be distinguished from indexes, which are territorial signs, but also from icons, which pertain to reterritorialization, and from symbols, which pertain to relative or negative deterritorialization. Defined diagrammatically in this way, an abstract machine is neither an infrastructure that is determining in the last instance nor a transcendental idea that is determining in the supreme instance. Rather, it plays a piloting role. The diagrammatic or abstract machine does not function to represent, even something real, but rather constructs a real that is yet to come, a new type of reality." *A Thousand Plateaus: Capitalism and Schizophrenia* (Minneapolis: University of Minnesota Press, 1987), 142.

9. The Doppler effect was discovered by the Austrian mathematician and physicist Christian Doppler (1803–53).

10. Michel Foucault, *L'Archéologie du savoir* (Paris: Éditions Gallimard, 1969).

11. Yve-Alain Bois citing *Webster's* dictionary, "A Picturesque Stroll around Clara-Clara," in *Richard Serra,* ed. Hal Foster with Gordon Hughes (Cambridge: MIT Press, 2000), 65.

12. Ibid., 66.

13. Dave Hickey, "Mitchum Gets Out of Jail," *Art Issues* (September/October 1997): 10–13.

14. Ibid., 12.

3

Starck Speaks:
Politics, Pleasure, and Play
Philippe Starck

In October 1997, Philippe Starck received the first Design Excellence Award from the Harvard University Graduate School of Design. His informal talk on that occasion has been adapted here.

It's strange that you invited me, because I am not an architect. Some architects hate me, and they're right. I agree. I am nothing. And I don't try to be more than nothing. I just try to merit existing, which is, I think, enough.

In English there may be nothing to explain the word *citoyen*. Citoyen is a very French concept. Citoyen is somebody who is deeply conscious of his responsibility in his world. I just try to do that. I am lazy, but I do what I can. I can do small things, like pens—no wait, I do something very well—I have a terrific nap every day. And in having this nap, which can go from one minute to three hours, sometimes it's boring—that's why you have to dream, and because I am not very intelligent, I don't dream about a new society, world, door, or window. . . . I dream about chairs and toothbrushes.

Through that, I try to exist. You must understand why. When I was young, I was better than today, a little more skinny, a nice guy, good family, good sports car—everything. And I had a problem *relationnel*,

34

a problem with other people. The girls didn't look at me, and it was a little difficult at seventeen, and I became a little schizophrenic. I spent a long time in my room, thinking, "My God, what must I do to exist?" And I remember my father, who was an airplane engineer, and he told me the only "clean" work is to find an idea yourself, and do it so that you don't take the work of somebody else. I remember a movie, *The Invisible Man*—you could see this invisible man when he put the white cloth strips around himself. And suddenly I had a flash: I must be like him. Nobody sees me, especially girls. But if I produce something, perhaps I shall exist and people will see me. And that's why after almost thirty years of work, I am like a Christmas tree because I've designed so many Christmas gifts. And what you see is not a designer or an architect but just a Christmas gift producer. That's life.

So how does somebody like that live? The life is very important, more important than the work. I live alone, almost. Last week I was in my office in Paris, a very small office with my small tribe of five, six people. It was the first time I was in my office for five months. I always spend my time in a collection of desert islands, where I am alone with my wife, with my new baby, sometimes with a few of the tribe who visit us. We live alone, alone, alone. I live like a monk. Either in the middle of a forest, or in the middle of the mud in my oyster farm, or in the middle of the sea, but alone. Why tell you that? Because if you want to make something a little personal, if you want to exist by yourself, it is very interesting to be always alone with yourself. Every morning I try to wake up at six o'clock—that means ten o'clock. And I go directly to my desk, and I put on very, very good music very loud. And I am in from the sea and alone like a beaver, and I do what I can do. It's not work, it's playing, playing with a project. Playing *alone* is very important, because the sort of work we see now is so trendy. A lot of young people think it's fashionable to be a designer or architect. You go to a cocktail party, and people say, "You are an architect at Harvard. Wow!" "You are a fashion designer in St. Martin's school! Wow!"

I go to bed after working. No cocktail. No reading *Domus, Wallpaper,* Rousseau, or anything else. It's working by yourself to find what you can do with your own tools to help your friends, your brothers, your society, your civilization. And to find how you can bring happiness and pleasure. The real honesty is to be always out of the trend, out of the mainstream. If you make things like everybody does, why do it? You must have your own responsibility, your own consciousness.

Now that is very serious, but now I can show you the bullshit I produce with this dutiful idea. I will show you less than 20 percent and explain why these things exist.

Alors. The Nani Nani (1989) is something strange. It's the first building I did. I'm sorry to show something so ugly in this famous architecture school. When somebody asked me to make a building in Tokyo, I was very happy. And I said, "But what can I do for these people, because they have Arato Isozaki, Shiro Kuramata, and others. They do beautiful work, and what can I do?" And I remembered something: I work only with intuition. I have the intuition that perhaps we can find a language, a common ground between them and us, using a symbolic monster. Remember Godzilla? Godzilla was the symbol of the atomic bomb; the Japanese people work only in symbols like that. That's why I think they like monsters. "OK, I shall make for them a monster." And I commit "nani nani"—the scream that the Japanese make when they meet a ghost. They scream "Naniii! Naniiii!" And I was waiting for people to do the same thing in the street when they saw my building.

The Nani Nani is just design. And if I am just making beautiful design, I definitely prefer a nap. You know, the idea is to make something special, to make an emotion, what I call "the fertile surprise." But it's very difficult to build in Tokyo, because space is scarce and because there are so many rules. So this building is strictly, purely functional. Some people said I was functionalist because—oooooo!—I made everything square. No. The Bauhaus was seventy years ago, and now there is a new way to be a functionalist with a lot of other parameters. When you are an architect, you will have dreams, and sometimes your dreams will be futile because nobody will pay for them. People say, "My god, your building is too costly—are you crazy?" When a developer tells you that, if you say, "I shall pay for it myself," then it's very easy. I have paid for all the buildings I designed. But I am not rich enough. That's why I made a strong image in Tokyo, so when the developer shows it in the magazines, everybody wants it. Or people want to spend money to be in this incredible building. A very easy way to pay for your dream in architecture is to make something that helps people find their image; then they create the money to build it.

The Asahi Beer Hall (1990) was made for the Asahi group in

Nani Nani, Tokyo, Japan, 1989. Courtesy of Philippe Starck.

Tokyo. It's big, 100 meters. It's mainly symbolic. As with everything, I am always not happy with what I do, and I come back to the bridge here, and I was crying a little, and a good friend from Mexico sees me very down and asks me, "Why do you cry?" I say, "Because it's an enormous bullshit." And he said, "No, no, . . . well, perhaps . . .

I cannot decide, but return and you will see." With something like this, either you hate it or you love it, but you must react. The worst thing is not reacting. Seriously, I don't know even today if it's really bullshit. But I know it's in a very poor area in Tokyo, and the people there are really proud of it—they have given it the name of a god, and I love this idea—that's why it's "The God Bullshit." And that's why you should never be afraid. Today this building is on the cover of the *Tokyo Guide*—it's a sign. Make what you feel, make what you want. Be free, and afterward society will decide; the city and society are self-cleaning: all the things they don't like will disappear. That's why you can make errors and take risks.

The Moondog (1990) we are building in Tokyo now. Somebody asked me to make a building for a bachelor. That's a strange Japanese idea—why make a building for a bachelor? OK, that's why I said, "Why not?" And, "What can I do for Japanese businessmen? They wake up, they go down the corridor, take the elevator, go into the street, go through the suburb, go into the office [Starck traces a path around the auditorium walls with a laser pointer]. Oooohhhhh, it's a *long* way in Japan. It's not very funny. And there is a sickness very known in Japan: people don't go back home; they sleep under their desks. That's why what I can do for them is to give them land. And that's why my bachelor, when he comes back from the office, walks on his own land. And suddenly he finds where he lives. There is a window.

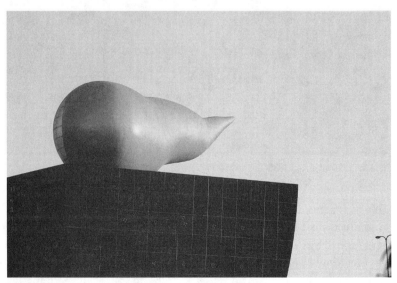

Asahi Beer Hall, Tokyo, Japan, 1990. Courtesy of Philippe Starck.

Bachelors, it's terrible to be alone; I cannot imagine that. I must help them to not stay bachelors. That's why I make this big room, so they can party, invite girls, and not stay bachelors. And I make this strange design, like old science fiction, bad utopia. Because in Tokyo, it's difficult to invite somebody—"Oh, perhaps we could have a blast tonight." "Yes, yes, yes, and with pleasure." "Where do you live?" "I live, I live, uh . . . at number 10,023, but there is no number, and it is between the gray building and the gray building. It's impossible to find." So people don't come to your house to have a drink. That's why I make it so: "Where do you live?" "I live in the strange building with big stairs and a rocket on top." "Oh, I'll see you tonight."

The Starck House (3 Suisses) (1994) is the best architecture I ever made, definitely the most advanced architecture. It doesn't look like something by Jean Nouvel or Zaha Hadid—it looks a little classic for the most advanced prototype of the modern house. This is because sometimes the modernity is not in the design but somewhere else, and it's in the "somewhere else" that it's interesting. Lots of good architects make lots of beautiful architecture. You can call them—they all have money problems, so they will be very happy to work for you. But a lot of these good architects will design only a big thing, beautiful and costly. But now, especially in Europe, you can buy a house that costs $100,000 that looks like bullshit. And a young couple will work all their lives to pay for this bullshit. Retired people will have

Starck House (3 Suisses), Rambouillet Forest, France, 1994. Courtesy of Philippe Starck. Photograph by Jacques Dirand.

worked all their lives to pay for this bullshit. That's why I have to find a way to say, "OK, every twenty minutes people buy a house like that at $100,000 with 1,500 square feet. Abomination."

And I said, "OK, I shall take the same budget, the same measurement, the same program, and I shall show that there can be something else." In the United States and in France you can make a cheap wood house with a strong image. This was intended to be the best design you can get by mail order; it was a solution to oblige the big companies to change their designs. This design caused a big scandal in Europe. I received pressure to not do it. That's why this house is not architecture but political action, not about architecture but about people. Now I am only interested in doing something like that. The main idea was just to make it different and more honest and more human than the bullshit they sell every twenty minutes. When you have a good idea, try in all ways to make the best things for the most people possible. If you succeed, that means the idea was good. Popular is elegant, and rare is vulgar.

The Bo Boolo table (1995) is more interesting for its history than as an object. Every seven years in Europe, there is a fad for wood that is supposed to be an ecology fad—they cut more and more wood "for ecological reasons," which is deeply stupid. That's why I made this table with the National Office of Forests, and said to people, "OK, once more you will see this picture in a mail order catalog," and you will say, "Oh, what a nice table—so chic." And you will pay for it, but you will receive just the top and the legs. "Oh, something's missing!" But you get a map of France, and on it is a letter that says you will receive the final piece of the table when you go with your map to this forest with an ax. You will have a discussion about the forest with the warden, and he will give you this branch. Then you go back home, and you will have your table. And it's interesting because people want wood, but they don't know what wood is, they don't know what a forest is, they don't know you have to get wood by cutting down trees. So they come back with a real piece of nature, and now they know.

OK, the Louis XX Chair (1992). I shall give you a history of my plastic chairs. You will see a good product, but the main idea is again not the product. I don't know if in the United States you have this disaster of a white chair that costs $5 and is sold along the road, and some terrible producer made this bullshit in millions. In Europe it's a disaster; it's like rats everywhere. And when I see that, I think,

"OK, I am in design. I must react. This chair is my problem." So I went to see my producers, and I said, "We produce good chairs that cost $700 or more in France. But why would people spend $600 for a chair when they can buy a chair for $5?" You can sit on the cheaper chair, it's comfortable, it's OK. I said, "We must now produce good products, the best we can, for everybody, and kill this product. To kill it we must produce it for $5." And they said, "Are you crazy?!" "Yes. Yes, we have no choice." "Nooooo!!! It's impossible." "We shall see."

Bon, the café chair, Dr. Glob (1990), at first cost $700, and I said, "I shall produce one nice, in plastic and metal, that will cost something like $300. Hup! Less money and big success." The producers come back and say, "Whoa, Philippe, do you remember your success with this café chair? Twenty thousand pieces per year, your biggest success. But can you make a new one that will be something like 100,000 per year?" "Yes, yes." That's why the year after, I produced this Louis XX Chair, with the blue molding, and it cost 30 percent less. Huge success. So, "Hey, Philippe, next year we can make another . . . ?" "Yes! No problem, I have time. I am vicious." And the year after, we produce Lord Yo (1994), which cost $140. Hooph. Huge success. Millions. Revolution of the market. And the producer says, "We want a plastic chair." Success. No design, comfortable, good looking, a variety of colors, good quality, very good product. But cheaper. "You do more?" "Yes. No problem." That's why the year after I produced Miss Trip (1996). Miss Trip was made to cost less and use wood, because everybody wanted wood. No problem. This cost $100. Success. One more. Dr. No (1996). Dr. No cost $80. Huge success. The factory must make four molds that operate night and day. They make a lot of money. But the chair we are fighting against cost $5, and this $80. There is a $75 difference. OK, we continue. The Prince Aha (1996) was designed four years ago. After this, a small stool, a sort of Brancusi in plastic, that cost $18. Success. Oh, perfect; we continue! And after the last chair, Cheap Chic (1997), that cost something like $50. Big success. And now we prepare for the next Milano exhibition with a chair that costs $40 and one that will cost $20. We are almost done. In ten years, I have cut the price of the object in half every two years. [Whistles.] The job was not to design the chairs. The job was to give a good product, an honest product, of high quality, something a little more, a better design, more poetic, for the price of the other bullshit, so that people can choose.

The Light Lite (1992) is interesting, because I did the same thing for the lamp as for the chair. One time I opened a box that my producer sent me, a box that held a lamp—"Wow, beautiful lamp." And then I saw the box, and it was beautiful and very interesting because it produced a vacuum that protected its contents. I called my producer and said, "What is the price of the box?. . . Wow, so costly! But perhaps we can design the lamp with the machine that produces the box, and thus we can lower the price." And he said, "It's impossible, my factory . . ." I said, "OK, OK, OK . . . we'll install a tent in the parking area. I'll take the machine that makes the vacuum. I'll design a collection of lamps using the machine." And the lamps cost the price of the box, and there is no box! And again, the work was about how to attack the problem freshly.

The Miss Sissi (1990) was a new beginning for me. It's what I call "low design." "Low design" is now a trend. This is why I *now* speak about the No Design and the No Product. You must always be in advance. You know the Tizio?—a beautiful black lamp. There are three thousand copies of that. And it's very intelligent . . . but what if you are sick of that lamp? I said, "Perhaps we can think about a schematic lamp. There is a game you play in the street when you are a child. You ask anybody, "Hey, name a color." And they always say, "red." "Name a tool." They say, "hammer." "Name a musical instrument." "A trumpet." "Name an animal." They always say, "a lion." And I think, "What is a lamp?" And I think, "a shade and a foot." I produced what everybody thinks in their unconscious a lamp is. It's interesting that it has been incredibly successful. Strangely, this was the most modern lamp you could design. It's more modern today to design this than to think for years about the most sophisticated, complicated lamp. You produce it in plastic with the best company, and you do it cheap, and it's OK.

Here is an Olympic Flame (1992). You remember Jean-Claude Killy, famous ski champion and president of the Olympic Games? He called me and said, "Philippe, do you want to make the torch for the Olympic Games?" I said, "You must be kidding—me with sports? I'm sorry, but no." "Yes, yes, yes, you will do it." And with me, when somebody says you must do it, I always do it. So I buy some books on the Olympics, and what I discover is terrible. The Olympic Games were supported by the Nazis, by the military. And I called Jean-Claude and said, "I cannot do it." He says, "You will find some way out." That's why I thought I had to find something that gives the idea but without all these terrible associations. I must speak of sports—somebody wants to use passion and energy and be victorious. OK, no problem. We shall buy a container of gas, and we shall put the hand of the athlete over the gas flame. . . . He will run faster. It was perfect, minimalist, elegant, inexpensive. But strangely they don't accept the idea. So I designed this simple thing, which is just the continuation of the arm, in organic harmony, just the person with his passion, without all the terrible Nazi competition. And reading the newspapers somebody says, "I ran with the Starck torch, and it was magic."

The boat, the First 41 S5 Volier L Coque (1989; exterior and interior), is for Beneteau, a big French company. When Mme. Beneteau asked me to design a boat, I came up with something very strange, a little "retro." And she writes, "Oh, Philippe, it's not new." I say, "Yes, I know, but do you think you need something new for a boat? You need new technology, but basically you need something that expresses the main dream about the boat." This boat is not a space lab—it's more organic, it's white, it looks as if it's fifteen years older than it was. Sometimes the modernity can look older than you expect, because it is not the problem to find where the modernity is. The problem is to find where the right action is, the right product for the happiness of people.

This is pasta, called Mandala (1987). Twenty years ago I was so naive. Panzani asked me to design a pasta. I was so happy because I'm very interested in things close to humans. I said, "OK, what can I do with pasta? Why do we love pasta? When do we love pasta? We love pasta when we are children, when we are sick, when we are stoned—ah!—or when we are old—in other words, when we are a bit regressed. But sometimes when you eat pasta, you become fat. Perhaps the thing I can do is to give the same pleasure, with a good mouthful of pasta, but without making people fat. How I can make a pasta that will be 10 percent pasta and 90 percent air? If you make a tube, you have 90 percent air, but when it's cooked, it collapses." That's why I thought of a spring that makes the pasta stay open. And because American and French people always overcook pasta, I made two wings that have a double thickness, so that when you overcook it, 80 percent of the pasta is still al dente. I asked a doctor, "What is in pasta?" and he said, "It's a perfectly well-balanced food." "Well-balanced: yin-yang! Perfect, that can be the spring!" This shows you that even in something small, everything can be functional. If you just make a nice design, it's nothing.

The Juicy Salif lemon squeezer (1990–91) is the biggest success of all. Strange, because it's a difficult object. Now it's well-known, but when it wasn't, you thought, "What is this?" A lot of people told me, "This object is stupid because electric *zinzinzin* costs half and works better . . . " "Yes it's true. There are one hundred electric things that work better. But sometimes you must choose why you design—in this case not to squeeze lemon, even though as a lemon squeezer it works. Sometimes you need some more humble service: on a certain night, the young couple, just married, invites the parents of the groom to dinner, and the groom and his father go to watch football on TV. And for the first time the mother of the groom and the young bride are in the kitchen, and there is a sort of malaise—this squeezer is made to start the conversation.

The Scooter Lama (1992) is the prototype of a motor scooter. When a company called me to design a scooter, I was happy because I drive only motorcycles—I have thirty-two. For me it was a dream. But I saw immediately a problem, because in Europe, scooters are mainly used by teenagers to go to school. The problem is that some stupid designer designed them like weapons: black like the moped of Batman, and that was especially stupid because at the time there was war in Yugoslavia. I said, "Why design weapons when a moped is just a very convenient, practical, nice object?" And I was sad when I saw that the guy who is lucky enough to have a moped was just saying, "Look, I have a bigger dick than yours." That's why I made my scooter a sex object. To exist, the object must have sexuality, or you don't have relations with it. The problem is that today, 100 percent of objects with engines have male sexuality; more than that, they are ridiculously, stupidly macho. Perhaps the macho look can be interesting if you want to fight dinosaurs. But *now* to survive, you need intelligence, not power and aggression. Modern intelligence means intuition—it's female. Products like this must follow the female intelligence. I've tried to work on that. This scooter doesn't look like a female, but it doesn't look like a dick either. It's just a simple animal with a soft skin and ears that are red because the winter is cold.

The Moto Aprilia 6, 5 (1995) is a motorcycle, definitely more male, but a lot less so than the terrible products on the market. The real problem is not sex for the motorcycle but marketing. The mar-

Scooter Lama, 1992. Courtesy of Philippe Starck.

keting sells to a fake person—"Buy a Harley-Davidson, and you will be a biker. Buy a Paris-Dakar, and you will be Thierry Sabine of Paris-Dakar." And it's terrible to buy a personality. It's especially terrible with a motorcycle, because a motorcycle is so intelligent, so minimalist—wheels, tank, engine, seat, *basta*. My design is just to say, "With this, you are yourself, not a fake Hell's Angel."

So, Della Valle shoe prototype (1996). This shoe, but better, will be on the market soon. This original model is just to say to Nike and Reebok almost the same thing as we said about the motorcycle: "Why must we be clowns? When you have Nike with the light flashing, you are not yourself; you are a clown." That's why, with the Italian company Superior, we developed a shoe that is more technical, but, in the spirit of the third millennium, not technical in look— the technical is hidden, discreet. We become the master of the technology, not its slave.

The Toothbrush (1989) is one of my best products, because, before, we were a bit ashamed of our ugly toothbrushes and put them in our drawers. When you make the toothbrush in this shape, suddenly millions of people want to get them for Christmas and are no longer ashamed.

The Mikli Eyeglasses (1996) are sunglasses; they are the prototype of modern products for many reasons. First, there is no name brand on the outside of the temples, no Chanel, no Gucci—the name is hidden on the inside. It's important because today people are not Mr. Smith but Mr. Gucci or Mr. Cardin. These glasses have no style, no gold, no fake Ray-Ban, because we need the minimum—we aren't interested in the glasses but in the person who wears the glasses. And on the temple piece is a chef d'oeuvre of microprocessing—a tiny human clavicle. We spent four years and something like $8 million to make this. We have created a new drug—when you wear this, it's so friendly, so in harmony, because the idea of the *bio-mechanique*. You are *bio-mechanique*.

The Toto car (1996) never existed, because when I proposed it to a big company, they said, "We love the concept, but we'll do it better." The main idea is not to make the power/sex car again—vroom, vroom. It's stupid. People say, "Look at my sports car! Ooooh!" Today, cars are just symbols of disgusting aggressivity and money. That's why Toto is the simplest car you can have. It's flat and small. The next Toto we design will be for the new consumer of the third millennium. The Toto costs nothing and just does its job of transporting people. Its only symbol is the symbol of "No," which means, "No, I'm not a consumer."

You are students; you will invent the future. That's why you must say about everything I show you, "This is all bullshit. This man is

Toto car, 1996. Courtesy of Philippe Starck.

old and stupid. He must go back to bed, and we must break all his products and reinvent the world." You are very lucky. In three years you will have a very potent symbol, the third millennium. The media will love that. Perhaps some people will say, "OK, it's time to make a sort of audit of our lives and propose new things. We must go into the third millennium like real citoyens with clean feet. To have clean feet, we must work now. I am not a philosopher; I am not a politician; I am not a socioeconomist. I work with little things. That's why I am trying to describe, through this stuff, what this citoyen must be. That is my theme. And I shall show what you must refuse—a lot—and what you don't need. And today I work a lot, with something like 220 projects at the same time, to arrive in the new millennium. But you can say, "Okay, Starck, I think the projects for this citoyen are okay. Everything you say is true. I don't need all this bullshit."

I have created an organic food company. I think to be a clean citoyen, you must first stop killing. It's incredible today that we continue to kill for food. We don't need to. Become vegetarian. When we say, "Become vegetarian," everybody says, "Aaaaah, my steak, my beef, my veal!" And you cannot say, "Become vegetarian"—it's taboo; it sounds goody-goody, altruistic, ethereal. You must have the inverse strategy and find something to appeal to people's selfishness, so you say "You *eat* all this shit, this poison? But it's so bad for you!"

But if you are responsible, if your ears and eyes are open, you would see that the main problem is that love has died. Today, the idea of status has replaced the idea of love. Nobody understands that the idea of love is unique to our species. And because we invent this concept, we can destroy it, and today we destroy it. It's the only thing important in our civilization. That's why now all our work is not to design one chair, it's to design something that can build a new relation between people, and between people and products. That's the main urgency—to see what I can do to start this third millennium as a new, clean, lovely phase. The first tool you must have is politics, politics, politics, politics, action, politics, action, politics. Don't think about esoteric aesthetics. Don't think about money. Think politics, action, for people, for yourself. [Starck raises both hands, making peace signs.] Peace and love!

1998

4

P.S./P.C.: On "Starck Speaks"

K. Michael Hays

Ten minutes into Philippe Starck's performance, I met the eyes of Peter Rose, a comrade in socio-aesthetic sensitivity and ideological correctness, and we exchanged a glance to the effect that, "This is not what we had expected." Not only did Starck offer us in person the model of a middle-aged, slightly overweight, white, heterosexual man *with taste* (we had almost lost hope it was conceivable), he also was suggesting that we could be rigorous cultural producers, avid consumers of objects (I thought about Peter's BMW 535) and still stay on the political left. This was better than Rem Koolhaas's shopping research project (conducted last year at the Harvard University Graduate School of Design, which sought to analyze various techniques of consumption as possible new urban experiences). This was better than even Walter Benjamin (who saw commodities as wish images reaching for future redemption in some genuinely new society). A refunctioning of sixties politics—"peace and love": we baby boomers still warm at the invocation; and, after all, isn't an aesthetics of delirious pleasure a properly sixties experience?—was about to be vindicated over and against all the cynical claims for the relevance of fashion, and from within the fashion system itself. I swear I had a lump in my throat.

Politically correct design has usually been formulated in the twin terms of resistance to the status quo of consumerism and estrangement

Philippe Starck. Courtesy of Philippe Starck.

from the normative techniques of the design professions. The most obvious version is a therapeutic puritanism, a blunt refusal to be tempted by a fashionable product or idea. There are high-end versions that stress esoteric, theory-driven work, the sheer intellectual difficulty of which blocks easy consumption and instrumentalization for profit. There are grittier, of-the-people, for-the-people versions that sacrifice "good form" for social activism. There are more recent

versions that indulge in the oversaturated, disorienting, hallucina-
tory intensity of global culture and seek not to stabilize their effects
but rather accelerate them toward some horizon where they will turn
into an ecstatic, schizoid ethics of total difference. In every case, the
relationship of the desired practice of design to the present culture
has been understood to be one of necessary dissonance.

What Starck was implying, however, was not dissonance but a con-
vergence of mass marketing, good design, and social service. "That's
why this house is not architecture but political action, not about
architecture but about people," Starck claimed of his affordable
house. "The main idea was just to make it different and more honest
and more human than the bullshit they sell every twenty minutes."
What is more, on Starck's model, strong form—from toothbrushes
to hotels—is not an esoteric or elite withdrawal from the triviality
and chattering of the tasteless masses but a genuine enrichment of all
our paltry, flattened-out experiences and a redemptive retooling of
the very "system" that had impoverished our lives in the first place.
This was better theory than that of the theorists, since, for all our
complicated accounts of the free play of signifiers and the subversive
potential of decentered subjectivity, we had never figured out a way
to buy designer furniture *and* save the rain forest. Now for the first
time, it seemed, we didn't have to hide our Alessi lamps when our
leftist friends came to dinner.

Thinking back, I still have no doubt about Starck's sincerity. It
derives, I think, from the more complex relation to what we might
call "the serious," a subversive but also campy attitude that he must
remember from Paris, May '68 (*Sous le pavé, la plage,* or something
to the effect that you must beat them at their own game); it is the
hope of someone nurtured on popular culture, schooled on contradiction and paradox, and instilled with the belief that things can be
changed, that design is a *practice,* and as such can and must make a
difference.

But there is a soft underside to his critique of the commodity system. For in a culture totally determined by consumerism, the transgressive, the brush against the grain, and above all the politically correct are as consumable as anything else. The eco-humanism of The
Body Shop has famously made a chubby Barbie and not hurting the
eyes of lab rabbits into a global profit-churning enterprise. Vegetari-
ans and paper recyclers dutifully pay a premium at the Bread and Circus food chain store. Ever since Nike used the Beatles' "Revolution"

in their advertisements, the neo-sixties style, including its libertarian rhetoric, has become a topos of the commodity fetish. And, oh yes, remember when Doc Martens were thought of as a work shoe? The rebel consumer is above all else a consumer, and the lesson of all these examples is the same: the next marketing niche lies within the very domain of those who have most resisted the market.

What Starck calls "No Design" is no different. For the brilliance of No Design, from a marketing point of view, is that it has a double appeal, an attractiveness to two groups thought incompatible: the sixties generation and the Slackers. Writing about the latter's refusal of the culture of the former, an article from 1992 in *Commodify Your Dissent* (the recent collection of essays from *The Baffler* magazine) titled "Twenty-Nothing" asserted, "We are a generation that finally says NO to your favorite institutions." There it is, the heretofore unattainable degree zero of niche marketing: the niche of nothing. The NO of the Slackers meets the political correctness of the Boomers. Starck's "symbol of No—which means, 'No, I'm not a consumer'" is a perfectly systematic progression from an earlier progressivist call for a pluralist design for a pluralist culture, to the realization and acceptance that pluralism is a massive wish fulfillment insofar as we have no really substantial choice about what we consume ("you want to go to Starbucks or Starbucks?"), to the end-of-the-line gambit so perfected by Slackers of sacrificing your very identity so that *that* becomes your identity, and hence a niche. Anyone who has seen the Volkswagen advertisement with the smelly sofa and the Trio overdub ("da, da, da") will recognize the enormous commercial attraction of not having a life. "C'est donc moi, c'est donc à moi!" as Gilles Deleuze would say.

Oh well, kick off your Nikes, Peter, and crank up that Billy Bragg CD.

Perhaps none of this is surprising, and, in any case, not worth the hand-wringing. But my skepticism notwithstanding, Starck's performance has the advantage of reminding us once again that design must strive to exist in nonconformity with the world that is its sponsor and must strive for that constantly. But a model of nonconformity other than that of dissonance might emerge from his work. Commodification must be ingested by designers like a homeopathic pill that, in small doses, might just produce its own antidote. Against the whole-grain puritanism that is the Cantabridgians' Volvo 240, but also against the sheer *jouissance* that is the BMW, does Starck's Toto represent the way the consumption system produces new demands and new needs that subvert the system itself? I'm still not sure.

In any case, that Starck takes his poison with some relish should not be refused him. For I believe it evidences but one side of a bipolar disorder many of us suffer from, one side of the mood swings between exhilaration and contempt with regard to commercial culture. The desires and pleasures of things, images, and events, which we ingest, it sometimes seems, through almost mindless consumption—all these cannot, I suggest, be dismissed offhand. They are but a reaction-formation against what history has dealt us—a totally commodified and leveled-out life—and they are but one side of a demand for something different. *The other side may well be design itself.* For to design entails the hope that the act will somehow manage to scandalously exceed what the designer is given to work with, converting the very complicity of the act into a proposition about how we should live and a critique of how we have failed so far.

1998

5

No More Dreams?
The Passion for Reality in
Recent Dutch Architecture . . .
and Its Limitations

Roemer van Toorn

It was once not considered foolish to dream great dreams. Imagining a new, better world energized thinkers and spurred their resistance to the status quo. Now utopian dreams are rare. Instead of chasing after elusive ideals, we prefer to surf the turbulent waves of free-market global capitalism. In our wildly prosperous First World—brimful of computerized production, technological and genetic applications, and commercial and cultural entertainment—reality can seem more exciting than dreams. Some even maintain that the ideals we strove for in the past have now become reality. According to Third Way politics, the neoliberal economic engine simply needs a bit of fine-tuning; late capitalism is the only game in town. Although social rights and a measure of equality are needed, corporate globalism can only be accommodated.[1]

From the perspective of this free-market fundamentalism, utopian attempts to change society lead to dictatorships. Not only conservatives think this. Neo-Marxists Michael Hardt and Antonio Negri argue that the organization of resistance in the margins is no longer necessary now that resistance is active in the very heart of society.[2] They believe that late capitalism is so complex and dynamic that it is capable of switching automatically from an alienating equilibrium of control into a potentiality for multiple freedoms. Everything is changing much faster than we ever imagined it could. Until the 1980s, mainstream cultural institutions condemned the transgressive operations of the avant-garde, whereas today they support and favor transgressive works, because they gain publicity from scandal. Time and time again, global capitalism has shown itself capable of transforming its initial limitations into challenges that culminate in new investments. One important consequence of this is that earlier forms of social criticism and social engagement are outmoded. Thus, many reflective architects believe that it no longer makes any sense to spend time constructing new ideologies or criticizing "the system." Instead, they draw inspiration from the perpetual mutations of late capitalism.[3]

During a symposium on "The State of Architecture at the Beginning of the Twenty-first Century" held at Columbia University, Sylvia Lavin, chair of the UCLA graduate department of architecture, uttered the provocation that architecture ceases to be "cool" when it clings to the critical tradition.[4] Nor is hers a lone voice; a whole cohort of American commentators is anxious to move beyond critical architecture.[5] One form of critical architecture—exemplified by the work of Peter Eisenman, Daniel Libeskind, Diller + Scofidio, and Bernard Tschumi—offers comments within architectural-social discourse and avoids looking for better alternatives in reality. The Frank House by Eisenman, for example, forces the couple living in it to think about the psychology of their cohabitation by placing a slot in the floor between their beds. Robert Somol and Sarah Whiting have argued provocatively that we should stop burning our fingers on this kind of "hot" architecture that insists on confrontations. Whiting and Somol discourage an architecture born out of pain or the need to sabotage norms. Instead, architects should initiate "projective" practices that are "cool."[6] (Why the word *projective*? "Because it includes the term *project*—that is, it is more about an approach, a strategy, than a product; it looks forward (projects), unlike criticality, which always looks backwards," according to Sarah Whiting in an e-mail.)

While Whiting and Somol focus foremost on American critical architecture that has been valorized by theories of deconstruction, Critical Regionalism in Europe, Asia, and Australia—exemplified by the works of Tadao Ando, Herman Hertzberger, Alvaro Siza, and Glenn Murcutt—tries, out of disgust with contemporary society, to overcome estrangement, commodification, and the destruction of nature.[7] Critical Regionalism does not strive to make difficult or playful comments on society but to invest in alternative spaces far from the wild city of late capitalism. It hopes to locate moments of authenticity—to calm the mind and the body—in order to survive in our runaway world. While critical architecture deconstructs the discourse of architecture, demystifies the status quo, and/or locates alternative worlds in the margin, it believes that constructing liberating realities in the center of society is impossible.

In contrast to both deconstruction and Critical Regionalism, Whiting and Somol's proposed "projective practices" aim to engage realities found in specific local contexts. Instead of hanging ideological prejudices (derived from utopian dreams or from criticism) on built form, the architectural project, in their view, must be rendered capable of functioning interactively. With a projective practice the distancing of critical theory is replaced by a curatorial attitude. This new paradigm in architecture, to paraphrase Dutch writer Harm Tilman, presupposes a continuous focus on the method (the "how") that leaves the "what" and the "why" undefined.[8] By systematically researching reality as found with the help of diagrams and other analytical measures, all kinds of latent beauties, forces, and possibilities can, projective architects maintain, be brought to the surface.[9]

These found realities are not only activated by the projective project but also, where possible, idealized. If all goes well in the realization of a projective design, the intelligent extrapolation of data, the deployment of an aesthetic sensibility, the transformation of the program, and the correct technology may activate utopian moments. But the utopianism is opportunistic, not centrally motivating.

Whereas projective projects are chiefly discussed in the United States, architects in the Netherlands, in other European countries, and in Asia have for some time pursued them in practice. Before we look at some examples, we must pause to consider the nature and failure of its predecessor, critical architecture. On the one hand, projective practice is inspired by personal and strategic motives. After all, if you want to succeed in a new generation, it is a good idea to contrast your own position with that of the preceding generation. On the other hand, the critical tradition has itself handed projective architecture the arguments against dreaming totalizing dreams, against designing speculative systems that offer a comprehensive picture of what reality should be.

Disenchantment

Between the end of the Second World War and the beginning of the 1970s, many architects came to the conclusion that Modern architecture, rather than fostering emancipation, encouraged repression and manipulation.[10] The depressing discovery that hopeful dreams can end in nightmares prompted prominent members of the architectural community—Kenneth Frampton, Manfredo Tafuri, Aldo Rossi, and Aldo van Eyck, among others—to mount a recalcitrant opposition to the commercial and populist city. They believed that instead of being a prisoner of modernity, architecture should mount continuous opposition to capitalist society. Quite apart from the fact that it operates in the margins of society and is often reserved for the elite, the creativity of critical architecture depends on dealing with the very things it finds repugnant.

As Theodor Adorno remarked, "Beauty today can have no other measure except the depth to which a work resolves contradictions. A work must cut through the contradictions and overcome them, not by covering them up, but by pursuing them."[11] The void in the Jewish Museum by Daniel Libeskind in Berlin memorializing the Holocaust is an example of the beauty Theodor Adorno is after. The horror of Fascism as a dark shadow of disaster present in this void gives the museum its symbolic meaning. Jean Nouvel avoids critique through the creation of symbolic meaning conveyed obliquely through form. Nouvel wants to break the enchantment of our mediatic world with a strong and strange presence that leads to a kind of seductive contemplation. His objects are unidentifiable, inconsumable, strange. This uncanny architecture must be developed, according to social theorist Jean Baudrillard, to reach the inexplicable, a reality so ineffable that it can counteract the oversignification of everything in our culture of transient junk images.[12] The alien language of Nouvel's architecture has the aura of nothingness, or, in the words of Paul Virilio, of a mute and silent space in radical opposition to the surfeit of our design culture. Instead of the negation of our broad cultural situation found in the work of Daniel Libeskind or Jean Nouvel, Diller + Scofidio, as analyzed by Michael Hays, "produce a kind of inventory of suspicion. They capture the salient elements of a given situation 'or problem,' register them, and slow down the processes that motivate them long enough to make the working perceptible, just before the whole thing again slips back into the cultural norm, beyond our critical grasp."[13]

Critical Regionalism, another form of critique, is a reaction against the rootlessness of modern urban life. It seeks durable values in opposition to our culture of mobility (it is no coincidence that Critical Regionalists see the car as a horror). Critical Regionalism locates its resistance in topography, anthropology, tectonics, and local light. It does not look for confrontation, as do Eisenman, Libeskind, Nouvel, and Diller + Scofidio, but is critical in its withdrawal from urban culture, and in its self-questioning and self-evaluating. According to Alexander Tzonis and Liane Lefaivre, its place-defining elements have to create a distance, have to be difficult, and should even be disturbing to overcome the regional illusions of the familiar, the romantic, and the popular.[14] Critical architecture supposedly does not compromise itself, since it tries to dismantle or distance itself from the logic that leads to exploitation. Yet, because of its constant need to unmask the forces to which it is opposed, it is condemned to engage with the scenes that threaten its effectiveness. As such, critical architecture is more reactive than proactive.

Critical architecture in general rests on a self-affirming system of theoretical and ideological convictions: "Look at me! I'm critical! Read me!" Somol and Whiting rightly remark that critical architecture proceeds from a preconceived legibility.[15] It is an architecture that brooks no alternative interpretations. Unless the critical theory and vision are legible in the object, the object fails. Critical architecture is opposed to the normative and anonymous conditions of the production process and dedicated to the production of difference. Criticism reveals the true face of repressive forces, and this view of power is supposed to promote political awareness. Criticism is critical architects' only hope. Much of this criticism is concentrated in formalist and deconstructive theory and has a textual and linguistic bias. Other critical positions, such as those of Van Eyck and the early Hertzberger, and of Critical Regionalism, try to create alternative worlds, "utopian islands" floating in seas of anonymity and destruction.

Although I have much sympathy for Critical Regionalism, it is too nostalgic for a lost, mainly rural landscape, too comfortable and marginal, too much in love with architecture (rather than the life that architecture can help script). Preferable, it seems to me, are works that operate with and within society at large and that set a collective and public agenda in direct communication with modernization. The victimology of critical theory leaves no room for plausible readings capable of completing a project in the mundane context of the everyday (including that of alienation and commodification). Estrangement must not be thought of as something to overcome but as a position from within which new horizons can open. Although the urban, capitalist, and modern everyday is pushing toward increased homogeneity in daily life, the irreconcilable disjunctions born in a postindustrial city full of anachronistic interstices make it impossible to think of modernization as only negative. Michel de Certeau's work confirmed the impossibility of a full colonization of everyday life by late capitalism and stressed that potential alternatives are always available, since individuals and institutions array resources and choose methods through particular creative arrangements. Often critical experts and intellectuals prefer to think of themselves as outside everyday life. Convinced that it is corrupt, they attempt to evade it. They use rhetorical language, meta-language, or autonomous language—to paraphrase Henri Lefebvre—as permanent substitutes for experience, allowing them to ignore the mediocrity of their own condition. Critical practices reject and react unsubtly to the positive things that have been achieved in contemporary society, such as the vitality of much popular culture, including its hedonism, luxury, and laughter.

After Critique

Instead of assailing reality with a priori positions or resistance, as critical architecture does, projective practices analyze the facts and, in the process of creation, make micro-decisions capable of transforming a project in concrete and surprising ways. The architect waits and sees in the process of creation where information leads him or her. As Michael Rock recently remarked,

> Much of the strange shapes of recent Dutch architecture can be attributed to the devotion to the diagram, and the authorial absolution it grants. By taking traditional Dutch pragmatism to absurd, deadpan extremes, the designer generates new, wholly unexpected forms. Some of Droog Design embodies this absurdist-hyperrationalism. The designer simply continues to apply the system until the form appears in all its strangeness. Dutch design seems intent on erasing the sense that any designer imposed any subjectivity.[16]

The touchstone here is not subjective vision but an addiction to extreme realism, a realism that is intended to show no theoretical or political mediation, a kind of degree zero of the political, without thought about the consequences of the social construction it would lead to in reality. The extreme realities the projective is obliged to confront are the cyborg; the information society; the global migration of money, people, and imagination; shopping; fashion; media; leisure; and the coincidence of the enormous effectiveness and absolute abstraction of digitization. In other words, this practice brings to its extreme the consequences of the processes of commodification, alienation, and estrangement that constitute the contemporary motor of modernity.

For projective practices, dreaming is no longer necessary, since even our wildest dreams are incapable of predicting how inspiring, chaotic, liberating, and dynamic reality can be. The intelligence a project is able to embody in negotiation with reality is what matters. According to the proponents of projective practices, involvement, even complicity with given conditions, rather than aloofness, is more productive than dreaming of a new world. Projective practices respect and reorganize the diverse economies, ecologies, information systems, and social groups present during the process of creation. Projective architecture also promotes a return to the discipline in a pragmatic and technical approach that takes account of the interdisciplinary influences that play a role in the realization of projects. Central to projective practice is the question of what architecture is able to express as material reality. The paternalistic "we know best" attitude that has long hindered critical architecture is a thing of the past. And architecture is allowed to be beautiful without any tortured worrying over accompanying dangers of superficiality or slickness.[17] We no longer have to say "sorry," according to Somol.[18] Often projective architects, like Foreign Office Architects, have no idea what they seek except apolitical architectural knowledge driven by technology and instrumentality. Others speak about beauty (the theme of the 2007 Documenta exhibition in Kassel), technical knowledge, and in some cases bottom-up self-organizing systems.[19]

The question now is what projective practices can affect in actuality. From my perspective, they come in three basic types in many recently realized projects in the Netherlands, types that display "projective autonomy," "projective mise-en-scène," and "projective naturalization." As we shall see, projective autonomy confines itself primarily to models of geometry. Projective mise-en-scène and projective naturalization, by contrast, experiment with architecture as infrastructure. Projective autonomy tries to restore contact with the user and the contemplator through passive experience, while projective mise-en-scène and projective naturalization seek interaction. While projective autonomy is interested in form—what the aesthetic by its own means is able to communicate—the projective mise-en-scène seeks the creation of theatrical situations, and projective naturalization seeks strictly instrumental and operational systems.

In the practices in the Netherlands I am about to discuss, architects are not theorizing their work as "projective"; rather they are practicing and making in ways that fit the projective concept.

Projective Autonomy

The architecture of Claus & Kaan, Rapp + Rapp, and Neutelings Riedijk reveals what I am calling "projective autonomy." The meticulously crafted forms (a return to the discipline) characteristic of their projective strategy offer comfort and reassurance. Projective autonomy revolves around the self-sufficiency of tasteful, subdued form, which, notwithstanding the vicissitudes of life or passing dreams, is in theory capable of enduring for centuries. In many cases it appears as a modest architecture that combines functional, economic, and representational requirements in an efficient, aesthetic, and sustainable manner. The preference for tranquility and harmony, for aloofness from change, means that in projective autonomy we are dealing with a conventional or limited projective practice. Projective autonomy is not concerned with movement, complexity, or any of the other dynamic processes that can be used to legitimize projects, but with relatively stable cultural and economic values.

Rapp + Rapp work with received architectural language, with the internal structure of architectural typologies as the residuum of the historical and the contemporary city, very much in the spirit of the early, less figurative work of Aldo Rossi, Hans Kollhoff, and Colin Rowe. Thus, the foyer in Amsterdam's Bos en Lommer district is a variation of the classic atrium typology. For Claus & Kaan, the organizing principle is not historical typology but the typographic autonomy of a building—I am referring not so much to the architects' fondness for letters and numbers as to the way they "interspace" the building, to the rhythm of thick and thin spaces by which the individual elements, from the smallest detail to the entire volume, are ordered. Just as the typographer selects his typeface and searches for the most appropriate spacing, so Claus & Kaan deal in a craftsmanly and repetitive manner with windows, columns, doors, facade panels, and volumes. They pursue a conventional architecture that inspires confidence and eschews controversy, that is about mass, boxy volumes, light, beauty, and style.[20] Radical chic and subversion are definitely not goals for them, but their buildings do possess some minimalist chic. The abstract language and meticulous detailing lend their buildings a self-satisfied, stylish gloss. The floating black bar with its sleek banded pattern in the main facade of the Municipal Offices in Breda reveals a certain kinship with the elegant profiling of Bang & Olufsen design. Minimal chic glosses over vulgarities with its abstract perfection.

While the buildings of Rapp + Rapp and of Claus & Kaan behave decorously and seriously, fun is given plenty of running room in the work of Neutelings Riedijk. No puritanical architecture for them but instead good strong shapes that tell a story. Architecture, like television, comics, and other manifestations of popular visual culture, must communicate with the public. In the case of Neutelings Riedijk it is once again possible to speak of "buildings with character." Neutelings Riedijk strive for dramatic effects that offer the viewer an "everyday architectural surrealism."[21] Their buildings are dramatis personae that have stepped into our carpet metropolis, turning their heads to survey their surroundings. Buildings in the landscape become part of the theater of life, although the leading player here is not the user but the architecture.

Neutelings Riedijk are interested not in life itself but in the autonomy of the decor against which it is played out. Their buildings may be brooding, robust, humorous, even bizarre. A critical architecture would use these powerful characteristics to sabotage the language of architecture or the norms and values of society. The "Pop Art" of Neutelings Riedijk, unlike that of Andy Warhol, for example, is free of ulterior motives. Their buildings are intended to be autonomous characters, to radiate a unique and subversively entertaining identity that we will not easily forget. Such narrative sculpture is ideally suited to the branding game so loved by clients and cities.

Projective Mise-en-scène

In the projective mise-en-scène approach favored by MVRDV and NL Architects, the user becomes an actor invited to take an active part in the theater choreographed by the architects. In these projective practices, projects are not to be contemplated; rather they throw reality forward through the help of scenarios inspired by the theatrical programs the architects write based on the data they find within contemporary "extreme reality." Because nobody really knows what the "appropriate" response is to the unprecedented degree of innovation and uncertainty in this reality, observing its many mutations "neutrally" is seen as essential.

In the projective mise-en-scène, the city is one huge datascape. The architects use a method based on systematic idealization, an overestimation of available clues in which it is possible to integrate even mediocre elements. The program of requirements, which sometimes seems impossible to comply with, is followed to the letter, as are the complex and stringent Dutch building regulations. But an experiment with the real world remains the basic aim: In the margins and gaps of late capitalism these architects hope to foreground unclassified realities easily seen as parts of the ordinary world, while turning them upside down by means of theatrical performances.

Usually theatrical performances allow us to dream of other worlds. Not so the theater of MVRDV and NL Architects: After observing and charting our dynamic society, they go in search of new shapes that, with the help of an inventive program and a fresh aesthetic, cater to actual and everyday demands of use. They turn life into an optimistic and cheerful play that generates new solutions while making jokes about our constantly mutating reality. Giving the flat roof of the bar in Utrecht an added function is not just a clever use of space; by putting a basketball court on the roof of this student bar, NL Architects also achieves a delightfully absurd juxtaposition of two quite different milieus. MVRDV makes "endless" interiors in which diverse programs are compactly interwoven. The architects call them "hungry boxes," boxes hungry to combine different programs in a continuous landscape.[22] Whereas Neutelings Riedijk create representational forms that tell a story at one remove from the user/observer, MVRDV translate the program into a carefully choreographed spatial experience that incorporates the user into science fictions hidden in the everyday. When you stack all the village libraries from the province of Brabant in one huge skyscraper with the looks of an up-dated tower of Pisa and make individual study rooms into elevators zipping up and down the facade of books, the user suddenly takes part in a futuristic mise-en-scène.

With NL and MVRDV, we can justifiably speak of spectacular effects, of "scripted spaces" that steer experience (especially via the eye) in a particular direction. While NL makes jokes and develops a trendy lifestyle typology without bothering too much about pro-viding the design with a data-based, pseudoscientific alibi, MVRDV looks for new spatial concepts capable of giving our deregulated so-ciety the best imaginable spectacular shape.

In projective mise-en-scène, it is not the autonomous force of the type, of chic minimalism, or of expressive decor that is given free rein—as in projective autonomy—but the daydreams alive in so-ciety. Objects are not important as things in a projective mise-en-scène; they are there to be used as a screen onto which fragments of our extreme reality can be projected. (On the Dutch pavilion at the Hannover world expo, MVRDV projected all kinds of Dutch data clichés—the artificial landscape, the dunes, tulip fields, a forest, and windmills.) As in the social sciences, objects are seen as the carriers of everyday culture and lifestyle. The architecture is a coproducer in the embodiment of cultural and social meaning. In projective mise-en-scènes, everyday life is magnified by the spectacular decor that the architect assembles from data that reproduce the hidden logic of contemporary society. Instead of continuing to hide the more than sixteen million pigs in thousands of pitch-roofed bioindustry barns spread over the picturesque countryside of the Netherlands, MVRDV proposes that it is more efficient and animal-friendly to house pigs in high-rise flats in the harbor of Rotterdam. Suddenly—without any value judgment—the facts that there are more pigs than people in the Netherlands and that pigs can be happy in high-rises with a view look plausible. The shock effect of such a surreal and pragmatic mise-en-scène—like the Benetton billboards by Olivier Toscani with an AIDS patient dying in a living room—will immediately grab our attention. But if this bewildering realistic mode of representation is interested in either a better world or in exposing our Brave New World remains uncertain. The fables that lie hidden in the everyday are made visible by MVRDV's opportunistic imagination and make users into lead-ing actors, as in the Maxima Medical Center "Pajama Garden" in Veldhoven. Instead of hanging around the sterile corridors and other

MVRDV, Maxima Medical Center "Pajama Garden," Veldhoven, Netherlands, 2003. Courtesy of MVRDV. Photograph by Rob't Hart.

introverted spaces typical of a hospital, patients can relax in their pajamas, daydreaming of the Mediterranean among olive trees and other surreal "Mediterranean" set pieces.

Dreaming about utopias has lost its appeal. The everyday is so rich in fantasies that dreaming of a different world outside the existing one is no longer necessary. Like Steven Spielberg, architects must provide new representations that everyone can enjoy.[23] Entertainment first confronts you with dystopias (e.g., sixteen million stacked pigs), then guarantees a happy ending by glossing them over with "pragmatic solutions," ensuring conformity. The attitude is the putatively cool "Whatever."

Projective Naturalization

The limitation of projective mise-en-scène is that while it is busily projecting meaning onto things, it forgets that things can themselves convey meaning, can be sensitive and active, and can activate processes in both the eye and the body. That performative capacity is at the heart of practices that follow the route of what could be called "projective naturalization." In the Netherlands, projective naturalizations have been developed by, among others, Oosterhuis.nl, UN Studio, Maurice Nio, and NOX Architekten. They featured largely in the recent "Non-Standard Architectures" exhibition in Paris.[24] Projective naturalization is not about signs, messages, codes, programs, or collages of ideas projected onto an object but about technologies that allow matter to be performative.

Architect Lars Spuybroek of NOX is not interested in technology as a way of regulating functions and comfort. He sees it as a destabilizing force whose function is to fulfill our craving for the accidental by providing a variety of potentialities and events. "With the fluid merging of skin and environment, body and space, object and speed, we will also merge plan and volume, floor and screen, surface and interface, and leave the mechanistic view of the body for a more plastic, liquid, and haptic version where action and vision are synthesized," he writes.[25] What geology, biology, and even history have taught the architects of projective naturalization is that mutable processes generate far more intelligent, refined, and complex systems than ready-made ideas ever can.[26] This nonconventional architecture comprehends many shapes and schools.[27] What these manifestations have in common with nature is that the shapes they produce exhibit similarities with the structures, processes, and shapes of biology. The properties of these buildings change in response to changing conditions, just as nature does. A facade is not simply a shell but a skin with depth that changes in response to activity, light, temperature, and sometimes even emotions.

A blobbish, interactive "D-tower" designed by NOX is connected to a Web site at which the city's inhabitants can record responses to a questionnaire, designed and written by artist Q. S. Serafijn, about their everyday emotions: hate, love, happiness, and fear. The answers are graphed in different "landscapes" on the Web site that show the valleys and peaks of emotions for each of the city's postal codes. The four emotions are represented by green, red, blue, and yellow and determine the colors of the lamps illuminating the tower. Each night, driving through the city of Doetinchem, one can see which emotion is most deeply felt that day. A host of measurable data and technologies gives rise to a sophisticated metabolism that, as in Foreign Office Architects' Yokohama Terminal, channels the flows of people, cars, ships, and information like blood cells through and near the organism of the building. The project tries to function without obstacles or other complications and avoids communicating cultural meaning through shock, as does the work of MVRDV.

Projective naturalization projects are not rough or unfinished like many projective mise-en-scènes but smooth and fluid. It is not ideology but the (wished for) instinct of artificial organisms that ensures that complex processes are operating appropriately. Buildings are intended to function like bodies without heads following complex biomechanical logic. When Foreign Office Architects exhibited their Yokohama Terminal at the Venice Biennale, they showed sections of a body scan parallel to that of the terminals, suggesting that the logic of a building should resemble the body's. The foreign presence of forms generated by the "genetic manipulation" of data and technology in projective naturalizations helps prevent instant categorization of these projects as good or bad, beautiful or ugly. Judgment is deferred. The building rebuffs immediate consumption as symbol or myth; instead, it invites people to use it, to interpret, to enter into relations, to step into a stream of stimuli organized by matter. More than ever a building is able—by means of the new digital design methods and computer-controlled production of complex 3-D elements ("advanced prototyping")—to behave like an organism.

In contrast to projective mise-en-scènes, projective naturalizations are not interested in projecting scenarios onto objects related to society, religion, power, politics, globalization, or individuals. Projective naturalizations possess a super-functionality that revolves around movement, self-organization, and interactivity.[28] The intelligence of the project does not reside in a capacity for reflection, in offering a representation for or against something, but in activating open processes that can supposedly function automatically in accord with the flows of the status quo. Projective naturalizations are about modulating precise and local decisions from a mechanistic perspective interested in open, self-organizing systems that allow flows of consensus to follow their different trajectories with the aid of advanced construction processes. Grand dreams and other paradigms—except those of advanced technology and design expertise—are of little relevance. While concentrating on organic abstractions, projective naturalizations totally neglect the fact that every appropriation of a project depends on narratives of use and is about the interaction between social behavior and a given objective condition. What projective naturalizations tend to forget is that our social actions and behavior, not our biological bodies, constitute our identities.[29]

Larger Ambitions

Breaking with criticism, a passion for reality and a return to what architecture as a discipline is capable of projecting are essential to make the most of the many possibilities inherent in the "second modernity."[30] Instead of predicting the future, we have to be attentive to the unknown knocking at the door. Projective practices also demonstrate that the question is not whether architecture should participate in late capitalism. That is a given. But what form this relationship with the market should take is an ethical and political question that cannot be curated only in pragmatic, technical, or aesthetic terms.

The projective practices described here create spaces cut from the same cloth as the garments of the ruling systems. As such they confine themselves to forms of comfort enjoyed in particular by the global middle class. Apart from fear of confrontation with the unknown, the chief concerns of this middle class are the smooth processes that guarantee its rights to power, individualism, career, identity, luxury, amusement, consuming, and the infrastructure that makes all this possible.

This totalitarianism of difference, of individual rights—celebrated as the "multitude" of neoliberalism—overlooks the fact that it is essential to pay attention to the collective interests of the world population (including that of the transnational middle class). Instead of the paradigm of difference, we should vivify a paradigm of sameness and supra-individual responsibility. Culture is now all about diversity, flexibility, and the search for permanent novelty and effect that a project initiates, about how an object can relate to the market as an open, supposedly neutral platform. This is a strategy without political ideals, without political or sociohistorical awareness, that is in danger of becoming the victim of a dictatorship of aesthetics, technology, and the pragmatism of the blindly onrushing global economy. Instead of taking responsibility for the design, instead of having the courage to steer flows in a certain direction, the ethical and political consequences arising from the design decisions are left to market realism, and the architect retreats into the givens of his discipline.[31] In that way, all three projective practices described here are formalistic.

The positive thing about projective practices is that in the making of a project, under the influence of the material, the economy, the construction, the form, the program, the specific context, and with the help of architectural knowledge and instruments, projections can be tested and developed. In the very act of walking, projective practices create their paths. In the making of work, reality projects itself.

What these projective practices fail to see, however, is that utopian dreams are necessary in order to develop in a project a perspective that reaches beyond the status quo. I am not suggesting that utopian dreams can be realized but that such dreams provide frames of reference for political action. Utopian dreams also enable us to make a detached diagnosis of the present. This moment of exile from the addiction to reality could make us aware of our own inevitable and implicit value judgments, of the fact that excluding political and social direction itself sets a political and social direction. It is the interaction between the dream of utopia and reality that could help a projective practice develop a new social perspective. What should fascinate projective practice is how it might inflect capitalism toward democracy.

The only problem is that so far almost nobody has been prepared to rethink the now eroded concept of democracy or to carry out research into what democracy could mean today in spatial terms.[32] Talking about democracy is simultaneously a taboo and a fetish. We treat the word *democracy* as a palliative that relieves us from having to think hard about its realization.

If we were to dream about new formations of democracy, we would develop visions that shake off the current political ennui, the blind pursuit of the market, and our incessant navel-gazing. But instead it looks as if we have nodded off. Do we really derive so much enjoyment from the addictive consumption of comfort, design trends, technology, and countless mutually indifferent differences? Isn't it time to wake from our deep sleep and again dream of utopias?

2005

Notes

Thanks to William S. Saunders and Dave Wendt for their input and remarks about this essay.

1. See Francis Fukuyama, *The End of History and the Last Man* (New York: Free Press, 1992); Anthony Giddens, *The Third Way: The Renewal of Social Democracy* (Malden, Mass.: Polity Press, 1999); Anthony Giddens, ed., *The Global Third Way Debate* (Cambridge, U.K.: Polity Press, 2001).

2. In Michael Hardt and Antonio Negri, *Empire* (Cambridge, Mass.: Harvard University Press, 2000); Gopal Balakarishnan, ed., *Debating Empire* (London and New York: Verso, 2003).

3. See also Zaha Hadid and Patrik Schumacher, eds., *Latent Utopias: Experiments within Contemporary Architecture* (Vienna and New York: Springer Verlag, 2002).

4. Symposium held to mark Bernard Tschumi's retirement as dean of Columbia University, New York City, March 28–29, 2003, now published in Bernard Tschumi and Irene Cheng, eds., *The State of Architecture at the Beginning of the Twenty-first Century* (New York: Monacelli Press, 2003).

5. More information about "postcritical" can be found in Sanford Kwinter, "Who Is Afraid of Formalism?" *ANY* 7/8 (1994); "Equipping the Architect for Today's Society: The Berlage Institute in the Educational Landscape" (dialogue between Wiel Arets, Alejandro Zaera-Polo, and Roemer van Toorn); Stan Allen, "Revising Our Expertise"; Sylvia Lavin, "In a Contemporary Mood"; and Michael Speaks, "Design Intelligence," in Hunch 6/7 (2003); Jeffrey Kipnis, "On the Wild Side" (1999), in *Phylogenesis: FOA's Ark/Foreign Office Architects,* Foreign Office Architects (Barcelona: Actar Editorial, 2004), 566–80. A robust debate about criticism among Hal Foster, Michael Speaks, Michael Hays, Sanford Kwinter, and Felicity Scott can be found in *Praxis: Journal of Writing and Building 5: Architecture after Capitalism* (2003): 6–23.

6. Sarah Whiting and Robert Somol, "Notes around the Doppler Effect and Other Moods of Modernisms," *Perspecta* 33 (2002): 72–77; reprinted in this volume, see chapter 2.

7. See Kenneth Frampton, "Towards a Critical Regionalism: Six Points

for an Architecture of Resistance," in *The Anti-Aesthetic: Essays on Post-modern Culture*, ed. Hal Foster (New York: New Press, 1999); and Liane Lefaivre and Alexander Tzonis, *Critical Regionalism: Architecture and Identity in a Globalized World* (New York: Prestel USA, 2003).

8. Harm Tilman, "Architectuur onder globalisering," editorial, *De Architect*, January 2004.

9. All data regarding location, program, use, and infrastructure as well as the economy, politics, art, fashion, the media, the everyday, technology, typology, and materials that might conceivably help to advance a specific "found" reality are documented in diagrammatic form, especially charts and graphs. Of course, ideology is implicit in the science of measurement and the way the hidden qualities of reality are communicated. Most projective practices are, however, not aware of this ideological dimension. In addition they are ideologically "smooth" because the veil of fashion and style hides the many contradictions through the deployment of the design. For more information on the ideological dimension of contemporary Dutch architecture, see my article "Fresh Conservatism: Landscapes of Normality," in *Artificial Landscape: Contemporary Architecture, Urbanism*, ed. Hans Ibelings (Rotterdam: Nai Publishers, 2000).

10. Manfredo Tafuri managed to convince the architectural world that the modern avant-garde, in overthrowing the past with its radical modernizing technology, had not only contributed to a progressive avant-garde program but had also and more particularly helped to accelerate capitalist modernization. The avant-garde's principle of montage anticipated—according to Tafuri—the assimilation process of the dynamic and mechanical capitalist revolution that every individual must undergo: permanent anxiety prompted by urban living and the loss of values.

11. Theodor Adorno, quoted in Hilde Heynen, *Architecture and Modernity: A Critique* (Cambridge, Mass.: MIT Press, 2000), 4.

12. For an excellent explication of the work of Jean Nouvel, see K. Michael Hays's introduction and the interview between Jean Baudrillard and Jean Nouvel in Jean Baudrillard, *The Singular Objects of Architecture*, trans. Robert Bononno (Minneapolis: University of Minnesota Press, 2002).

13. K. Michael Hays, "Scanners," in *Scanning: The Aberrant Architectures of Diller + Scofidio*, Aaron Betsky, K. Michael Hays, and Laurie Anderson (New York: Whitney Museum of Art, 2003), 129–36.

14. Lefaivre and Tzonis, *Critical Regionalism*.

15. Various observations on criticism versus the projective are set out clearly by Somol and Whiting in "Notes around the Doppler Effect and Other Moods of Modernism."

16. "Mad Dutch Disease," Premsela Lecture by graphic designer Michael Rock at Premsela Dutch Design Foundation, Amsterdam, February 11, 2004, available from the Premsela Foundation, www.premsela.org.

17. As long ago as 1995, Hans van Dijk noted a tendency in Dutch architecture toward a kind of "aestheticized pragmatism" that combines realism (with respect to the terms of reference, regulations, budget, etc.) with a desire to produce a good-looking building (but without reference to any particular aesthetic theory). See Hans van Dijk, "On Stagnation and Innovation: Commentary on a Selection," in *Architecture in the Netherlands: Yearbook 1994–1995*, ed. Ruud Brouwers et al. (Rotterdam: Nai Publishers, 1995), 138–52.

18. See also Robert Somol, "12 Reasons to Get Back into Shape," in *Content*, ed. Rem Koolhaas and OMA-AMO (Cologne: Taschen, 2004), 86–87.

19. Research done by offices like Stefano Boeri and Multiplicity and Raoul Bunschoten and CHORA investigates the territorial transformations taking place in contemporary society. With the help of new observing, representing, and curating tools, they map and work with the processes of self-organization of inhabited space rather than in typological prototypes. The inherent rule in their design projects aims at constructing itself in relation to the dynamics already operating in the territory, which are not all necessarily controllable by centralized planning practices. See also Stefano Boeri, "Eclectic Atlases," in *USE: Uncertain States of Europe* (Milan: Skira Editore, 2003), by Multiplicity; and Raoul Bunschoten and Chora, *Urban Flotsam* (Rotterdam: 010 Publishers, 2001).

20. "We do not believe in designing aesthetic objects with complicated forms that can only be built through craftsmanship. Instead, we use standard industrial materials, spans, and constructions: ordinary products and ordinary techniques." Claus & Kaan, *Hunch* 6/7 (2003): 140.

21. Willen Jan Neutelings and Michael Riedijk, *At Work: Neutelings Riedijk Architects* (Rotterdam: Uitgeverij 010, 2003), 7.

22. "The Hungry Box," a traveling exhibition about the work of MVRDV, at the Netherlands Architecture Institute from November 2, 2002, to January 5, 2003.

23. Winy Maas mentioned Spielberg in a call to architects during the presentation of a research studio at the Berlage Institute, March 2, 2004.

24. See *Non-Standard Architectures*, catalog and exhibition curated by Zeynep Mennan and Frédéric Migayrou at the Centre Pompidou, Paris (December 10, 2003–March 1, 2004), which featured work by Asymptote, dECOi Architects, DR_D, Greg Lynn FORM, KOL/MAC Studio, Kovac Architecture, NOX Architekten, Objectile, Oosterhuis.nl, R&Sie, Servo, and UN Studio.

25. Lars Spuybroek in a 1998 essay outlining the philosophy of NOX Architekten at www.archilab.org.

26. See also Manuel De Landa, *A Thousand Years of Nonlinear History* (New York: Zone Books, 2000); and Manuel De Landa, *Intensive Science and Virtual Philosophy* (London and New York: Continuum, 2002).

27. The pavilions by Oosterhuis.nl and Asymptote in the Floriade Park (in *Architecture in the Netherlands: Yearbook 2002–2003*, ed. Anne Hoogewoning, Roemer Van Toorn, Piet Vollaard, and Arthur Wortmann [Rotterdam: NAI Publishers, 2003], 38–40); and the saltwater pavilion by Kas Oosterhuis and the freshwater pavilion by Lars Spuybroek at Neeltje Jans (in *Architecture in the Netherlands: Yearbook 1997–1998*, ed. Hans Van Dijk, Hans Ibelings, Bart Lootsma, and Ron Verstegen [Rotterdam: NAI Publishers, 1998], 42–47).

28. Projective naturalizations also aspire to be operational. See also what Rem Koolhaas has to say about this in a reaction to the manifesto of Ben van Berkel, Sanford Kwinter, Alejandro Zaera-Polo, and Greg Lynn (during the 1997 Anyhow conference in Rotterdam): "They had fresh and new ambitions and postures—antisemantic, purely operational—represented in virtuoso computer (in)animation. I remember being critical of their claim, then, that they had gone beyond form to sheer performance, and their claim that they had gone beyond the semantic into the purely instrumental and strictly operational. What I find (still) baffling is their hostility to the semantic. Semiotics is more triumphant than ever—as evidenced, for example, in the corporate world or in branding—and the semantic critique may be more useful than ever." Rem Koolhaas in "Spot Check: A Conversation between Rem Koolhaas and Sarah Whiting," *Assemblage* 40 (December 1999): 46. See also Felicity D. Scott, "Involuntary Prisoners of Architecture," *October* 106 (Fall 2003): 75–101.

29. I am always surprised when Van Berkel & Bos (UN Studio) show their "Manimal" metaphor for a new architectural practice—an image hybridizing a lion, a snake, and a human—and talk only about the process of generating the Manimal but never about its cultural, ideological, and symbolic implications. For them, it's all about form and not how social practices of use unlock such a metaphor.

30. The idea of a "second" or "reflexive" modernity was first developed in Ulrich Beck, *Risikogesellschaft: auf dem Weg in eine andere Moderne* (Frankfurt am Main: Suhrkamp, 1986), translated as *Risk Society: Towards a New Modernity* (London; Newbury Park, Calif.: Sage Publications, 1992).

31. For the role of the market in architecture, see also Roemer van Toorn, "Lost in Paradise" in *Architecture in the Netherlands: Yearbook 2001–2002*, ed. Anne Hoogewoning, Piet Vollaard, and Roemer van Toorn (Rotterdam: Nai Publishers, 2002); and Roemer van Toorn, "Propaganda," in *Architecture in the Netherlands: Yearbook 2002–2003*.

32. At times, the practice of Rem Koolhaas (although he refuses to talk about it) seems to experiment with new notions of democracy in space. Alongside the three projective practices mentioned in this article are also "projective juxtapositions," in which the permanent crisis of late capitalism is a source of inspiration. Projective juxtapositions are characterized

by an indefinable critical detachment that continually places the program and with it the organization of society in a state of crisis. In projective juxtapositions—such as those of OMA—a project never reaches a conclusion but instead provokes a never-ending subjective interpretation and inhabitation. The early projective juxtapositions of OMA were a vessel to experiment with new freedoms, as, for example, in the Kunsthal, resisting the current idea that a museum needs to be a temple with quasi-neutral white exhibition spaces. There a projective juxtaposition is combined with what Immanuel Wallerstein calls Utopistics (Immanuel Wallerstein, *Utopistics, or, Historical Choices of the Twenty-first Century* [New York: W. W. Norton & Company, 1998]). With Utopistics, Wallerstein is not referring to a progressivism that already knows what is to come but is pleading for a science that seriously assesses liberating historical alternatives—what best possible path for a far (and uncertain) future can be followed. Reassessing utopistic examples—which proved successful in creating freedom in the past—can help in the creation of new situations of freedom. Such an approach can be found in the OMA's Seattle library, which to a large extent reworks the public library of Hans Scharoun in Berlin (among other examples from the catalog of utopistic examples). When utopistics are combined with a projective juxtaposition, we come close to what I am after. But the OMA experiments with Prada and the Guggenheim in Las Vegas went no further than a projective mise-en-scène, which Salvador Dalí would have loved: "It is not necessary for the public to know whether I am joking or whether I am serious, just as it is not necessary for me to know it myself" (Salvador Dalí, *Diary of a Genius* [London: Creation Books, 1964]).

6

No More Tabula Rasa: Progressive Architectural Practices in England

Lucy Bullivant

Instead of carrying the heavy utopian baggage of the twentieth century, a new generation of British architects promotes realism—working with what is rather than with a tabula rasa. In a spirit of pragmatic adventure, this generation uses architecture as a tool and promotes collaboration with the powers that be. Everything is negotiable. Every win counts as some kind of improvement, however temporary.

Responses to the volatility of change brought about by global capitalism and the struggle between public and private interests over urban space have made microplanning an art in British architecture. Questioning the social codes that prescribed earlier generations of built form, especially in housing and education, and above all carefully modulating their behavior in contexts of complex vested interests, younger, self-reflective British architects are willing to engage political and social forces and are comfortable with contingencies and multitasking. They are gradually reinventing the role of the thoughtful architect. Maneuvering in a commercially branded landscape and manipulating givens through microplanning in order to create a more open-ended public-private environment—this is the new, modestly utopian face of British architecture.

Recent conditions favor these tactics: The public urban realm is the subject of countless new central and local government policy initiatives

75

Microflats (rendering). Courtesy of Piercy Connor Architects.

to make developers fund what were once government-funded facilities and locations, and of more sophisticated mechanisms to promote
urban regeneration. These initiatives include the government's £22
billion Sustainable Communities plan, launched in 2003, and the

new Urban Regeneration Companies established by local partners,[1] as well as social schemes geared to ameliorating children's safety, play, and education.[2] All these provide potential work for the rising generation. Many offer considerable potential for speculation on preconditions for increased common ground among local governments, commercial clients, development agencies and firms, and architects: the Olympic 2012 bid plan for the regeneration of the Lower Lea Valley, a major swath of East London, by a multidisciplinary team including FOA and Fluid, being a case in point.

Cutting their teeth on small- and occasionally large-scale competition wins and highly varied commissions, potent younger firms—FOA, S333, Adjaye Architects, Alison Brooks Architects, Sergison Bates, muf, Gross.Max, East, FAT, dsdha, Allford Hall Monaghan Morris, de Rijke Marsh Morgan, Piercy Conner, Urban Salon, McDowell Benedetti, and KDa, in particular—have taught themselves to be adept at resourceful thinking and microplanning about critical urban problems. The coincidence of increased government concern for urban and environmental conditions and the change to a more socially engaged younger generation is serendipitous and could not have been anticipated at the beginning of the 1990s, when many practitioners first chose to avoid a traditional career route as employees of bigger practices and set up their own offices, some (in the style of Microsoft or *Dazed and Confused* magazine) in their own front rooms. Through their processes of making, their ethos, and their redefinition of the public-private topography, these practices reflect how far the definitions of the fabric and the functional categories of our society have changed.

Transparency in architecture's social role and hence in the process of making architecture is common in the Netherlands but far less pervasive in the United Kingdom, with its erratic record of urban policy management and labyrinthine planning legislation. Although advanced architectural thinking now coexists in the United Kingdom with episodes of huge client bravery, a failure of political will on the part of too many clients prevails when it comes to adding architectural value on larger scales. Yet the incremental effects of smaller-scale schemes and strategic thinking of an entire generation are likely to increase the leverage of fresh architectural thinking substantially in the next decade.

Diverse larger-scale multidisciplinary strategies (particularly master planning and urban research) evolved by younger practices have an increasingly holistic approach in common, with socioeconomic factors given as much emphasis as spatial ones. These practices witness regeneration plans in developers' and government's hands driving for value-adding results but frequently grinding to a halt, and yet they see that the reflection allowed by delay means that the results are better for not being too reliant on one-size-fits-all iconic solutions.

Confidence about transport infrastructure design took a leap forward with the completion of London's Jubilee Line extension, which engaged many exceptional practices. Yet few younger firms get the chance to make waves in this field. Transport is in the hands of Rogers, Foster, Grimshaw, and more anonymous large-scale firms. But British transport design will eventually pass to the thirty- and forty-something architects, because they understand how transport infrastructures—airports, especially—are morphing into new pieces of the city, and they maintain these luminaries' thirst for complex urban design. Provision has always lagged far behind need, and failure of political will often eases out the best architectural solution: proof of the value of the high-quality Jubilee Line has not meant a high-profile name will design the new Eurostar Terminal at King's Cross (a design and build solution by the railway company is due for completion in 2008). Nonetheless—and perhaps this is inevitable due to UK designers' and engineers' facility with structure—younger practices are quickly developing a skills base in transport infrastructure design. Foreign Office Architects (FOA), in particular, is noted for its hugely accomplished infrastructure design submissions to international competitions and its specific focus on circulation, on creating permeable boundaries between interior and exterior, and on the material orders of the contemporary world. In spite of the relative lack of options now, it can only be a matter of time before British clients more widely embrace schemes involving the interpenetration of building and landscape in urban centers, whether or not they are transportation buildings—a type that FOA has tested through commissioned and realized work in Japan (Yokohama International Port Terminal) and in Barcelona (with its park for the Forum 2004).

Architecture has become as fluid as the social orders it is entrusted to accommodate. To ask younger British architects or interior designers, engaged as they inevitably are by consumer brands, to define the sense of place in their work is a loaded request now that so many projects have a short life cycle. It may well not affront architecture's contemporary social role to emphasize "experience"—a sense of occasion instead of place. But these are only words. The conceptually powerful architecture of the younger implementers described here deploys words, but much more an arsenal of strategies covering process, program, technique, and so on. They ask not what architecture represents but what it *does*.

The fluidity of these young practices also broadens the bandwidth of formerly narrow building typologies into things more holistically and credibly urban with the scope to grow in the future: Housing—representing memory, property, attachment, solitude, communality, and social ties—is one area in which new productive processes are maximizing designers' desired material and social effects.

S333

S333, a multidisciplinary studio of architects and urbanists founded by Dominic Papa, Jonathan Woodroffe, Chris Moller, and Burton Hamfelt, generates instrumental operating strategies drawing on architecture, landscape architecture, urbanism, infrastructural design, and socioeconomics. S333 is determined to "rediscover architecture within contemporary cultural conditions," as Papa put it, rather than representing reality through physical form. The firm is interested "in manipulating program to create a sense of place. . . . Driven by social concerns, it treats *form* as a verb rather than a noun," said Woodroffe.[3]

Formed in London at the height of the recession of the early 1990s out of shared concern over the need to generate debate about contemporary European urbanism through workshops, publications, and competitions, S333 has evolved socially driven master planning techniques. In 1994 they won the Europan 3 international housing competition for Groningen's Circus site in the Netherlands and moved to a permanent base in Amsterdam. Now they are increasingly involved in the United Kingdom's urban renaissance. Ten years ago, this would not have been feasible, but a new force field—combining the influence of Richard Rogers and his Urban Task Force, new lobbying bodies (such as the Commission for the Built Environment) actively seeking optimum processes for master planning, proactive agencies (such as the Architecture Foundation) and people (such as Richard Burdett, director of the Cities Programme at the London School of Economics and a ubiquitous presence on competition juries), and the pervasive media exposure of design and architectural activities—has created a much more welcoming environment.

Although S333 frequently finds itself labeled "Dutch," now that the public sector bodies behind Thames Gateway, the major urban regeneration project in the United Kingdom's southeast, have given Dutch architects and planners West 8 and Maxwan a key master planning and development role, S333's UK refocus, taking advantage of this fluidity in intellectual trading based around the regeneration of place, is a tactically productive strategy playing on the blurring of national boundaries.

CiBoGa Terrain in Groningen, S333's winning scheme for Europan 3, embodies a modus operandi that in many of their projects takes the site as the generator of ideas. Groningen's local authorities were well known for inviting architects including Daniel Libeskind, Zaha Hadid, and Rem Koolhaas to build in the city but had failed over the prior seven years to find a new way of perceiving the site. The fourteen-hectare marginal zone of CiBoGa, once the northeastern industrial area, traced the city's original medieval walls in a ring. Formerly open land for a circus, freight storage, and a gas works, it was a nebulous area that the city initially hoped to capitalize on by creating an edge condition with offices but later came to see as a potential residential area once the national government agreed to provide twelve million euros to clean up pollution there. From the 1970s onwards, the compact city plan, along with an interest in master plans, increasingly came back into favor in the Netherlands as well as the United Kingdom, and S333 was able to combine compactness in its design for CiBoGa while triggering an ecological rebirth for the entire area, a rebirth that edge-city adherents of earlier times would doubtless have pooh-poohed.

The competition that resulted, "At Home in the City: Urbanizing Residential Neighbourhoods," requested proposals for the design of thirteen blocks of new housing, specifying that the architects "rethink the relationship between the city's private and public spaces and the spatial scaling from domestic intimacy to urban collectivity." S333 was struck by the fact that while the developers wanted a high density of residential units, the city wanted an ecological corridor through the site connecting the park to the west and the canal to the east. Responding to the conflicting demands of a commission is part of an architect's job, but for S333 these demands—including those stated by city dwellers—established the organizational cues for the project to bring about what Papa called "a three-dimensional over-lapping of program and landscape elements."

Owing to the complexity of the area, the city's department of urban planning predicted long delays in the development and realization stages and asked S333 to draw up a master plan for the entire CiBoGa site to include 1,000 housing units, 1,000 parking spaces, and 30,000 square meters of mixed-use and recreational areas. This expanded remit gave S333 the opportunity to conduct intensive research to make a set of propositions. The firm initiated studies, forums, and typological research, working with urbanists and other architects to explore contemporary living and working patterns, time-sharing, security, and privacy. On-site workshops led by Foreign Office Architects and members of the Architectural Association's Housing and Urbanism Unit mapped movement and spatial links. Research projects by environmental engineers and workshops with developers and local business groups explored the potential conflicts of the new commercial programs and the leisure-based facilities on the adjacent urban fabric. Working with the city's ecologists and with landscape architects, S333 also examined how sustainability can direct the development of a large mass of housing.

The emphasis—and this is the crux of this new form of practice—was on the performative, the topographical, the local, and the incremental, rather than on the typological, the singular, or the visionary. The practice's work here introduced a level of prolonged informal as well as formal public consultation that British architects associate with the participative style of Will Alsop, who has received mainland European commissions for some time. However, it cannot be said that the United Kingdom is simply importing from the continent a custom of architects' being accessible to their public, for such a re-valorization of different types of public consultation is at the heart of the work of more indigenous practices like FAT (which is working on two Dutch commissions) and "muf," which has worked mainly on public sector schemes in the United Kingdom. Both practices have public identities as architects-artists, and their style of working adds new functions or experimentation with the brief.

It is likely that no Europan competition win other than CiBoGa Terrain has resulted in such an intensely prolonged and public-involving form of scrutiny. Basing itself on a specific discourse about social change—in this case an emphasis on individual freedoms—the project centered on the fact that "urban dwellers, in establishing new parameters for the appropriate use of public and private space, are promoting spatial usage that is more time-based, aligned to individual work/living patterns, mobility, and their own personal choice," explained Papa.

S333 was commissioned to design the first two of the urban blocks for which the city used the concept of Schotsen (icebergs), "a compact building volume eroded by views and desire lines that negotiate between the public and private realms," in Papa's words. With three levels oriented in many directions to take advantage of the sun, their composition is clearly defined by movement flows, sight lines, and oblique open public spaces rather than the kind of geometric restraint that working in a historic center would have imposed. Shops and housing entrances are all at ground level, and houses and apartments are in U- and L-shaped blocks oriented at the middle level around a courtyard, with private roof terraces and gardens on top. "Unlike the tradition in Britain of architecture focusing on itself, Schots 1 and 2 don't form an isolated object but rather respond to their surroundings," Papa explained. It is not a self-contained, isolated suburb or edge condition but instead a new hybrid that diversifies the living environment in an area with very little housing provision. The housing and shops have density, but they do not prevent openness and high-quality public space so that the site acts as a link

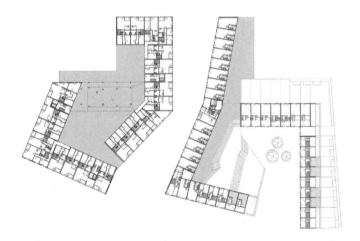

S333, CiBoGa, plan, Groningen, Netherlands, 2003. Courtesy of S333.

between the park to the west and the canal area to the east. A series of stepped galvanized steel sloping walls leading up to flat "tables" create three large climbing terraces that break the public court into more intimate areas.

While the rare incursion into mixed use in the United Kingdom often gets developers and local councils nervous about aesthetics and siting, the Schots, completed in summer 2003, not only innovatively mix housing and retail but also contain a range of terrace houses, courtyard blocks, and apartment towers. They offer an instrumental architectural response to increasingly shifting and fragmenting patterns of living in the city: Inhabitants can move between the rented dwellings as their aspirations, family size, and finances change. The design prompts a break with the time-honored tradition in the West of leaving the city for the suburbs and countryside for more living space.

Each Schot is overlaid by a new surface landscape interweaving with the architecture: Large areas of ivy, patios, roof gardens, ramped surfaces, courtyards, and playgrounds add to the sense of a variegated environment and promote biodiversity. While a 0.5 car-parking policy (only 50 percent of the housing units can have a parking space on the perimeter, and public transport was boosted to compensate) bans cars from the site, pedestrian routes through it link the park and the canal, integrating the scheme within the urban landscape. "The multi-layering of activities and landscape offers an alternative to the interiorized and hermetic world of the traditional urban block," explained Papa. "Context, nature, and urban ecology reposition themselves here as generating forces in the reevaluation of housing in cities."

Research by S333 into housing typologies, energy alternatives, and ecological soundness gave the CiBoGa project recognition as a national pilot scheme for sustainable urban renewal. In a reversal of the British norm that disseminates marketing imagery to sell shell and core space, the collaborative ethos established by the city council, development consortium client, and S333 enabled an innovative design approach delaying emphasis on the final aesthetic form. "Instead, far more emphasis was placed on the project's organization and strategic development," Papa said. "What has resulted is a series of investigations in which we the architects have played an intermediary role, mapping a process of events and shaping forces." Crucially S333 has made fundamental issues of community drivers of this benchmark project.

Housing: Alison Brooks Architects, Piercy Connor, Sergison Bates

Architect Alison Brooks's overriding interest lies in extending architecture into landscape, giving it new character beyond the boundaries of tectonic convention. Working and living in Toronto until 1989, when she moved to London, Brooks craved "the intensity and density" of London as a place where "eccentricity is nurtured."[4] Becoming a partner of Ron Arad Associates in 1991, she and Arad designed the firm's One Off studios (now Ron Arad Associates) on Chalk Farm Road (1991), the Tel Aviv Opera House foyer (1994), and, in the mid-1990s, Belgo Noord restaurant and the three-hundred-seat Belgo Centraal restaurant in Covent Garden. After seven years, she left and set up Alison Brooks Architects (ABA). "I was determined to get out of interiors and into urbanism. I hated the idea that housing was a ghetto: Housing is city-building. It should be a site for experimentation."

The eight years of ABA work have seen a proliferation of opportunities to shoehorn new ideas into the repertoires of house builders in both the social and the commercial sectors. In an area with few guarantees that speculative proposals will be built, the firm has generated ideas that manipulate program and draw out the potential of a site without depending on a tabula rasa. Moreover, in this climate of multidimensional cultural collaboration, architects have turned into business speculators. One young practitioner, Piercy Connor, proposed Microflat prefabricated housing in pod form, which was first shown at real size, occupied by temporary inhabitants, in the windows of Selfridges Department Store. The practice then took on the challenge of finding a backer and suitable sites: A supermarket parking garage, even the space above a supermarket—tiny, vacant, central urban interstitial sites—were ideal for the future occupants of the Microflats, twenty-somethings otherwise not able to live close to their work. The Microflat represented the potential for the micro-generation of urban life. Again we see the pursuit of idealistic goals combined with a realistic modesty of means.

ABA has also thrown its energies into competition schemes, including urbanDNA (Diverse Neutral Accommodation) for Britannia Basin in Manchester (1999)—a prototype exploiting fast-track production systems, economies of scale, and the urban character of a brownfield site. ABA has cross-fertilized the speculative thinking applied in competitions for public housing schemes with more lucrative private housing commissions. The semidetached house, the terraced house, live/work spaces, social housing, homes for public service employees such as nurses and teachers—these housing typologies demand reassessment in the wake of intense social changes such as escalating property prices putting house purchase increasingly out of reach for younger people; a growing trend for self-employment, with the home expanding its identity to include work; as well as the desire to limit time spent traveling to work and the proliferation of households without traditional nuclear families. The retreat to the countryside—increasingly undertaken by middle-class families with small children (from London in particular) to escape urban crime— or to the larger spaces of suburbia does not make these developments any less pressing. They offer younger practices the chance to reinvent the fabric of the everyday, spurred by the questions, "What can domestic building do in the twenty-first century? How can you pull domestic built form away from anachronistic social codes while integrating the residual validity of its design?"

Sergison Bates's design for a prototype house for the William Sutton Trust, built in Stevenage, Hertfordshire, in 2000, notably addresses this challenge. It became a means for speculating on the house-like image of the ubiquitous semidetached dwelling without merely tampering with representation. Reinforcing the form through a minimum expression of joints and overlaps between materials and surfaces, Bates makes the roof and wall cladding continuous and freely arranges the windows to allow walls and roof to appear in a seamless flow, something the traditional semidetached house prevented through compartmentalization into a constricted structure of small, boxy spaces. This tactic manipulates the language of protection in a metaphorical stance that promotes the experience of "dwelling."

Reworking the normative in commercial housing schemes is still an uncommon opportunity for many younger architects. However, Wayne Hemingway, founder of the Red or Dead fashion label, was commissioned to design houses for volume house builders Wimpy on Merseyside a few years ago—a sheer fluke, given Wimpy's conservatism up to that point—and this commission kick-started a huge media discussion about the desperate lack of real choice offered by the appearance, spatial composition, and quality of housing designs monopolizing the market. An increasing fluidity in the design of housing architecture was not being matched by a commercial openness to new designs, but suddenly one key builder awoke to niche marketing.

Undoubtedly this debate had a rousing effect on the clients of an emerging scheme ABA is designing (one that has already won a RIBA Housing Design Award). Ahead of completion, it is increasingly recognized as an exemplar in relation to the PPG3 (Planning Policy Guidance) guidelines issued by the British government in 2000 and to its sustainability agenda. Brooklands Avenue (2002–), Brooks's housing scheme in Cambridge for Countryside Properties, will be the largest housing development in the city since 1965.

Countryside wanted to achieve a high eco-home rating with courtyard houses at high density in car-free streets. Brooks describes her involvement as "participating in a process of city-building rather than house-building per se." Forty units within three different building types, each with its distinct condition, sit within a four-hundred-unit master plan designed by Feilden Clegg of Bath and London. In the tradition of Cambridge academic morphology, the buildings appear to be part of a campus landscape with a central boulevard. However, what is certainly not normative is their copper-clad fractured facades, not something house purchasers in the United Kingdom have seen before among the volume house builders' limited styles. The units are excellent test cases for the exploration of individuality within communal building forms and for new spatial models of the single-family house. "We take a completely site-specific approach," Brooks adds, aiming to create "architecture that has the potential for non-specific occupation."

The first model is a new loft building with "spaces interlocking like those of a Rubik's cube." Brooks not only orients individual spaces to the sun but also expresses each flat as a piece in the overall structure: Occupants can "read" their flat on the outside through the detailing on the copper. On the ground floor are four apartment unit types; all the other floors have, repeated over two levels, five different maisonette types (in a total of four stories), containing one to three bedrooms. Each has a void "to provide a visual link between the different levels and accentuate the open-plan layout," L-shaped sky patios on the north side of the balconies, and sun-catching screens in a shape developed out of the structural element of the concrete wall/slab that provide a continuation of interior to exterior. "I gave the building something that transforms as you go around it."

The second model is a semidetached house three and a half stories high with a flexible open-plan layout that has spaces of varied heights and orientations achieved with a split-level staircase and a central void. It is clad in fair-faced yellow stock brick with a curved copper-clad roof and entrance portico. Interestingly, Brooklands Avenue is a design-build project, but the process has honored custom-designed architecture, bucking the trend toward a dilution of design concept. Also, although the architects considered tunnel-form concrete with Kajima Construction, they opted for precast concrete panels that are quick to assemble: "It's halfway towards prefabrication, a good compromise allowing more interesting configurations addressing contemporary issues of how families work in a space and providing chances for moving walls to enlarge bedrooms."

The third building is a ten-flat, six-story apartment clad in faceted copper. "People call it the giant copper crisp [potato chip] packet. The idea was to angle the facade so each one had oblique views across the landscape and long views of the space surrounding the building." The "woven" effect of the facade comes from the alternation of the floor slabs. The external amenity spaces are not separate elements but part of this geometry—notably, the cantilevering floor slabs of the levels below create the external spaces for the balconies above. Brooks does not want to create "an apparition between the greenery," but instead "to try to dissolve the overall form into the canopy of trees. Sometimes the building will be light and transparent—at night it will dematerialize into little scattered cubes of light. I think of the whole thing in movement."

Brooks is intent on producing a radical new vision for housing and urban design in the United Kingdom. The way she sees it, British people "have already bought into the idea of modern flexible spaces—the loft was part of that shift. They are more open-minded." She thinks the house-building industry is "ripe for new models and experimentation," citing the willingness in mainland Europe to see housing as a territory for exciting ideas. "There are pockets of enlightened developments in the UK. The challenge is whether the agenda of the master plan filters through to the buildings." Brooks sees the paradigm shift that has come about in the past twenty years in the use of digital technology, computer modeling, software, and structural analysis as key in any housing debate. "We produce three-dimensional models at a very early stage. You can test everything you do—the ideas against the virtual model. And clients are starting to want to respond to such modeling."

I have explored "emergent models of practice" (as Stan Allen describes them in "Stocktaking 2004," chapter 9, this volume) that break and melt any boundaries already falling. They do not need to wait for change: Social change is their raw material. They have not lost their predecessors' taste for theory, but to them it cannot be theory distanced from society or from engaged practice. They fuse theory and practice in an intense parallel program both heuristic and experimental. This is easier to do if you are drawing out the potential of a site rather than stamping it with your interpretation. The process of public collaboration is perceived as central in the creative evolution of projects, not purely a management duty.

Reflecting social change without being socially determinist and allowing the process of production to transform the initial idea for the project—these are some of the design parameters that distinguish the finest work of this rising generation from that of any generation that asks too much or too little from architecture. The predetermined, self-referential sculptural presence of building is no longer the means to architecture's communications: That has been transcended by the wedding of process, sociospatial concerns, and adaptation to new information and uses. The professional vulnerability of architecture brought on by its loss of its master-mason status is counteracted by an intensely multivalent strategy of engagement in the world. Why, after all, with our pliable sense of time and place, should abstraction still be of much value?

2005

Notes

1. Catalyst Corby was the first. Richard Rogers, Rafael Vignoly, Feilden Clegg, and young architects Hawkins\Brown have been short-listed to regenerate Corby, an ailing Midlands town.

2. The New Deal for Communities (which includes funds for architecture) and the Schools for the Future scheme (geared at creating templates for new educational environments).

3. This and subsequent quotations come from an interview I conducted with S333 on February 20, 2004, in Amsterdam.

4. This and subsequent quotations come from an interview I conducted with Alison Brooks on April 20, 2004, in London.

7

Not Unlike Life Itself: Landscape Strategy Now

James Corner

The notion of "design intelligence," defined by Michael Speaks as "practices [that] allow for a greater degree of innovation because they encourage opportunism and risk-taking rather than problem solving,"[1] is pertinent to this particular moment and fundamental, I believe, to the advancement and larger cultural efficacy of landscape architecture, architecture, and urban design. The idea of strategy, more generally, invokes the art of engagement, typically in battles, but also in any activity that requires a certain finesse, careful positioning, and intelligent, informed, coordinated actions to ensure success (advantage rather than disadvantage, survival rather than death). However, to think solely in terms of ends is perhaps not accurate, for a good strategy remains dynamic and open and thereby assures its own longevity. It is more conversational and engaging than it is confrontational or assertive. A good strategy is a highly organized plan (spatial, programmatic, or logistical) that is at the same time flexible and structurally capable of significant adaptation in response to changing circumstances. Too rigid a strategy will succumb to a surprise or to a logic other than that for which it was designed, and too loose a strategy will succumb to anything more complex or to anything more highly organized and better coordinated.

Life scientists will tell you that a resilient system must be both robust and open. Such suppleness is essential for successful adaptation, which is in turn necessary for survival in an evolving open system. In order to grow and develop, life forms must both persist and adapt, their organizational structures sufficiently resilient to withstand challenges while also supple enough to morph and reorganize. These principles are as topical today in business and management as they are in biology and ecology, urbanism and the design of public space. And, importantly, these principles describe not only pathways and processes but also specific forms of organization, specific arrangements, configurations, and relational structures that are essential for constructing both resilient and adaptive capacities. In this case, a "fitness landscape" is one best disposed toward and best adapted to certain conditions. It is both healthy (or physically fit) and synthetically symbiotic (or "fitting") because of its specific organizational and material form. Now, because architectural, landscape, and urban projects are inevitably formal (both geometrical and material), durational (subject to time and process), and complex (subject to multiple forces and relations), strategy is fundamental to contemporary design practices.

Moreover, the increased marginalization of design from public life—architecture and landscape are valued more as symbolic, aesthetic, or emblematic works rather than as modes of practice directed toward larger urban issues, physical planning, and social/public improvement—necessitates a stocktaking of the field, a revamping of professional orientation toward future practices. In an increasingly unregulated, dispersed, global, and pluralistic world, projects have become more complicated, more difficult to pull off, more difficult to maintain in quality. Without kings, autocratic presidents, singular corporate leaders, or similarly single-minded "clients with power and authority," it is very difficult to produce significantly innovative work, especially at a larger, urban scale. The kind of ad-hoc, inclusionist populism that passes as participatory public process today typically leads to dull projects, bland politics, and general cultural inertia.

Now, not wanting to return to hierarchical societies and wanting instead to more fully, effectively, innovatively engage urban public life in the realization of complex projects, how exactly might one act professionally?

Landscape, Ecology, and Propagation

Both landscape and ecology serve as useful strategic models for three primary reasons: (1) they accept the often messy and complex circumstances of the given site, replete with constraints, potentials, and realities, and they have developed techniques—mapping, diagramming, planning, imaging, arranging, and so on—for both representing and working with the seemingly unmanageable or inchoate complexities of the given; (2) they both address issues of large-scale spatial organization and relational structuring among parts, a structuring that remains open and dynamic, not fixed; and (3) they both deal with time open-endedly, often viewing a project more in terms of cultivation, staging, and setting up certain conditions rather than obsessing on fixity, finish, and completeness. Landscape and ecology understand projects as dynamic, grounded temporalities, as context-specific unfoldings—becomings, durational emergences, themselves seeding potentials that go on to engender further sets of effect and novelty. Landscape architects tend to view the specificity of a given site—its environment, culture, politics, and economies—as a program unto itself, a program that has an innate tendency or propensity with regard to future potentials. This is why practices of agriculture, silviculture, horticulture, and other techniques of adaptive management of material systems are so interesting and pertinent to urbanism.

Subsequently, once seeded, set up, or staged, ecological succession presents one site state that establishes the conditions for the next, which in turn overwrites the past and precipitates a future, not necessarily in foreseeable or prescribable ways. In a sense, the landscape project is less about static, fixed organizations than it is about—to borrow biologist Stuart Kauffman's terms—"propagating organizations," provisional sets of structures that perform work to construct more of themselves in order to literally propagate more diverse and complex lifeworlds. I use *lifeworld* intentionally here to invoke imaginative, programmatic, and urban, as well as the natural or biological dimensions.

A single cell or unit working to produce a second copy from small building blocks is literally propagating not only an organization of material but also an organization of process, a process that goes on to gradually construct increasingly diverse sets of emergent forms, generating novelty, distinctive forms, and programs that never existed before. Self-constructing organization propagates and evolves—our globe is covered by propagating organizations—life and its consequences.

In design terms, landscapes and field organizations set up the conditions for life to evolve. Any landscape configuration inevitably has an inherent potentiality. Design strategy involves understanding that potentiality, and shaping or deploying form in order to maximize effects. The notion of a propagating organization is totally enmeshed in unfolding the potentials of real things over time. The evolution of circumstances in fact renews potentials and hence the efficacy of the disposition.

Dispositions: Materiality, Form, and Design

This brings me to my third point: Design practices that are contextually responsive, temporal and open-ended, adaptive and flexible, and ecologically strategic do not imply that formal, material precision is irrelevant. Proponents who argue for strategy over form, for strategic modes of practice over formal, material practices, or even for a kind of objective naturalism over subjective creativity are misguided. First, as landscape architects, architects, and urban designers, we give physical shape and form to the world—geometry and material are fundamental. We draw from strategy and from various disciplines that deploy strategic and organizational thinking not to become master strategists per se but rather to find greater efficacy and potential for the physical reshaping of our world. Strategic technique—research, survey, mapping, projecting, decentralizing, bundling, networking, testing, shaping, sounding out, and so on—are of enormous value to designers trying to expand the scope and efficacy of their work. At the same time, however, form, geometry, and material are precisely the physical media, the substrate if you will, through which any strategy plays itself out. In other words, there is no general strategy of battle, only a specific unfolding of battle as dictated or afforded by the specific contours and local conditions of a particular terrain.

Similarly, in designing pathways, corridors, patches, fields, matrices, meshworks, boundaries, surfaces, mats, membranes, sections, and joints—each configuration highly specific in dimension, material, and organization—we are constructing a dynamic expanding field, literally a machinic stage for the performance of life, for the propagation of more life, and for the emergence of novelty. In other words, arguments for staging uncertainty, for indeterminacy and open-endedness, for endless scenario gaming and datascaping—in fact anything to do with the whole notion of free flexibility and adaptation—do not make sense in a world without specific material form and precise design organizations.

The very performance of life is dependent on a highly organized material matrix, a landscape ecology both robust and adaptable, strategic by virtue of its material cunning in diversification and survival. Fluid, pliant fields—whether wetlands, cities, or economies—are able to absorb, transform, and exchange information with their surroundings. Their stability and robustness in handling and processing movement, difference, and exchange derive from their organizational configuration, their positioning, their arrangement, and relational structuring: in sum, their "design intelligence."

Contemporary urban projects demand a new kind of synthetic imagination—a new form of practice in which architecture, landscape, planning, ecology, engineering, social policy, and political process are both understood and coordinated as an interrelated field. The synthesis of this range of knowledge bases and its embodiment in public space lie at the heart of a strategic landscape practice. Working inclusively and collaboratively across multiple scales and with broad scope, strategic design intelligence can surely move toward a more effective and powerful form of urban design. But while strategic thinking aids design intelligence, it is design intelligence that ultimately gives shape and form to the grounds—the very landscape substrate (or the fuller environment more broadly)—that both supports and instigates future emergent forms and novel effects. In this sense, both strategy and design are crucial for evolving new forms, new programs, new publics, new natures, and new urbanisms. That is design intelligence, with its broad reach and its extraordinary creativity, not unlike life itself.

2005

Notes

1. Michael Speaks, "Theory was interesting . . . but now we have work," *arq* 6/2, "perspective," June 26, 2002.

8

On Not Being Governed

Dave Hickey

This essay was originally a speech at the GSD 2005 conference "Loopholes," organized by Ashley Shafer, Brian Price, and Jonathan Lott.

Let me be candid. I decided to come here today because I found the title of this symposium so mysterious. "Loopholes," I thought. "Loopholes through what?" What possible barrier might we be peeking or sneaking through by virtue of these loopholes? We do, after all, live in the least regulated, most permissive, most self-indulgent, most expressive culture in the history of humankind. We have, by definition, more technical resources today than at any point in the history of the built environment, so what's the barrier? What are we looking through into this utopian construction site? Then I got here and heard a new architecture buzzword: *postcriticality*. Even though I like anything new, I found the term daunting.

Foucault's great definition of critique presented itself immediately: "The art of not being governed quite so much." This axiom has been the linchpin of my own practice for forty years, and yet, even so, I understood the angst, guilt, and restlessness that almost certainly gave birth to the term *postcriticality* in the domain of architecture. Foucault himself identified these emotions as the consequence of a critique that, rather than resisting governance, has become a form of governance itself—an idiom of critique that, rather than setting us free, oppresses us. Today I would like to discuss the permutations that the idiom of structuralist critique has undergone since the late 1950s that have transformed it into an idiom of governance. My smaller, more specific agenda here is to address a moral eccentricity that pervades American "high architecture," the ABC principle—ABC standing in this case for "Anything But Commercial." This principle holds that a really serious, well-connected, metaphysically sound architect in the early twenty-first century will work for any government, however repressive, any corporation, however predatory, and any private client, however reprehensible, rather than just design a department store.

So let me be clear here: I have been identified in the past as the art critic who defends beauty and commerce. This is ridiculous. It's like saying that I am the gnat who defends Godzilla and T. Rex because in the colloquium of forces that impact contemporary culture, beauty and commerce are the monsters at the table. Beauty wins, and commerce works, nearly always and by definition. I am merely the critic who argues that any theoretical model that fails to come to terms with these facts of life is probably trivial. I am, in fact, no more in favor of commercial architecture than I am of institutional architecture. I am only arguing that the "order of commercial architecture" is absolutely distinct from the "order of institutional architecture"—that commercial architecture is a coherent, complementary, and contrapositive discourse, and that as a consequence, the prim, moral exceptionalism that derides discussing it and practicing it debilitates the larger discourse of architecture by half.

To cite a specific case, I found it beguiling and quaint that Bob Venturi and Denise Scott Brown's decision to integrate attributes of commercial architecture into their work on the National Gallery in London should have been considered a radical architectural maneuver. I found myself wondering what protocol had been breached, and this brought me back to a remark that Morris Lapidus made to me in conversation. Morris insisted that there are only two primal kinds of building: the corral and the souk. The corral is in a fence around a space; the souk is a carpet on the ground and a cloth ceiling. In other words, there are structures that prioritize the walls and insist on the vertical relationship between the sky and the earth, between God and Nature; and there are structures that prioritize the floor and ceiling, that block out God and Nature and that insist on the horizontal space of human commerce. Institutional architecture is about walls and control, about keeping out time and change, aliens and foreigners. Commercial architecture is about no walls, about that eight-foot space of human interaction that encloses the planet. In this space, there is a floor to protect you from Nature and a ceiling to protect you from God.

There are only two books, to my knowledge, that seriously address this interface in the realm of architecture, Benjamin's *Arcades Project* and Ruskin's *Stones of Venice,* and they are both anticommercial screeds. Beyond that, there is silence, and the only explanation I have ever been given for this pedagogical deficit was offered to me by an architecture professor who explained that professors were bound to be commercially disinterested. Leaving aside the fact that architecture professors are not commercially disinterested, I must note that commercial disinterest applies to making money. It doesn't mean that you're not supposed to be interested in commerce itself or its products. As any economist can tell you, academic life provides an ideal platform from which you might exercise an interest in and influence on the commercial world without the taint of self-interest.

Anyway, back in the 1960s, when I was a young maven of French structuralism, in the early days of America's reign as the premier designer and exporter of packaged desire, I saw in the principles of structuralist thinking a model for a renewed vision of commerce and high culture. I was half right. Structuralist principles over the years have informed the redesign of American business, have created Silicone Valley and the new Las Vegas. They have created a new array of nonhierarchal, decentralized, dynamic business models, but with the exception of Warhol's Factory, they have not produced any high cultural equivalent. High culture talks about structuralism, it doesn't apply it.

The question I would like to address is why not, and I'd like to begin by quoting two of my old adversaries on the single points upon which we agree. My first adversary is Hilton Kramer, who now runs a right-wing—but very well-edited—magazine called *The New Criterion.* At the time of this quote, Hilton was a senior editor and art critic of the *New York Times.* I went to see him lecture at a ceramics conference, and he gave a nice talk about Peter Voulkos. During the question period after the talk, a dusty ceramics dude got up and asked, "Don't you want to comment on the joys of ceramics as a human endeavor—on the pleasures of the wheel, the importance of touching the earth?" Hilton's response is emblazoned on my wall of primary axioms. He said, "I don't care how you make it, Bub, or even if you did."

Since then, this has been my position on the joys of creation and of "being an artist." First, I really think it is dangerous to equate the wish or the process or the job description with the act because, in truth, there are no artists, no architects, and no men of letters. There is only art, architecture, literature, and a lot of hapless, confused people trying to make objects or texts that will someday be recognized as art or architecture or literature by the citizens who make those decisions well after the fact. It is not architecture because an architect made it. It is not art because an artist made it. It is not literature because a writer wrote it. Architecture is the consequence of a building having been made and subsequently valorized. It is not a privilege of the title, and the whole idea of accepting the mantle in advance of the act mitigates ambition and cheapens our endeavors.

The second quote is from my old philosophy professor at the University of Texas, who now denies he said this, although he did. The occasion was his assigning us the famous Yale *French Review* issue on structuralism that introduced the discipline to America—an important publication and a very influential one for me. What my professor said in class was that "the worst thing about this criticism [of Lévi-Strauss, Derrida, etc.] is that it has no heart. It seethes with contempt for the most ordinary social sentience." Then he turned around and said, "The best thing about this criticism is that it has no soul." By which he meant it had no woozy Heideggerian effervescence.

You can't imagine yourselves in the 1960s, I know, but you should try to image how heartless it seemed then to insist that the cultural modalities of words, signs, and symbols are nothing more than an ideological shorthand, radically disconnected from the world beyond us. Think how heartless it was to insist that there's no meaning outside the text, to assert the absolute contingency of reference, as Derrida did. Think how heartless it was to announce the death of the author as the primal site of cultural production. Think how heartless it was to detonate utopia and all ideas about the narrativity of history. How heartless to declare our alienation from nature and our fellow human beings to be an irrevocable condition of human society.

How heartless to reconceive human communication as an elaborate ritual of social correlation and authoritarian coercion. Heartless, indeed, but heartlessness has its virtues.

For all of us who were actively engaged in the flowering of structuralism in America, there was a kind of joy in this emptiness, a heady dose of liberation in the deconstruction of authority and coercion. I embraced it so heartily, in fact, that I immediately left academia to deal in art and then to play rock and roll. Which is to say that I took structuralism as a serious permission. I didn't depart from academia unthinkingly, because at this time we were talking structuralism in its primary form, as critique of institutions, and of language as an institution. The difficulty of critiquing institutions from within institutions was obvious then, since it is very difficult to raise issues about the authoritarian, coercive nature of institutions when one has had one's tenure bestowed by the largesse of that coercive structure. So it seemed to me that there was no academic future for French structuralism in America, and I was right. It was a practice that by definition had no footnotes, that was bound to the world and not to books.

So I went away for about ten years and came back to a theoretical environment that had been completely transformed. The university was still the same, but structuralism had been adapted. I would hear Derrida's phrase "there is no meaning outside the text" bandied around as an occasion to "raise our consciousness," as if Derrida's last-ditch formalism, his bedrock statement of the absolute conditions of our tragic and contingent relationship with the world around us, were a problem that we just had to solve. Even more dangerously, I thought, Foucault's radical critique of the human sciences had been suppressed in favor of Frankfurt School sociology that trafficked in crypto-Freudian psychology and some sort of vaguely Marxist critique. And I'm not really attacking Frankfurt School theory, here. It's just a theory, like structuralism. I'm talking about a radical shift in fashionable ideas that during the 1970s reaffirmed the traditional thrust of American academic thought, which has been German since jump street.

In any case, heartlessness was gone, and, God help us, aura was back, not the aura of authenticity of course, but the aura of the nostalgia for authenticity that pervades all of Benjamin and that I find kind of dopey and sentimental. Also, the freakin' apocalypse was back, best embodied by Adorno's similarly sentimental remark about there being no lyric poetry after the Holocaust, when there are numerous reasonable arguments to be made that, after the Holocaust, lyric poetry is exactly what we might need. Anyway, I'm looking around this new academia. Everything that my heartless colleagues and I had so assiduously shoved into the sea had magically reappeared. The author was back! Reincarnated as an avatar of "identity," *Herr auteur* had been returned to his position of high privilege. His or her intentions were presumed, once more, to matter. So we had nostalgia back. We had sentiment back. We had soul back. Architecture schools and liberal arts schools brought back all this crap, even though nobody in economics is much worried about Marx anymore, and nobody in psychology is much worried about Freud.

All this utopian romance has returned to us, I think, because contingency and dynamic systems are hard to teach and heartless, and as a consequence, practice in its presentness is dead. The flowering of American culture in the 1950s and 1960s withered as the present was transformed into a damaged site that we would fix tomorrow, or maybe next week. And since this fix was perpetually deferred, the future, as imagined by a coercive bureaucracy, took precedence. And it's hard to work while you're waiting for utopia, because optimism and joy are verboten. They are, after all, attributes of the imperfect present and not the perfect future. They are manifestations of a presumption that the future can be handicapped like any other bet. Real optimism, in fact, doesn't even require that you win your bet. One's position today is empowered by not being governed by an implacable future. If we all drown tomorrow when a giant tsunami covers Cambridge, today will be none the worse.

So we have utopia back, but not, I must note, a dynamic utopia. We have a kind of suburban, pre-Raphaelite utopia that is little more than pessimistic nostalgia for a failed idea. The surest sign of this is that there are no new utopias. There are socialist utopias, Marxist utopias, and a selection of faith-based Neverlands, all of which are showing their age, and all of which imagine the future as a world run by large, central institutions. So if we are preparing our students for this future and we are Marxist utopians or theocratic Jesus freaks, we will teach them to make institutional architecture. That is the normal thing to do. The courthouses, churches, art museums, and Kunsthalles—we will teach them to build all these so they will be ready when the revolution comes. I, however, am betting on a different future.

What I see is an ongoing collaboration and antagonism between the imperatives of institutional and commercial culture. What I hope for is that neither side wins. What I wish for is that practitioners of architecture will learn from the distinct attributes of the corral and the souk. What I fear is that the "postcritical" will throw out the baby with the bathwater, that it will become the post-theoretical and the postintellectual. If this happens, we are lost. We are mere academics and mere businessmen, and there will be no reason henceforth to call anything architecture again.

2006

9

Stocktaking 2004: Questions about the Present and Future of Design

Stan Allen, Hal Foster, and Kenneth Frampton

What do you think are, in your country, the most important current issues or challenges for architects, landscape architects, and/or urban designers, and why?

STAN ALLEN: There was an astonishing moment last spring at the Columbia University design conference organized to mark the end of Bernard Tschumi's tenure as dean of the Graduate School of Architecture, Preservation, and Planning. Michael Sorkin, our most passionate and articulate advocate of architecture's avant-garde tradition of radical experimentation, presented a sharp critique of Daniel Libeskind's proposals for lower Manhattan. Sorkin's comments, later published in the May 2003 *Architectural Record*, began by asking: "Is there anything new here?" "The final Libeskind scheme," Sorkin went on to say, "is simply conventional, its putative avant-gardism occlusive rather than innovative, offering up poignant, if familiar symbols to 'balance' the real investment to be made and the major uses to which the site is to be restored." Now this is not, in itself, surprising. Architecture's more radical wing has publicly and privately derided Libeskind's "sellout" of his avant-garde origins. What *was* unexpected was Robert A. M. Stern's quick defense of Libeskind's scheme as reasonable and pragmatic urban planning. An interesting new fault line has opened up, and it may require some rethinking.

Many of the younger audience members at the Columbia conference—those born, let's say, in the 1970s or later—may not remember the history. In those years Libeskind was a student of John Hejduk, that paradigm of resistance and withdrawal, whose most significant projects awaited realization by others. At Cooper Union and later as a teacher at Cranbrook, Libeskind emerged as a forceful advocate and exemplar of a radical architecture that began and ended in drawings, intentionally disengaged from the complexities and compromise of implementation. Stern, then, as now, was a defender of traditional architecture and conventional means of realization. That he would emerge as an advocate of Libeskind or, conversely, that Libeskind would be producing work that Stern could comfortably stand behind represents a significant realignment.

Of course, time and circumstance have changed, and to see this simply as sellout on Libeskind's part is too easy. Many other architects once committed to experimentation, critique, or alternative practices have made their peace with the intricacies of a more or less conventional building practice. Architects as diverse as Diller + Scofidio, Bernard Tschumi, Peter Eisenman, and Zaha Hadid are all focused on active building commissions, and it would be a mistake to view this as some sort of massive retreat from theoretical ambition and avant-garde experimentation. If anything, the stakes for both theory *and* practice are higher now. What is interesting to watch are the various intellectual and practical struggles that this shift has set off and the curious realignments it now sponsors.

The issue here is that in the United States at least, two equally unacceptable alternatives appear to be on the table. On the one hand, there is the trajectory implicitly favored by Stern: experimentation and design research are fine, but when it comes to getting something built in the real world, you have to play by the rules. This may be realistic, but it is ultimately cynical. On the other hand, we have Sorkin's call for continued resistance and experimentation, even at the risk of marginalization—the familiar strategy of many generations of avant-gardes. But the problem with the avant-garde model is that any departure from the narrow path of resistance can only be construed as a compromise that leads to the inevitable cry of sellout or retreat. For those actively committed to realizing complex projects while maintaining a high level of design ambition, neither path seems promising. The successful models from Europe—innovative architectural practices such as UN Studio, MVRDV, Abalos + Herreros, or Foreign Office Architects, all of which are committed to innovative strategies of realization, to high levels of design practice, and to parallel operations of research and publication—have so far resisted translation to the United States.

So, to answer the question directly: the most important issue facing architects, landscape architects, and urban designers today is how to construct a viable, progressive project capable of incorporating the innovative design research of the past decades into a productive new model of practice. This would be a form of practice committed to public legibility, to the active engagement of new technologies, and to creative means of implementation. It would be an experimental practice that takes as its object not self-referential theories but real problems—the difficult moments when architecture takes its place in the world. It would be a practice open to innovation and play, capable of confronting the complexities of realization without facile compromise. This means going beyond the traditional avant-garde models, with their suspicion of practice, to engage the complexity of architecture's techniques, procedures, and protocols of implementation as legitimate material for creative experimentation. Far from retreating from the complexity of the problem, such a practice would find material for experimentation, critique, and theoretical speculation in the methods and procedures of day-to-day architectural practice.

Theoretical reflection can help here because a period of critique and skeptical examination of received practices necessarily precedes innovation. But critique cannot be an end in itself; we need to imagine a form of practice at once more agile and more effective. The point here is that architecture needs to confront serious issues—from the ecological crisis, to the globalization of practice, to architecture's place in the contemporary city, or the impact of digital technologies on design—and the present toolbox of theories and practices has simply proven inadequate. The old opposition that pits the tired dogmas of yesterday's avant-garde against the cynical platitudes of conventional professional practice is enormously unproductive. (Theory, too, needs to be reexamined, so that it can become a creative field that engages in lively dialogue with history and practice.)

What exactly would such a practice look like? In broad strokes, it would be an architecture open and sympathetic to popular culture and the creativity of the marketplace. The emergence of what Michael

Speaks has called "Design Intelligence," which implies a creative use of design expertise in a looser, more entrepreneurial relationship to the market, is a promising development.[1] Speaks's suggestive formulation plays on two meanings of the word *intelligence*. On the one hand, it recognizes that architects and other design professionals possess a specific form of expertise, a synthetic and projective capacity unique to their own discipline. On the other hand, just as military intelligence is necessarily composed of rumors and fragmented information, often from suspect sources (with a high noise to signal ratio), it implies that architects need to be open to the "chatter" of the world outside of their own field and alert to new ways of interpreting, or putting that information to work. As in intelligence work, with immense quantities of information now simultaneously available, it is no longer access to information but the ability to process, organize, and visualize information that is crucial.

These new models of practice would therefore no longer oppose conventional practice to the established strategies of the avant-garde (critique, narrative, or negation). Instead of being conventionally unconventional in this way, or just conventionally conventional (like unexamined practice), they would look for unanticipated potential in the unconventionally conventional. They would examine new forms of collaboration and be open to the innovations of allied disciplines. They would make creative use of new technologies while remaining skeptical of the extravagant claims made for those very technologies. As Robert Somol and Sarah Whiting have argued, these new practices would be less invested in difficulty and more comfortable with the speed and intensity of contemporary urban life—not interrogating their tools but putting them to work. This "projective" program, Whiting and Somol argue, "does not necessarily entail a capitulation to market forces but actually respects or reorganizes multiple economies, ecologies, information systems, and social groups."[2]

These emergent models of practice are anticipatory, rather than hermeneutic. They are less concerned with interpreting the history of the site and more concerned with strategies to activate the site's potential. They draw freely from other disciplines, being less concerned with what architecture is, or what it means, and more with what it can do, that is to say, what effects it can set in motion, regardless of their origin. They are robust, information-dense, and open to change and revision. Its practitioners realize that the new reality of technology and the city is one of continual obsolescence and that the only way to survive change is to change themselves. Finally, they trust the intelligence of architecture's audience, understanding that architecture has many publics and that the significant work of architecture is one that allows continual revision and rereading, teasing out new meanings as the context changes.

In contrast to the established model that has traditionally used a teaching career as a jumping-off point for experimental work, many young architects today are impatient with the implied slow path to a mature practice that this implies. They have moved into practice earlier and embraced commercial development and the public realm instead of the standard pattern of competitions and small private commissions. Young architects such as SHoP, Open Office, and Lindy Roy have all developed practices that have internalized the academic work of the recent past. They are design driven, technologically adept, and agile—capable of making rapid tactical adjustments that the project or the market requires. But these small firms also use new technologies and strategic collaborations to leverage their expertise in order to respond effectively to larger and more complex commissions. The prominence of United Architects in the World Trade Center competition last year is another sign that new models of practice are emerging. This global, interdisciplinary collective brought the combined expertise of several decades of experimental design research to bear on a problem that demanded both innovation and plausibility. They understood very well that, as opposed to an avant-garde provocation, which need not be fully worked out, design innovation requires not only creativity but also a high level of technical resolution. If you are going to propose something new, you take on the added responsibility of proving that it works. These architects responded to the constraints of the site and program with a solution that was formally complex, not out of an arbitrary desire for complex form but rather as a realistic response to a complex problem and to the multiple publics necessarily represented at the World Trade Center site.

Innovation and critique now form part of the everyday landscape of professional practice—it's rare that an RFP or Q for a public project goes out that does not ask for "innovative design." But what is really meant by this? Would anyone know it if they saw it? True innovation, almost by definition, would likely go unrecognized; it might register, instead, as an unfamiliar use of familiar strategies, or as Roberto Unger has suggested in another context, "the vindication of repressed solutions, of yesterday's missed opportunities, today's forgotten anomalies, and tomorrow's unsuspected possibilities."[3] Innovation is different from the Modernist ideas of absolute newness on the tabula rasa. It works incrementally, building on what is known. But it is also capable of setting off a cascade of effects—architectural, social, and perhaps political—that over time, create the potential for more significant change.

HAL FOSTER: I want to highlight four issues. Not all are new, but even the old ones remain pressing.

1. The first concerns the small fraction of the built environment that can be considered architecture. For all the massive attention given a few projects, reflective architecture appears ever more marginal to the actual construction of our everyday world. There are many reasons for this situation—from the old separation of architecture and engineering to the more recent domination of big construction firms—but some blame must be laid to the self-involvement of the architectural vanguard. (Self-involvement is hardly the same thing as creative research, let alone self-critique, and it should not be pinned on the usual scapegoats—academy and theory—as even some academic theorists do.) This relative lack of reflective architecture permits the proliferation of what Rem Koolhaas calls Junkspace and what Luis Fernández-Galiano calls the "horizontal Babel."[4]

Obviously some of the forces in play here far exceed the control of the architectural profession. Driven by a Fordist economy, the modern city was a relatively fixed world of factories and warehouses, skyscrapers, railways, bridges, and highways. However, as capital began to flow ever more rapidly in search of cheap labor, innovative manufacture, financial deregulation, and new markets, the life expectancy of many structures fell dramatically. This post-Fordist process is evident enough in the United States, but it is blatant where development is even less restricted. How can architectural design adapt to such a rapid rate of physical turnover? Advocates of Pop architecture like Reyner Banham and John McHale responded forty years ago with the proposal of "throwaway architecture." But throwaways don't necessarily go away, and plastic has a half-life that rivals that of the Parthenon; in part Pop architecture becomes another recipe for Junkspace. The same is true of the decorated shed of Postmodern architecture à la Venturi and Scott Brown, which was explicitly offered as an accommodation to "the ordinary and the ugly"; today the periodic adjusting of the sign out front and the structure behind is standard practice everywhere. Recently Sylvia Lavin has updated this Pop-Postmodern position with a call for a "reorientation of architecture toward a field of [special visual] effects" (296); perhaps this is what Learning from Las Vegas means today.[5] It is hard to resist the common sense of "market realism," but must it mean obeisance? Why not issue a challenge instead? How might master developers and architects alike be induced to pay more attention to everyday building, to average architecture, in a not-so-throwaway manner that neither reiterates the ordinary and the ugly nor opts for special visual effects?

2. Architectural discourse today often oscillates between opposite demands: on the one hand, to follow the forces of technological dematerialization; on the other, to recover the experience of architectural materiality. Thus, for example, Mark C. Taylor insists, "All architecture must become network architecture" (445), while Kazuyo Sejima states, "In an age in which people communicate through various media in nonphysical spaces, it is the architect's responsibility to make actual space for physical and direct communication between people" (407). Perhaps, like all antinomies, these two positions belong to one another, even partake of one another. What, then, is the stake that lies beneath this opposition, and how can we both grasp that stake and move beyond this opposition?

3. One such stake is the role of architecture in what is still sometimes called, optimistically, "the public sphere." (After all, both aforementioned positions insist on "communication," which suggests that a felt lack of community is held in common.) The difficulty of the public sphere—it was always a mostly heuristic concept—is only deepened by the ever greater complexity of the population and the ever greater indifference (malevolence?) of its institutional mediators—from media corporations to nation-states. Nevertheless, since 9/11 the question of architecture in the public sphere is back on the table (if it is not obscene to speak of a "good effect" of this event, this is one). Anthony Vidler has articulated the present predicament exactly: on the one hand, "there has never been a more propitious moment than now to revisit the question of architecture's social responsibilities" (469); on the other hand, "the gap that exists now between the specialized discourses of planning, architecture, political process, and the public has never been so great" (472).

4. A further problem in this regard is the veritable attack on the public sphere, under the cover of "security and surveillance," by our

own, and here again architecture might figure importantly. For some historical perspective here, consider the old Modernist image of skyscrapers and airships conjoined (of a dirigible, say, set to dock at the spire of the Empire State Building). This is an image of the city not only as a spectacle of commercial tourism but also as a utopia of metropolitan space—of people free to circulate from the street, through the tower, to the sky, and back down again. (And it is not a strictly capitalist image: similar ones appear in revolutionary Soviet designs of the 1920s.) The attack on the World Trade Center—of the two jets flown into the two towers—was a dystopian perversion of this old Modernist dream of free movement through urban space. New fears cling to the skyscraper as a terrorist target, and the values of urban density and "delirious space" are overshadowed by calls for surveillance and "defensible space." Those values need advocates like never before, for, to paraphrase the Surrealists, cosmopolitan beauty will be delirious or will not be.

Here again most of the forces in play exceed the terrain of the architectural profession, but architects are still involved in the disposition of bodies in space and time (even, perhaps especially, when they have gone "network"); that is to say, they are still involved, crucially, in security and surveillance—and not only with structures that might be deemed panoptical. With every new project, every new proposal, architects must decide how to intervene in this political realm.

KENNETH FRAMPTON: Whether one addresses oneself exclusively to the United States or to the developing world at large, two fundamental approaches in the field of environmental design ought to be emphasized: first, architectural practice should surely focus much more urgently on sustainability, while, second, it ought to recognize the salient importance of landscape, not only because it has the capacity to integrate one-off buildings into their surrounding topography, but also because landscape intervention is possibly the sole remaining agent capable of mediating the chaos of the megalopolis. Notwithstanding the occasional bucolic suburb, it is surely overwhelmingly evident that our suburbanized dystopia is fast becoming a universal condition. The chances are that little of this will ever be rebuilt or even reformulated in a culturally significant way. Urban sprawl seems to be irreversible, and apart from the possibility of modifying it on a piecemeal basis through earthwork interventions of various kinds, one can readily envisage its eventual long-term ruin and abandonment. Given what has happened to the "brownfield" legacy of the past century, one can hardly be sanguine about its future demolition and/or restoration.

It is becoming increasingly evident that we should reduce the amount of energy consumed by built form. If the latest statistics are to be taken at face value, it is somehow shocking to discover that while commutation by automobile, aircraft, and public transport are jointly responsible for some 40 percent of our annual energy consumption, the built environment currently accounts for an equal amount or more, with the remaining 20 percent being used in various modes of primary and secondary industry. As Michelle Addington informs us in *Harvard Design Magazine* 18, a large part of this "built consumption" stems from our profligate use of electric light, with air-conditioning coming a close second.[6]

At the same time, it is clear that the prospect of attaining a truly sustainable architecture is an extremely subtle affair. It depends (as the legacy of the vernacular should have long since informed us) not only on the climate and topography but also on the resources of the region in which a building is situated. When it comes to the vernacular in the original sense of the term, we also need to recall the mores of the particular society within which it once emerged. One thinks in this regard of the complementing "sustainable" role of the siesta in the pre-industrial culture of the Mediterranean and the Middle East.

As Peter Buchanan puts it in his seminal catalog essay "Ten Shades of Green," there is no such thing as green architecture, by which he means that there is no universal mechanistic formula, such as the blanket application of photovoltaic cells, with which to mitigate the environmental shortfall of current building practice.[7] Instead there is the ongoing culture of building, which should be properly regarded as an evolving craft rather than as an art or an applied science, although this obviously does not mean that it is not susceptible to scientific technique or that it cannot avail itself of advanced environmental technology. Indeed, one needs to acknowledge that engineering verges on becoming culture at exactly that point where architecture encroaches on engineering, and vice versa. At the same time, one needs to bear in mind that building remains, in many respects, a hybrid, quasi-anachronistic activity, in which there is no automatic prestige accruing to the latest technology as an end itself. One should rather look for a judicious and subtle mixture of old and new techniques, for, as the late Aldo van Eyck put it years ago, what antiquarians and technocrats have in common is a sentimental attitude toward time—for him, where the former were sentimental about the past, the latter were sentimental about the future. One way or another, sentimentality (or should we say "spectacular rhetoric"?) tends to be our nemesis, while more often than not the "timeless" resilience of building culture continues to elude us.

One thinks in this regard of all those curtain-walled, high-rise office structures that somehow managed, through various technical ruses, to eschew sunscreening of any kind, so as to proclaim their indifference to the greenhouse effect. It is as though no one had ever thought of *brise soleil* or adjustable louvers, or, for that matter, shutters or blinds, and, above all, electronic servo-mechanisms. Here we encounter the unfinished Modern project in more ways than one. One thinks in this regard of the multiple options offered to the occupant in Le Corbusier's Maison Clarté of 1933. It is ridiculous to claim that sliding windows, adjustable horizontal shutters, and roller blinds are expensive to install and difficult to maintain, when the energy savings they would achieve over the long haul would more than compensate for their cost, not to mention provide the liberative sensual pleasure of being able to modulate both light and ventilation manually at will.

For its part, landscape design is rapidly becoming the remedial art par excellence, for without its critical application, the nature-culture interface can never begin to approach any kind of "homeostatic" resolution, ecologically or culturally. In this context we should surely tell ourselves that, with a few exceptions, we do not need any more freestanding objects, irrespective of their aesthetic quality. The megalopolitan domain is already overburdened with a surfeit of freestanding objects of every conceivable genre, proliferated by the production-consumption cycle of the free-market strip economy, without our voluntarily adding yet another object that is not closely integrated into the contiguous topography.

I am convinced that landscape proffers itself as a creative-cum-remedial modus both literally and metaphorically. The long-standing ideological division of labor between urban planning, urban design, and architecture can only be overcome, in my view, through what I can only call the self-conscious encouragement of a topographic/phenomenological disposition on the part of architects and planners, one that, while being against conventional expectations, is both technically adept and economically realistic. Ultimately, it is obviously a matter of imposing restrictive legislation on future development. I am thinking of such utopian provisions as the blanket prohibition of urban sprawl or, let us say, a seemingly less utopian sanction against impermeable, blacktop parking lots, both of which could be said to fall under the rubric of landscape. At another, possibly less contentious level, it is a matter of recognizing the scope of potential strategic interventions within the urban continuum, having precisely limited spatial and temporal aims, such as of fairly large, "place-creating" hybrid megaforms, or dense, limited land settlement patterns, or heterotopic quasi-urbanistic concentrations spun off public transport infrastructures. Each of these options could be said to fall under the rubric Manuel de Solà-Morales has brilliantly characterized as "urban acupuncture."[8] Irrespective of the degree of investment, public transit is surely a key catalyst in all this, as we may judge from the success of the urban policies pursued by Jaime Lerner in Curitiba, Brazil, and Enrique Peñalosa in Bogotá, Colombia, not to mention the interregional, transcontinental role played by high-speed rail in Europe and Japan, and the pioneering of the German Maglev train system—the world's first magnetic levitation railroad line—in the Shanghai region. Landscape architecture may contribute to such strategic interventions in many ways, from the provision of light-rail links with compensatory earthworks to the conservation and irrigation of storm water, or the equally sustainable construction of reed beds for the filtering and purification of gray water and the provision of shade trees.

What recent architecture, landscape architecture, and/or urban design projects or kinds of projects do you consider best and/or most important, and why?

FOSTER: My choices are literally "projects," not realized as structures but exhibited as interventions in the past two years at the Storefront for Architecture in SoHo (a small but important venue). I select these two projects because, indirectly, the first challenges the current fatigue with critical architecture, while the second questions the Postmodern suspicion about utopian architecture.

The first project—*A Civilian Occupation: The Politics of Israeli Architecture* by Rafi Segal and Eyal Weizman—is precisely an architectural intervention in the political terrain of security and surveillance. This ensemble of plans, maps, photographs, and texts examines the settlements in the West Bank in many dimensions—architectural, urbanistic, environmental, historical, military, and political. The conclusions are damning: "The mundane elements of planning and architecture have been conscripted as tactical tools in the Israeli state strategy, seeking national and geopolitical objectives in the organization of space. . . . Space becomes the physical embodiment of a matrix of forces, manifested across the landscape in the construction of roads, hilltop settlements, development towns, and garden-suburbs." For Segal and Weizman, the settlements are war continued by other means—architecture and planning in the service of conquest and colonization. For all the specificity of the West Bank, these Israeli architects suggest that the settlements might not be entirely unique, that they might serve as prototypes for militarized societies of the near future, "a worst-case scenario of capitalist globalization and its spatial fall-out."⁹

The second project—*Wave Garden* by Yusuke Obuchi—is a 480-acre field designed to float, like a Suprematist rectangle, off the coast of California. Made up of 1,800 piezoelectric sheets supported by 1,800 buoys, it is an electrical generator during the week and a marine park on the weekend. In its first mode the sheets of the garden are bent by the sea waves in a way that generates electricity that is then transferred to the energy grid of the Golden State. In its second mode, electricity is run through the sheets in a way that shapes them into a metamorphic island of coastal leisure and maritime play. Neither entirely fantastic nor quite practical, *Wave Garden* is precisely utopian: it forces us to think "Why not?" in a way that questions what is.

Obuchi calls up precedents from Gaudí to the earthworks of the late 1960s and early 1970s. However, he does not partake of the fascination with entropy so evident in Robert Smithson's work; on the contrary, *Wave Garden* generates alternative energy rather than submitting to its dissipation. At the same time, the project is not as redemptive as it may first appear. Early on New York artist Robert Morris was sensitive to the ideological recuperation of the earthwork idea—that despoilers of the environment might use earthworks as so much artistic camouflage. *Wave Garden* skirts this danger: unlike many designers today, Obuchi does not seek to naturalize—to vitalize or to animate—his architecture; rather, his project is continuous with the greater human project to acculturate nature, which it proposes to tame rather than pervert. In the era of Enron, Obuchi conjures up a vision of energy, physical and social, in a way that rivals in its utopian force the proposal for a *Monument to the Third International* (1920) by Vladimir Tatlin.

FRAMPTON: Our mediatic popularizers seem to have no compunction whatsoever about their compulsive cultivation of the archi-star. By virtue of this all-but-somnambulist consensus, certain spectacular works are continually being overvalued, while others, of a less immediately gratifying nature, remain undervalued. These mediatic distortions seem all the more arbitrary and absurd in the face of the fact that the global quality of normative architecture has never been higher or more sophisticated, notwithstanding the blanket barbarism of speculative development that prevails virtually everywhere.

This ascendancy of a global, nearly anonymous architecture of high quality is perhaps partially due to the paradoxically positive effects of the media—to the fact that today young architects habitually judge their work in accordance with global standards, even though their architecture, at its best, remains highly responsive to local circumstances. While highly aestheticized, spectacular building is the architectural lingua franca of the so-called First World, invariably sponsored by regional capitals that compete with each other at the level of sensational civic patronage, once one casts one's net somewhat wider, one invariably encounters a surprising breadth and depth of architectural culture worldwide. If one assesses this seemingly spontaneous development in terms of the number of architects of quality practicing in a given region at a particular time, then certain geographical domains seem to emerge into prominence. As I have remarked elsewhere, the built architectural culture of France, Spain, Finland, and Japan seems to me to have been particularly fertile in this regard. Over the past quarter of a century, these countries have been able to realize works of exceptional quality and density on a remarkably broad front, and now much the same may surely be claimed for the architects of Australia.

When it comes to the architectural culture of North America, it seems to me that it would be more ecumenical and critically productive to include both Canada and Mexico under this rubric, for then one could embrace within the normative North American architectural spectrum figures as distinguished in their own way as Dan Hanganu (Montreal), John and Patricia Patkau (Vancouver), and the rapidly ascending practice of Howard Sutcliffe and Brigitte Shim

(Toronto), not to mention the rising talent of Alberto Kalach (Mexico City). Would this not leaven, as it were, the received, somewhat restrictive scope of what we currently accept as prestigious American architecture as disseminated by the media? Within a broader rubric, might one not recontextualize, as it were, the work of our archi-stars and thereby permit us to accord value, for example, to such underestimated architects as Will Bruder, Rick Joy, and Wendell Burnette in the American Southwest, or, let us say, Carlos Jimenez in Houston, or the even less familiar practice of Lake/Flato in San Antonio?

There are, of course, in Latin America, many other distinguished architects that more than merit our renewed attention—Ricardo Legorreta (Mexico), the late Eladio Dieste (Uruguay), Paulo Mendes da Rocha (Brazil), Clorinda Testa (Argentina), Jesus Tenreiro (Venezuela), Christian de Groote (Chile), and Rogelio Salmona (Colombia), to name only the leading members of a certain generation.

After all this, I find that I have still not responded to the tenor of the question, so let me cite four works that seem to me to be of particular significance. At the urban scale, I attach particular value to two relatively recent works: L'Illa Block, realized on the Avenida Diagonal in Barcelona in 1994 to the designs of Rafael Moneo and Manuel de Solà-Morales, and Peter Walker's 1988 Marina Linear Park, San Diego. The first is a hybrid, multiuse megastructure simultaneously pitched at the scale of both Ildefons Cerdà's Ensanche and the chaotic urban sprawl that surrounds the nineteenth-century core of Barcelona on every side. The other is the embellishment of a light-rail system that, at the hands of a master landscape architect, has been rendered as an urban boulevard lined with palm trees and exotic shrubs. Obviously I value these interventions as paradigmatic urban ameliorations rather than as sublime works of architecture.

When it comes to architecture, I would opt for two exceptional exercises in timber construction at a relatively large scale. I have in mind the realization of the Seabird Island School, in Agassiz, British Columbia, to the designs of Patkau Architects in 1990, and the completion some three years later of Renzo Piano's Tjibaou Cultural Center in Noumea, New Caledonia. While both seem exemplary tectonic pieces that manifest particular sensitivity to their sites and their specific climates, I find it equally significant that they are highly inventive, modernizing constructs conceived by "outsiders" for the reaffirmation of native cultures. Thus in both instances a symbolic evocation of a lost aboriginal vernacular is matched by a commitment to the modernization

Patkau Architects, Seabird Island School, Agassiz, British Columbia, Canada, 1991. Courtesy of Patkau Architects.

Renzo Piano, Tjibaou Cultural Center, Noumea, New Caledonia, 1998. Photograph by Tim Griffith/ESTO.

of a rooted culture. Further, one should note that both buildings make an all-but-exclusive use of wood, which, from a sustainable standpoint (as long as forests are sustainably managed), is the singular building material with the least embodied energy of currently available materials.

What recent design projects or kinds of projects do you consider overrated, and why?

FOSTER: I want to underscore two overrated tendencies in contemporary design, the first of which might be called "spectacle architecture," the second, "trauma architecture." Once more the economic ideologies and political myths in play here exceed the architectural profession; what interests me, however, is how architects respond to these forces.

In *The Society of the Spectacle* (1967), Guy Debord defined spectacle as "capital accumulated to the point where it becomes an image." Of course, spectacle has become only more intensive in the past four decades, to the point where media—communications—and entertainment conglomerates are the dominant ideological apparatuses in our society, powerful enough to refashion other institutions (such as architecture, not to mention art) in their guise. Today, then, the corollary of the Debordian definition is true as well: spectacle is "an image accumulated to the point where it becomes capital." This logic is so pervasive as to appear almost natural: consider, as but one example, all the cultural centers that, alongside theme parks and sports complexes, assist in the corporate "revival" of the city—that is, in its being made safe for shopping, spectating, and spacing out. This is the true "Bilbao Effect," and architects like Frank Gehry have designed accordingly, not in any suspicion of spectacle but according to its specifications. (It is indicative of our political condition that "liberal" media organs like the *New York Times* continue to conflate this spectacle logic with a democratic architecture of a public sphere.)

Gehry Partners, Walt Disney Concert Hall, Los Angeles, California, 2003. Photograph by Roland Halbe.

As the example of Gehry alone suggests, spectacle not only governs the use of architecture but also becomes internal to its design. Today, for example, many prominent architects delight in the projective skins and luminous scrims permitted by new materials and techniques (Herzog and de Meuron come to mind). Yet often these skins and scrims only dazzle or confuse, and the architecture becomes an illuminated sculpture, a radiant jewel. However beautiful, it can also be spectacular in the Debordian sense—a kind of commodity fetish on a grand scale, a mysterious object whose production is mystified. This is not a plea for structural transparency; it is simply a caution about a new kind of Potemkin architecture of conjured surfaces driven by computer design.[10]

The second tendency—architecture dedicated to a traumatic view of history—is not as pervasive as the first, but it is no less problematic. Of course, the exemplar here is the work of Daniel Libeskind, and the latest instance is his design for the World Trade Center site.[11] Such trauma architecture, with its allegories of rupture and discontinuity, might work well in his Jewish Museum Berlin, but that is a museum, not an entire section of a city, and it was built when the commemorated event was in the past—that is, when the museum could truly serve as a memorial. However horrific, the World Trade Center atrocity can hardly be compared with the Holocaust. That "our lives were changed forever by the events of 9/11" seems true to many Americans, even ones who are not history challenged, but this statement is also deeply ideological (it was originally credited to John Ashcroft), and Libeskind has adapted its rhetoric to support his trauma architecture. "From now on architecture will never be the same," he has proclaimed, with the implication that his architecture will best register this supposed fact.[12]

Should urban architecture be rethought in terms of trauma? Libeskind argued so for Berlin: "The lost center cannot be reconnected like an artificial limb to an old body, but must generate an overall transformation of the city."[13] But should New York be remapped through Ground Zero? The memorial elements of the Libeskind design—the foundation walls, the open wedge, the symbolic spire—want to fix lower Manhattan in monumental terms, terms alien to a city defined from its beginnings by its embrace of change. Such traumatic monumentalism is problematic enough, but there is another motive here as well. "Build them higher than before," one often heard after the fall of the towers, as if our problem were

Studio Daniel Libeskind, World Trade Center, study, 2002. Courtesy of Studio Daniel Libeskind. Photograph by Jock Pottle.

penile dysfunction—and, perhaps, imperially speaking, it is. If the hole in the ground figures the tragedy for Libeskind, his spire "will let the world know that the terrorists have failed." A large part of the great attraction of his scheme is disclosed right there: it gives us both commemorative prop and imperial thrust, both the traumatic and the triumphal. Or, more exactly, it gives us trauma troped as triumph, a site of civilian tragedy turned into a symbol of militaristic defiance. This is a dangerous concoction; certainly the historical precedents when the wounded have linked up with the hubristic are not savory to contemplate (think of the German Right after World War I).

FRAMPTON: To venture upon revealing one's prejudices as to the overvalued works of our time is somewhat invidious. As everyone knows, the subject of such attention is not inclined to appreciate the so-called positive value of negative criticism. Nevertheless I find a few lauded works of recent date sufficiently arbitrary as to border on the totally irrational. I have in mind, I regret to say, most of the submissions for the World Trade Center competition, which, in my view, save for the singular design submitted by Foster Associates of London, were each more gratuitous and cacophonic than the next.

However much one might have misgivings about the sociopolitical, not to say economic viability of reasserting the global prowess of Wall Street by building back a "twin" high-rise structure of even greater capacity and height than the ill-fated World Trade Center, Foster, at the very least, posited a structurally lucid, heroic design that was reciprocally linked both symbolically and otherwise to the familiar twin footprint of the former World Trade Center. These paired square openings, opening to an elevated, landscaped ground plane, would have provided zenithal light for commemorative reflecting pools, bounded by promenades beneath. Foster had the acumen to explain the nuanced intentions of his design with comprehensive diagrams indicating that no one working in the rebuilt twin towers would be able to overlook those visiting the memorial pools below grade.

Whatever the shortcomings of the World Trade Center fiasco, your question prompts me to touch on the expressively spectacular line assumed by Frank Gehry in what we might call his triumphant maturity, and here I find myself broaching the vexed question of the difference between what I perceive to be "large art," on the one hand, and the sociocultural destiny of architecture, on the other, or rather, the ethics of building culture versus pre-emptive attempts to compete with the ever more pluralized individual expressivity of art. Most of my reservations about the later work of Gehry stem from this disjunction, namely, a situation in which an idiosyncratically expressive talent manifests its apparent indifference to the more socio-phenomenological aspects of building at its best. Thus, notwithstanding the undeniably spectacular aspects of the Guggenheim in Bilbao—one that seemingly has assured this ex-shipyard city its current cultural kudos—I fail to see the intrinsic virtues of a work in which there seems to be no alternative but to climb up from the river walk and then, having done so, immediately descend through the same difference in level in order to access the main entrance, let alone other infelicities such as a riverfront gourmet restaurant that, owing to the formal necessity of maintaining the plastic continuity of the titanium shell, is denied any fenestration overlooking the river. Or have I missed something? These seemingly "minor lapses" that will no doubt be dismissed by the aficionados as trivial objections are symptomatic in my view of an aestheticized indifference that, unfortunately, informs, or should we say deforms, a great deal of late Modern architecture.

Do you think the social and cultural influence and power of designers are increasing, decreasing, or steady? How would you describe the level and kind of that power and influence? How far apart are the realities and the ideal?

ALLEN: Though we often blur the social and cultural when we talk about architecture, I believe it is important to be more precise. My dictionary defines *social* as "of or relating to human society, the interaction of the individual and the group, or the welfare of human beings as members of society," whereas it speaks of *culture* as "acquaintance with and taste in the fine arts, humanities, and broad aspects of science as distinguished from vocational and technical skills."[14] Thanks in part to the massive media coverage of the World Trade Center competition and to the high visibility of figures such as Rem Koolhaas and Frank Gehry, it is safe to say that "acquaintance with and taste in" architecture as a "fine art" is probably on the rise. The irony is that architecture, which is nothing if not a social art form, loses effectiveness precisely to the degree that it becomes exclusively a cultural phenomenon. The same public that happily patronizes the new Disney Concert Hall in Los Angeles more than likely lives quite conventionally in traditional houses. Its patterns of work, everyday life, and leisure, while superficially modern (commuting to work on the freeway, shopping in the mall, linked up to the Internet, etc.), exist in an unformed and uninflected relationship to modernity's new spaces.

The paradox here is that we live in a time of unprecedented penetration of high design into everyday life. Design is everywhere. Michael Graves, Philippe Starck, and Isaac Mizrahi design for Target, and Karim Rashid wants to change the world. Today's design-conscious consumers may drive new Volkswagen Beetles and work on iMacs; they dress in Prada and Helmut Lang when they can afford it and Banana Republic when they can't. They buy their furniture at Ikea or Design Within Reach, their coffee at Starbucks, and clothes for their child at Baby Gap. In every aspect of their lives, the distance between "highbrow" and low is closing, with the probable exception of their house. Whether they live in the city or suburbs, chances are good that they live in a traditional house. At precisely the point where the effect of design might become social, that is, might sponsor alternative lifestyles or new forms of domestic life, it disappears.

Tom Wolfe has quipped that only the very rich or the very poor live in Modern architecture—the former by choice, the latter by mandate. This may have once been true but seems much less so today. What we are seeing is a leveling of the field of "taste" with a default setting of vaguely traditional (e.g., Modernist masterpieces torn down to make room for McMansions) and an overlay of modernity—those same McMansions wired for the most up-to-date electronics and designer kitchens and marble bathrooms as selling points in urban "luxury" apartments. To a small degree (see *Dwell* and *Real Simple*), serious efforts have been made to bring affordable, well-designed architecture to a mass market. Perhaps this marks the beginning of a shift in which design consciousness does not stop at the walls. Nevertheless, at present the paradox remains—serious architecture is gaining presence on the cultural stage and in the details of private life, while it is still pretty much absent from the key sites of everyday life: the workplace, the freeway, the mall, houses, and housing.

In part this may be the effect of a lingering concern that the "social" has been the scene of some of Modern architecture's most spectacular failures. The midcentury experiments of social housing so derided by Wolfe and other critics are today held up as evidence of architecture's inability to contribute productively to the public realm. (W. H. Auden's 1946 dictum still seems pertinent: "Thou shalt not sit / With statisticians nor commit / A social science."[15]) Moreover, historians now suggest that architecture in any form would have been powerless to resist the social and economic forces that led to failure of Modern architecture's social project. It is therefore not surprising that architects today hold social issues at arm's length and concentrate their attention where architecture can actually be more effective. Perhaps we can say that *architecture will become an effective public art form at the moment when it can leverage its cultural efficacy toward social ends.* The most promising areas would seem to be those moments in the urban and suburban realm where mixing and exchange occur—the mall, the market, transportation hubs, and our small stock of collective housing—where there are moments of genuine, cooperative social innovation, now happening without much help from architecture. If architecture, in its role as a public art form, can begin to accelerate or intensify these effects, it might regain some of its social impact.

FOSTER: Clearly architecture has a new centrality in the culture at large. Although this prominence stems from the initial debates about Postmodernism in the 1970s, it is clinched by more recent developments, some of which I have mentioned above (spectacle and traumatic monumentalism). Yet this new importance also has a compensatory dimension: in many ways the architect is our latest dream-figure of a magisterial vision and worldly agency that the rest of us cannot hope to possess; in a sense the mythic architect is a contemporary substitute for the mythic artist. (Perhaps this is why vanguard architecture sometimes seems "popular" today—the person on the street is likely to come up with the names of a few architects but not of a few artists—despite the great gap between such vanguard architecture and our everyday environment.) The often paranoid structure of architectural discourse today—the manner in which visions of grandeur seem to alternate with feelings of abasement at every turn—also points to this compensatory dimension. "Since the early 1990s the 'market' has ruled, so the only tool we seem to have left is seduction," Kamiel Klaasse remarks. "This creates the unpleasant condition of dependency. Architects combine arrogance with impotence; we are beggars and braggarts" (269). "These days architects can do everything—and, at the same time, nothing," Maarten Kloos adds. "Architecture has become an amorphous, evasive concept that just hangs like a scent in the air or the latest fad . . . " (276). It is not just the market that places architecture in this ambiguous position; it is also political constraints (building codes, urban zonings, and environmental laws, to name only a few). Moreover, when all is said and done, architecture is not the problem, and as such it can only be a small part of the solution.

FRAMPTON: Despite the ever-ascending popularity of spectacular architecture as media hype in the press and even, to a degree, on television, the influence of architects on progressive environmental culture in general seems to me virtually negligible, or certainly less than it was in the European welfare state during the three decades after the Second World War. Even at the level of popular dissemination, it is not clear that the increased "visibility" of architecture as a mediatic theme has necessarily led to a general elevation of either public or institutional taste. Symptomatic of the limitations of architecture with regard to the public discourse at another level is the current British environmental predicament as analyzed by the Urban Studies Task Force chaired by Lord Rogers and commissioned by the British Labor Government, published in 1999 under the title *Towards an Urban Renaissance.*[16] Among its many recommended strategies, this report advocated that 60 percent of the estimated British housing need for the next two decades—3.8 million households—be accommodated on "brownfield" sites of which, as of now, there are some 45,000 hectares available, along with 250,000 vacant housing units, mostly in built-up urban areas. As elsewhere, much of this is a product of industrial decline combined with underinvestment in public transport, plus greenfield suburbanization and the corresponding exodus of retail shopping from established urban centers. Architects were, of course, part of this task force, but it is doubtful, given the current track record of New Labour, that the Blair government will adopt and pursue the necessary legislation and public policies to enact anything like the full range of the report's recommendations. A similar impasse, at a local rather than a national scale, confronts the urban planning technocracy of Atlanta, which would like to introduce legislation that would effectively eclipse any further expansion of this ten-mile-diameter, low-density conurbation. A consequence of this current boom, as Ellen Dunham-Jones reminded us, is that over the space of the past decade Atlantans have doubled the number of hours they spend each year in their automobiles.[17]

What seem like promising new roles, activities, and territories for architecture, landscape architecture, and/or urban design in the next decade?

ALLEN: Architecture's traditional alignment with the culture of cities is undergoing a change. Just as the elevator, fireproof construction, and urban mass transit transformed the city in the first half of the twentieth century, the interstate highway system, federal loan programs, and new communication technologies made it almost unrecognizable in the last half of that century. One consequence of this is that our entire notion of what constitutes a city has to be revised. On the one hand, vast global cities have emerged in both developing and developed countries, while in the developed West, a decentralized network of edge cities and residential suburbs has become the norm. The megalopolis and the suburb are two sides of the same coin: both unplanned and uncontrollable assemblages that sprawl across political jurisdictions and thrive on mobility and networked economies. Architects have recently become fascinated with the megalopolis, which offers a kind of exoticism, and the endless creativity of displaced populations making do under difficult circumstances. But the banal everydayness of suburbia, while it has been well documented and studied by economic historians, urban geographers, and social scientists, has so far been avoided by architects.

It is not that architects have entirely ignored these new, decentralized urban formations. The European discourse of the *terrain vague* has examined the periphery of the traditional western European city, where immigrants and other underprivileged populations have accumulated, while the New Urbanists have turned their attention to American suburbs. But this is just a start: one of the most urgent new roles for architecture, landscape architecture, and urban design is to engage this new suburban territory. Interestingly enough, it is a challenge that can only be met through the collaboration of all three disciplines.

In part, this might involve giving up our cherished preconceptions about American suburbia. We tend to think of the suburbs as primarily residential, but that is changing. In 1979, 85 percent of the office space in the United States was located in cities; today the city and the suburbs share the market 50/50. Suburbs were once a pastoral adjunct to dense city centers, but today it is hard to tell the difference. Greater Phoenix, which hardly has a "downtown," will have ten million inhabitants by 2004. Metropolitan Los Angeles, considered as a region, actually has a higher average density than greater New York City. These "sprinkler cities" (sprinkled across the landscape and relying on lawn sprinklers) are often knowledge-driven and arise independent of an older hub. Moreover, the social character of the suburban landscape is changing. The majority of Asian Americans live in suburbs; 50 percent of the Hispanic population and 40 per-cent of African Americans live in these new "lite" cities.[18] All of this suggests an interesting opportunity as well as a significant challenge for architecture, landscape, and urban design, a challenge requiring enormous creativity and a rethinking of architecture's traditional role in the city.

One of the most significant consequences of the rapid acceleration of suburban sprawl has been irreversible environmental damage. In New Jersey alone, fifty acres of land are lost to development every day. While I am somewhat skeptical of the potentials of a "green" architecture (which seems, on the one hand, anti-ecological in its limited, building-by-building approach, and on the other hand, too easily co-opted by institutions and corporations looking to market an environmentally sensitive image), I do feel that architecture and urbanism have something to contribute in helping to imagine alternative patterns of development that might begin to mediate the impact of continued development. With the emergence of the Smart Growth movement, some environmentalists have shifted from an opposi-tional stance to one directed at channeling the inevitable growth in more sensible directions.

To date, this movement has been informed by an implicit New Urbanist agenda that advocates dense "town" centers as an alterna-tive to sprawl. While gaining political momentum, this alignment with traditional urban forms would seem to limit their long-term effectiveness. The transformations that have taken place in the sub-urban landscape over the past fifty years are simply too radical to be effectively addressed with the design technologies of the nineteenth century. What we need are innovative new propositions that take into account the complexity of modern life and contemporary tech-nologies, the real needs and desires of the diverse populations that now live in suburbia, and the intricate ecological web into which de-velopment must be inserted: a feedback loop between the social and natural ecologies of suburbia. Architects and urbanists uniquely have the capacity to imagine viable new models for suburban development that incorporate advanced ecological principles that might in turn provoke architectural invention. Meanwhile, creative solutions for the vast number of brownfield sites created by the movement of heavy industry offshore can relieve the pressure on the remaining greenfield sites and redirect development to abandoned urban areas adjacent to the traditional city centers.

This is an optimistic scenario that clearly we will not see if architects continue to ignore the suburban landscape. For me, the conjunction of new social and spatial formations emerging in suburbia, combined with the urgency of environmental questions, suggests that an active, interdisciplinary engagement on the part of architects, landscape architects, and urban designers, working in collaboration with ecologists, transportation planners and engineers, social scientists, retail consultants, marketing, communication, and branding experts (among others), may well be the most significant new territory for design in the next decade.

FOSTER: There is another reason for the prominence of architecture today: the inflation of design and display in art, fashion, and business—indeed, in advanced consumer capitalism as a whole. The architect is redefined as a designer who can do "everything and nothing"; as architecture expands into total design, it also runs the risk of dissolution. "It seems that it will soon be necessary for architects to offer a complete array of services," Hani Rashid writes, "and to do so with a seamless integration of all aspects of the process" (391). Apparently, if you don't have an acronymed design consultancy (an AMO to complement your OMA), you no longer count as a major architect.

Some architects celebrate this condition of total design. "The architect is going to be the fashion designer of the future," Ben van Berkel and Caroline Bos state. "The new architectural network studio is a hybrid mixture of club, atelier, laboratory, and automobile plant, encouraging plug-in professionalism" (90). Others decry it. "Architects have transformed themselves from creators into coordinators and managers," Mario Botta remarks. "They have become directors of sorts, shackled by consultants and specialists from multiple sectors; their duties have become limited to mediating diverse technical, economic, juridical, and functional requirements" (112). Here a dialectical view might help, one that differentiates between the progressive aspects of the tendency toward total design (the way, for example, in which architecture, landscape design, and urban planning are no longer so divided in practice or in pedagogy) and its problematic aspects (for which this comment by Kas Oosterhuis might stand as an example: "We architects must focus now on emotive styling. . . . We give shape to the flow of data; we sculpt information" (371).

What do you consider the strengths and weaknesses of design education? How might it be improved?

ALLEN: I want to answer this question—which for obvious reasons [he was a new dean at Princeton] has become a preoccupation of mine—not with specifics of programs and curriculum but with a story about the recent past. In the late 1970s, a major shift occurred in the relationship between the schools and the profession. Before that time, it was rather unproblematically understood that the job of the schools was, for the most part, to train practicing architects. The precepts of Modern architecture were widely accepted, and they formed the basis of a common language that both practitioners and educators spoke. Major practitioners—Eero Saarinen or Paul Rudolph, for example—were important educators as well as active practicing architects.

The emergence of Postmodernism, in its multiple guises, changed that relationship in complex ways. Although largely discredited today, the historicist Postmodernism of the 1970s—the writings and buildings of Robert Venturi in particular—served as a stunning critique of the failures of institutionalized, postwar Modernist practice. This critique, which had its origin in the academy, was directed primarily against a mainstream professional practice that still uncritically held to the somewhat shopworn principles of Modernism and, in the view of those critical of it, was producing an architecture bereft of meaning and ignorant of the traditional structure of the city. Parallel to this populist critique, the more complex propositions of Eisenman and the Five Architects (also sponsored by the schools) held that architecture needed to reexamine its own intrinsic formal conditions as an autonomous discipline, free of the social and economic constraints that dominated professional practice.

The force of these two competing critiques was such that by the end of the 1970s, an atmosphere of antagonism and distrust characterized the relationship between the schools and the profession. This was the moment in which Leon Krier could declare, "I do not build because I am an architect," and Daniel Libeskind would assert that an architect's work began and ended in drawings. Libeskind and Krier could agree on little else, but they were united in their distrust of the profession and their dependence on the academy.

However, by the 1980s, all that had changed. The profession itself had embraced Postmodernism and, somewhat later, even a stylized version of deconstructivism. The more intelligent elements of the profession reacted to this critique preemptively. Rather than resist it, they absorbed the terms of the Postmodernist critique into their own practice, understanding that it threatened their professional survival. But also they managed to rework it on their own terms. They understood the market potential of the populist Postmodernism, and they moved quickly to capitalize on it. This is the period of the phenomenal success of a firm like KPF, for example, which went from something like three partners to three hundred employees almost overnight and in turn began to be seen by other corporate firms as a competitive threat, requiring them to shift their own stylistic orientation. These firms had discovered the market value of the image, and they moved quickly to find the design resources necessary to produce the new images. Above all, they turned to the schools, and those who had studied with Graves, Krier, or Stirling hired young graduates and gave them unprecedented design freedom. For their part, by the late 1980s, both Krier and Libeskind, along with Eisenman, Raimund Abraham, Koolhaas, et al. (the heart of the academic vanguard that had turned its back on the profession a decade earlier) were all actively pursuing building commissions.

In a few short years, the mainstream profession had realized that they could profit from the new design expertise being taught in the schools and began to think of them as their own personal research and development branches, never-ending reservoirs of new design ideas ready to market to clients who had themselves tired of Modernism. This was a fundamental realignment between the schools and the profession: instead of reflecting the concerns of the profession, the schools were now moving in advance of the profession, which reacted by looking for new ways to incorporate that design research into their own production.

There was, however, an important difference in the way this new design expertise was incorporated into mainstream practice. In its critique of the totalizing logic of Modernist transparency, Postmodernism had sanctioned a split between surface and structure—divorcing image from execution and meaning from technique. In its most obvious manifestation, a thin classical skin stretched over a Modernist structure was perfectly acceptable, a kind of dumbed-down version of the complexities and contradictions outlined by Venturi two decades earlier. In mainstream practice, this separation of image from technique was also manifest in the organization of offices. The young designers hired at corporate firms were brought in as image experts. They were not expected to know how to build, and it didn't matter, because these firms had the technical expertise, still thoroughly steeped in Modernist traditions, to realize anything these young designers could imagine. The split between image and execution was reinforced by the lack of technical knowledge on the part of designers and a lack of design expertise on the part of the technical experts. There was no common language within which real innovation might occur.

Now all that may seem like ancient history. Nobody is particularly interested today in historicist Postmodernism. But we are still living with the consequences of this realignment between the schools and the profession, and the subsequent split between image and technique. The profession continues to look to the schools for something "useful" from an image and marketing point of view. I think that part of our present impasse—in which the profession complains loudly that the schools are out of touch and not serving the profession, when the regulating boards and accrediting agencies are at odds with the best schools—has little to do with trivial complaints like not teaching enough AutoCAD. In my analysis, it is the expression of a frustration that much of what is coming out of the schools cannot be easily digested by the profession looking for a packaged and commodified "design." They don't really want to change the way they work; they just want to plug into the latest image.

The schools, for their part, have continued along the path of critique. Reacting to the mainstream co-option of Postmodernism, they moved into ever more difficult and sometimes esoteric territory. In an attempt to resist absorption by the market forces, critical theory borrowed from literary theory, philosophy, and cultural studies. In the schools, architecture was aligned with other practices: film, media, and critical art. Its operative, technical capacity was minimized. This is not to dismiss the serious work done in the 1980s and 1990s, but rather to point out that in the end the collective effect of that work was to further marginalize the schools by insisting that image and meaning—discourse and interpretation—were the proper purview of the academy and, in effect, to cede technique and practice to the profession. I find this a very troubling situation, one that is going to require a major rethinking on the part of the schools. Architects cannot allow themselves to be relegated to the role of producers of consumable images, prevented from participating in the actual process of production.

If we really want to have a meaningful impact on practice (which is, I believe, an appropriate ambition for a professional school), we have to embrace the technical and operative expertise necessary to innovate in a rapidly changing world. By applying the pragmatist criterion of "differences that make a difference," we can actually outpace a profession that is, in its own way, stuck in outmoded habits. Architecture today is made within a complex social exchange involving large numbers of individuals, agencies, and institutions. In addition to needing the traditional skills of design, craft, and fabrication, increasingly, the architect must be a manager and a negotiator, especially now that information and images seem more and more to dominate over hard matter. This does not mean, however, that because architects manipulate images in order to realize buildings, manipulating images is the same thing as making architecture. The realization of architecture requires a complex process of calculation and translation, paying close attention to the practical and worldly consequences resulting from the manipulation of these abstract codes. We have to equip our students with the intellectual and practical tools to work effectively in this paradoxical environment—at once immersed in the world of images and abstract notations, yet intimately connected to the hard logics of matter and forces. In this regard, I think there are promising signs: If we look at the contemporary scene, we see that many highly innovative young practices are embracing new technologies, investigating new materials, inventing new forms of practice, and developing new forms of collaboration. These new practices are constructing a new relationship to the profession and incrementally redefining the practice of architecture.

However, it is worthwhile remembering that if the practice of architecture is an ongoing conversation, it is also the obligation of the schools to teach each student the fundamentals of the discipline so that they can participate actively in that conversation. We have to pay close attention to the intricacies of our own discipline and not get lost in the seductions of image, media, and discourses only marginally related. As the Russian Formalist critic Victor Shklovsky once remarked, "In trying to understand a motor, one must look at the drive belt as a detail in a machine—from the mechanic's point of view—and not from the point of view of a vegetarian."[19]

Does this imply a return to Modernist orthodoxies, with the schools serving the profession? No, because the techniques themselves are always changing. Digital media, global markets, and the changing conditions of our cities all require continual innovation and creativity to devise new techniques, and these are areas where academics have specialized knowledge and thus the ability to move faster than mainstream professionals. The schools earn the right to run in advance of the profession and need not fall back on stable rules and conventions. They can play a critical role, holding up the generic norms of professional practice to strict performative criteria, testing their effectiveness against multiple criteria. The schools are well positioned to look for fresh solutions and new ways of working in response to the challenges of changing technologies and new demands on the discipline. Reality always moves faster than our own ability to understand or control it—we have to respect that reality, which means paying close attention to the world outside the academy. As educators, we have the responsibility not to try to tame that process of innovation with a set of rules but rather to teach the young designers the technical and intellectual tools that will allow them to do something creative with their own reality.

FOSTER: The tendency toward total design might participate in the greater revenge of consumer capitalism on Postmodernist culture—a recouping, even a routinization, of its interdisciplinary transgressions and transformations. Perhaps it is time to recover a strategic sense of disciplinary autonomy and its contestation. This is not to turn against critical theory and interdisciplinary work; on the contrary, it is to see them in historical perspective so as to practice them anew. Today one often hears that we have too much theory and interdisciplinarity; I think we have never had enough. In my experience at the Princeton School of Architecture, which is known for its emphasis on these kinds of inquiry, the critiques are not often well informed in relevant philosophy or other pertinent fields (including art). We are not sufficiently theoretical, and we have not yet been critical.

It is a funny time—a tragically funny time, architecturally as well as politically—to give up on critique. This is why the call for a "postcritical" architecture seems so misguided to me. Sometimes this call is specific enough—a complaint about an instrumental, hit-and-run application of theory in design—and here I agree entirely. But why drown the baby in the bathwater and pronounce all dialectical thinking, critical distance, and "resolute negativity" dead? What is the difference, politically, between such postcritical affirmation and the dominant neoconservativism? "There are vested interests that want us to believe that 'there is no alternative,'" Hilde Heynen comments (242). "We should not denounce this dimension [of seeking alternatives] but rather seek to reevaluate and resuscitate it" (243).[20]

Often implicit in postcritical discourse is a futurist faith that new materials and media are somehow progressive per se. Certainly they hold great possibilities—an immense expansion in techniques for designers and a partial recovery of the means of production for architects—but they also invite some precritical naïvetés as well. (A small instance: no one seems to question the return of perspective in the computer images that have become standard in architectural presentations.) Also often implicit in postcritical discourse is a willful opposition between "critique" and "invention," as if the two were really opposed, and an equally willful narrative in which "pragmatism" comes "after theory," as if pragmatism were not also a theory and theory not also pragmatic. What is meant by pragmatism here? An innovative reengagement, through "design intelligence," with the world. "Innovation operates by an affirmative, nonlinear process of continuous feedback," Michael Speaks argues, "through which opportunities are discovered that are exploited and transformed into designs not posed or unforeseen by the problem" (417). Yet this formulation could also lead to a new kind of design formalism or to process fetishism.[21]

FRAMPTON: Needless to say, my views on environmental design education vaguely follow the lines of my response to the previous questions; I want to emphasize above all the issue of sustainability and the recently invented synthetic discipline currently subsumed in the Architectural Association School, London, under the title Landscape Urbanism. It seems to me that both of these environmental agendas ought to be strongly emphasized by architecture and urban planning faculties in any categorical reformulation of the curricula and methods obtaining in the design studio. In this regard I find myself in total accord with the *Harvard Design Magazine* essay of Susannah Hagan, who fails to see why sustainability should be any more constraining of the designer's freedom than any of the other pragmatic limitations that architects have to cope with.[22] Indeed, as an erstwhile advocate of "critical regionalism," I feel that the rooted, tectonic expressivity of a work can only be enriched by taking the impact of the specific local environment (i.e., climate, topography) into consideration. In my view we have to attempt to return to the unfinished Modern project, thereby to aspire, despite the demise of the Enlightenment, to a more mediated rationality, one that takes into consideration our inevitable dependency on nature, including our own intrinsic nature, at both biological and psychological levels. In other words, we have to readdress exactly what kind of rationality we have in mind, much as Alvar Aalto evoked this theme in his 1935 lecture "Rationalism and Man," wherein he argued that a truly rationalist architecture must take into consideration the psychological and corporeal susceptibility of the user.[23] There should be no cultural incompatibility between this and the category of sustainability. *Ars sine scientia nihil est* ("art is nothing without science") is the maxim recently echoed by Winfried Nerdinger in writing on the exemplary work of Thomas Herzog[24]—the other Herzog, so to speak. And this brings me, while focusing on design education, to touch on the somewhat taboo topic of the uses and abuses of the computer, for while the computer, in terms of simulation, is essential to the evolution of subtler forms of sustainable architecture, it is questionable whether it should be formalistically exploited for the arbitrary gestation of spectacular forms, derived from digital morphologies having no other aim than the production of fashionable imagery.

2004

Notes

1. Michael Speaks, "Design Intelligence: Introduction," *A+U*, December 2002, 11–18.

2. R. E. Somol and Sarah Whiting, "Notes around the Doppler Effect and Other Moods of Modernism," *Perspecta* 33 (2002): 77; reprinted in this volume, see chapter 2.

3. Roberto Mangabeira Unger, *Social Theory: Its Situation and Its Task* (New York: Cambridge University Press, 1987), 166.

4. From Luis Fernández-Galiano's talk at "Doors of Perception 7: flow," Amsterdam, November 14–16, 2002. The phrase was earlier used by Pico Iyer in "Imaging Canada: An Outsider's Hope for a Global Future," a lecture at the University of Toronto, April 5, 2001. "Junkspace" may be found in Chuihua Judy Chung and Sze Tsung Leong, eds., *The Harvard Design School Guide to Shopping* (Los Angeles: Tashen America, 2002).

5. Lavin: "Of paramount importance, especially with respect to pedagogy, is the de-emphasis on volume, the logic of the plan, and the ethics of rationalism in favor of atmospheres produced through the curation of the surface. . . . Contemporary architecture embraces the quixotic pleasure and designed obsolescence of consumer culture" (296). All quotations followed by page numbers in my comments refer to contents in *hunch* 6/7, 109 *Provisional Attempts to Address Six Simple and Hard Questions about What Architects Do Today and Where Their Profession Might Go Tomorrow*, published by the Berlage Institute in 2003.

6. Michelle Addington, "Energy, Body, Building: Rethinking Sustainable Design Solutions," *Harvard Design Magazine* 18 (Spring/Summer 2003): 18–21. More dire percentages are given by Ed Mazria in *The Passive Solar Energy Book* (New York: Rodale Press, 1979); his breakdown is building, 48 percent; transportation, 27 percent; industry, 25 percent. See *Metropolis*, October 2003, 1–7.

7. This exhibition, curated by architecture critic and writer Peter Buchanan and organized by the Architectural League of New York City, made its debut in spring 2000 at the Urban Center Gallery. It has since traveled widely. A catalog of the exhibition is in production and is available online at http://www.archleague.org/tenshadesofgreen/10shades.html. See also Buchanan's "Invitation to the Dance: Sustainability and the Expanded Realm of Design," in *Harvard Design Magazine* 18 (Spring/Summer 2003).

8. Probably from "Un'altra tradizione moderna dalla rottura dell'anno trenta al progetto urbano moderno," *Lotus International* 64, 1989, 6–31.

9. Rafi Segal and Eyal Weizman, *A Civilian Occupation: The Politics of Israeli Architecture* (New York: Verso, 2003).

10. In his seminal analysis of the spectacle logic of "late capitalism," Fredric Jameson used the vast atrium of the Bonaventure Hotel in Los Angeles as a symptom of the kind of architectural sublime that results: a sort of hyperspace that deranges the human sensorium. Jameson took this spatial delirium as a particular instance of a general incapacity to comprehend the late capitalist universe, to map it cognitively. Strangely, what Jameson offered as a critique of Postmodern culture has been taken by architects like Gehry as a paragon: the creation of extravagant spaces that work to overwhelm the subject, a neo-Baroque Sublime dedicated to the glory of the Corporation, the Church of our age. See Fredric Jameson, "The Cultural Logic of Late Capitalism," in *Postmodernism, or, the Cultural Logic of Late Capitalism* (Durham, N.C.: Duke University Press, 1991).

11. The two tendencies—spectacle and trauma architectures—are not mutually exclusive, as this design attests. Here a pessimist might glimpse a Trauma Theme Park in the making, with Libeskind a contemporary cross between Parisian filmmaker Claude Lanzmann and Walt Disney, the perfect maestro for a time when historical tragedy can be turned into urban spectacle.

12. For these citations see my "In New York," *London Review of Books* 20 (March 2003), from which this section is adapted.

13. Originally in the *New York Times*, quoted in my essay "In New York."

14. *Webster's New Collegiate Dictionary* (Springfield, Mass.: G. & C. Merriam Co., 1974).

15. W. H. Auden, "Under Which Lyre: A Reactionary Tract for the Times," Phi Beta Kappa poem, Harvard University, 1946.

16. *Towards an Urban Renaissance, Final Report of the Urban Task Force,* chaired by Lord Rogers of Riverside, Great Britain, 1999.

17. Ellen Durham-Jones, "Smart Growth in Atlanta: A Response to Krieger and Kiefer," *Harvard Design Magazine* 19 (Fall/Winter 2003): 63.

18. These statistics are from John B. Judis and Ruy Teixeira, "Where Democrats Can Build a New Majority"; and David Brooks, "Brawl in the Sprawl," both in *Blueprint: Ideas for a New Century,* September/October 2002, 14–27.

19. Cited in Fredric Jameson, *The Prison-House of Language* (Princeton, N.J.: Princeton University Press, 1972), 83.

20. Interestingly, the theory not dissed today tends to be vitalist—a reading of Gilles Deleuze in particular. This is in keeping with the most dominant discourse of all—biology—even as it also speaks, alongside the traumatic view of history, to a new kind of metaphysics. As usual, Charles Jencks is refreshingly, straightforwardly ideological in this regard: of the "organi-tech architects" he writes: "My belief is that the universe story will become a shared metaphysics . . . an iconography based on Gaia and cosmogenesis" (266, 268).

21. Lucas Verweij: "Designers at this moment prefer to study their own obsessions—formulating and answering their own questions—than to answer questions asked by their clients or society" (466, 467).

22. Susannah Hagan, "Five Reasons to Adopt Environmental Design," *Harvard Design Magazine* 18 (Spring/Summer 2003): 5–11.

23. Alvar Aalto, "Rationalism and Man," in *Alvar Aalto in His Own Words,* ed. Göran Schildt (New York: Rizzoli, 1998), 89–93.

24. Winfried Nerdinger, "Architecture and Science" in *Thomas Herzog: Architecture of Technology* (Munich: Prestel, 2001), 16–21. The Latin phrase was made famous by Gothic architect Jean Vignot in 1392.

10

"Criticality" and
Its Discontents

George Baird

S hortly before his untimely death, the Spanish theorist and critic Ignasi de Solà-Morales commented to me that "if European architects or architectural scholars wished to study contemporary architectural theory, they would have to come to the East Coast of the United States."

Is it still true that theory on the American East Coast holds such preeminence? I realize that it is one of the intentions of the Berlage Institute's new doctoral program and of the creation of the new Delft School of Design to challenge this American hegemony—and recent events suggest that these challenges are meeting with some success. If America does retain some prominence in these matters, then it may be of interest to readers to know (or know more) about a significant divergence now appearing in the territory of contemporary theory there, a divergence that is triggering increasingly intense discussions such as have not been seen since the beginning of the polemical attacks of the protagonists of deconstructivism on Postmodernism a decade and a half ago. The matter now coming into question is the concept of a "critical architecture" that has been promulgated in advanced circles in architectural theory for at least two decades. The conception can probably be said to have received a definitive early formulation in a text by my Harvard colleague Michael Hays, a text that Robert Somol and Sarah Whiting (two of the prominent recent participants in the discussion) have labeled "canonic": "Critical Architecture: Between Culture and Form," published in *Perspecta* 21 in 1984.[1]

Today "criticality" is under attack, seen by its critics as obsolete, as irrelevant, and/or as inhibiting design creativity. What is more, the criticisms that are increasingly frequently being made come from an interesting diversity of sources. To start to make sense of this emergent situation, we might try to locate the beginnings of the evident shift of opinion against this once-so-dominant theoretical discourse in architecture. One interesting precursor of current comment was an outburst by Rem Koolhaas at one of the series of conferences organized by *ANY* magazine, this one at the Canadian Centre for Architecture in 1994: "The problem with the prevailing discourse of architectural criticism," complained Koolhaas, "is [the] inability to recognize there is in the deepest motivations of architecture something that cannot be critical."[2] But if Koolhaas's complaint was a harbinger of things to come, probably the first frontal challenge to criticality was a text published by Michael Speaks, the director of Graduate Studies at the Southern California Institute of Architecture, in the American magazine *Architectural Record* in 2002.[3] In a startlingly revisionist text, Speaks explicitly abandons the "resistance" that he had learned from his own teacher Fredric Jameson in favor of a model of a new, alternative, and efficaciously integrated architecture that would take its cues from contemporary business management practices.[4]

Before the dust from Speaks's polemic had settled, two other American theorists, Robert Somol of UCLA and Sarah Whiting of Harvard, mounted a subtler challenge. Their text, "Notes around the Doppler Effect and Other Moods of Modernism," appeared in *Perspecta* 33 in 2002 (and is reprinted in this volume; see chapter 2).[5] In it, Somol and Whiting argue against the conception of a "critical architecture" that had been long promulgated by Michael Hays. In the place of the hitherto "critical" architecture, Somol and Whiting propose one that would be "projective."

Since Somol and Whiting's publication, the pace of publications on this theme and the number of participants in the discussion have increased. At the end of 2002, for example, Michael Speaks followed up his polemic with a longer text published in *A+U*.[6] Since then, additional partisans, such as Stan Allen, dean of the School of Architecture at Princeton, and Sylvia Lavin, chair of the Department of Architecture at the University of California, Los Angeles, have joined the fray.

I have set myself the task of attempting to briefly clarify how the divergence I have described has unfolded to date and to summarize what is at stake in it, since it is my view that a great deal indeed is at stake.

Let me begin with a short account of the lineage of "criticality." One of its most cogent and internally coherent renditions has been that of the practitioner—and no mean theorist himself—Peter Eisenman, accompanied by Hays. Together, over the past two decades, these two have developed a position that has consistently focused intellectually on concepts of "resistance" and "negation." For Eisenman, the position derives primarily from the work of the Italian historian and critic Manfredo Tafuri, but it has been fleshed out in Eisenman's own mind by other prominent figures in contemporary thought, including Jacques Derrida, Gianni Vattimo, and others. For Hays, Tafuri is as important a figure as he has been for Eisenman, but he is accompanied by additional figures such as Georg Lukács, Theodor Adorno, and Fredric Jameson.

For Hays, following Tafuri, the paramount exemplar of negation in late Modernism was Mies van der Rohe. Like his mentor, Hays has seen the late Mies as embodying a "refusal" of the terms of contemporary consumer society in the very surfaces of his built forms. (In this regard, the Seagram Building is as important a case study for Hays as it is for Tafuri.) For his part, Eisenman has, over his career as a designer and thinker, welded precepts from Tafuri to others derived from the theories of minimalist art practices, as they have been articulated by figures such as Rosalind Krauss. In his hands, this has produced not so much a series of built forms embodying refusal or resistance but rather a design method that for Eisenman is more important as a process than it is for the architectural products resulting from it. Notwithstanding these differences in nuance, for the past two decades Eisenman and Hays have formed a formidable pair of advocates of "resistance" in contemporary architecture and architectural theory.

But an enumeration of participants in a recent *Harvard Design Magazine* "Stocktaking" symposium makes clear that Eisenman and Hays do not exhaust the modalities of "criticality" that have had influence in recent years.[7] For example, Kenneth Frampton's commitment to "resistance" to consumer society has been as resolute as that of Eisenman and Hays during the period in question, even if his intellectual lineage leads back more to Adorno and Heidegger than to

Tafuri. Then there is Michael Sorkin, much more of a New York City "street fighter," politically speaking, than any of the figures I have discussed so far. Sorkin is renowned in American design circles for his long-standing courage in having mounted compelling attacks on prominent figures on the American design scene, from Philip Johnson to Daniel Libeskind. But despite widespread admiration for his critical writings, the substantive theoretical form of Sorkin's "resistance" is not seen to be centrally embedded in his own design production, as Mies's has been seen to be by Tafuri, or Eisenman's has been seen to be by Hays. And this has meant that Sorkin's criticism, powerful as it has been, has nonetheless been limited in its impact on the evolving forms of American design practice.

Perhaps the most distinctive "critical" American design practice has been that of two figures who did not take part in the *Harvard Design Magazine* "Stocktaking": Elizabeth Diller and Ricardo Scofidio. For almost as long as Eisenman and Hays's collaboration, Diller + Scofidio have produced a remarkable range of projects that have succeeded in embodying "resistance" in a fashion that bears comparison with the one Tafuri admired in the late work of Mies. Still, most of the work in question has comprised museum and gallery installations rather than buildings. And the museum has continued to be a more receptive venue for critical work than the street during the period in question, as witness the parallel art practices of the Belgian Marcel Broodthaers, the German transplant to New York Hans Haacke, and so on. How interesting, then, that the first major exhibition convened by the recently appointed architecture curator of New York's Whitney Museum, Michael Hays, should be of the work of Diller + Scofidio: surely a recent and, can we perhaps say, "late" triumph of American "criticality"? What is more, it is interesting to note that in their Whitney show, Diller + Scofidio chose to exhibit many of the museum gallery projects that have made them famous and almost none of the building projects on which their recent design practice has focused, projects that will have to meet the more difficult test of being critical "in the street." It will be interesting to see how successful this firm will be in sustaining its compelling "resistance" in buildings rather than in installations and in the now-changing climate of American architectural theory.

What, then, can we say about this changing climate? What reasons can we adduce for the increasingly threatened state of "criticality"? And what are the key features of the approaches to architectural theory that are being offered up in its place? It seems to me that there are a number of strands to the story, most of them interesting, if not all of equal historical consequence.

One of them, as far as I can tell, is a purely biographical—not to say generational—predicament. It is a commonplace to note that Peter Eisenman has been a major influence in American architectural education since his founding of the New York–based Institute for Architecture and Urban Studies and of its in-house *Oppositions,* some three decades ago. By now I think it can be said that Eisenman's influence on his protégés can be compared with that of his own mentor Colin Rowe on his. But Rowe, it would seem, was a more easygoing mentor than Eisenman has been able to be. As a consequence, getting out from under the influence of the master has been a much greater challenge for the protégés of Eisenman than it was for those of Rowe. I do not think it is a coincidence that so many of the protagonists of the currently proffered alternatives to "criticality" are former protégés of Eisenman, or at least figures at the edge of his circle. Stan Allen, Robert Somol, and Sarah Whiting all fall into one or the other of these categories. To the extent, then, that Eisenman himself has maintained such obdurate loyalty to "criticality" over a long span of time, he has produced a corresponding tension among his followers in respect to their understandable career efforts to cut loose from him. I suspect that we could go even further and speculate that to the extent that he has also maintained a stance of continuing contempt for what he, following Rowe, has called *"décor de la vie,"* he has opened the door to a revived interest in surface and texture—even decoration—on the part of some of his revisionist followers. Whatever the final answers to these intriguing biographical questions turn out to be, it is clear that an effort to transcend a certain Eisenmanian hegemony in the upper echelons of American architectural culture is one of the more personal current tendencies evident to observers such as myself.

What is more, it is probably no less coincidental that an alternate referent frequently turned to in the various discourses of "postcriticality" is Rem Koolhaas. For example, Koolhaas performs a crucial bridging role in Somol and Whiting's "Doppler Effect" text, enabling them to shift from a "critical" stance to a "projective" one. Then, too, it is almost inconceivable that the post-utopian pragmatism so pervasive in leading Dutch architectural circles nowadays (and which one suspects, to some extent, has been imported to the United States by Speaks) cannot be tracked back to the influence of the stormy young Koolhaas himself on the early generations of his own protégés, in the late 1970s and 1980s.[8]

But this reference to Koolhaas brings me back to the short quotation from him I cited early in this text, which will serve to move us from biographical and generational considerations to more substantive ones. In the commentary in question, Koolhaas went on to speculate, "Maybe some of our most interesting engagements are uncritical, emphatic engagements, which deal with the sometimes insane difficulty of an architectural project to deal with the incredible accumulation of economic, cultural, political but also logistical issues."[9] Here we see Koolhaas the ambitious realpolitiker once again exhibiting his intense belief in the necessity of a professional, architectural efficacy. And for him, if it turns out that "criticality" constrains efficacy, then to that extent "criticality" must give way.

What is more, as the 1990s wore on, as it became apparent that Eisenman's own design interests would increasingly focus on process rather than products, and as it became apparent that the putative tropes of the then ascendant "deconstructivism" were much less "critical" than many had expected them to be, all this contributed to a dissipation of the robust energy that had earlier been embodied— theoretically at least—by the project of "critical architecture."

Then, too, it is probably the case that the trajectory of the life of Manfredo Tafuri, from his retreat from contemporary criticism in the mid-1980s to his death in 1994, contributed further to this shift of mood. After all, Tafuri had been the most assertive contemporary advocate of an architecture that would not accept the terms of reality as they were presented. Indeed, in an extended series of essays over the span of the 1970s, he formulated an utterly distinctive conception of the architectural "project," one that would at one and the same time propose a new architectural form, would do so on the plane of the entire urban entity in which it was to be located, and would, by inference, transform that entire urban entity itself into something new. Needless to say, there were not too many successful historical examples of this bold and ambitious method that he could point to (Le Corbusier's *Plan Obus* for Algiers being one of the few). Given that before he had retired to Venetian Renaissance history, he had already dismissed American avant-garde architecture as "architecture in the boudoir," it cannot be denied that by the time of his death his overall theoretical stance was a somewhat disheartening one—especially for American audiences, who had had the dystopic side of Tafuri's sensibility so predominantly emphasized to them in earlier years.

In any event, with Speaks's polemic of early 2002, there commenced a stream of "counter-critical" texts that has continued up to the present day. Speaks's *A+U* text of late 2002 is probably the most developed argument that he has contributed to the ongoing discussion to date. Titled "Design Intelligence," it starts off with a calculatedly particular usage of the term *intelligence*—that of the American Central Intelligence Agency—and then moves on to argue that in the contemporary design world, "visionary ideas have given way to the 'chatter' of intelligence."[10] Speaks then goes on specifically to dissociate himself from a whole series of design tendencies he saw as obsolete, disparaging the influences of both Derrida and Tafuri along the way: "Post-modernism, Deconstructivism, Critical Regionalism and a host of other critical architectures in the late 1980's and 1990's posed . . . as false pretenders to Modernism. Whether effetely Derridian or ponderously Tafurian, theoretically inspired vanguards operated in a state of perpetual critique. Stuck between a world of certainty whose demise they had been instrumental in bringing about, and an emergent world of uncertainty into which they were being thrown headlong, theoretical vanguards were incapacitated by their own resolute negativity."[11] Instead, Speaks argued for what he called a "post-vanguard" professional practice defined by "design intelligence, and not by any formal, theoretical or professional identity." He went on: "Accustomed in ways that their vanguard predecessors can never be to open source intelligence (OSINT as it is called by the CIA) gathered from the little truths published on the web, found in popular culture, and gleaned from other professions and design disciplines, these practices are adaptable to almost any circumstance almost anywhere."[12]

Compared to the strongly pragmatic—even antitheoretical—stance advocated by Speaks, Somol and Whiting's "Doppler Effect" remains a model of enduringly "theoretical"—not to say "philosophical"—nuance. They summarize their concern about what they label "the now dominant paradigm" by observing that in recent years "disciplinarity has been absorbed and exhausted by the project of criticality."[13] They employ the design production of Peter Eisenman together with the theory of Michael Hays to attempt to demonstrate this. In this respect, perhaps their most important claim is that "for both [Eisenman and Hays], disciplinarity is understood as autonomy (enabling critique, representation, and signification) but not as instrumentality (projection, performativity, and pragmatics). One could say that their definition of disciplinarity is directed against reification rather than toward the possibility of emergence."[14] And they conclude this part of their argument by observing: "As an alternative to the critical project—here linked to the indexical, the dialectical and hot representation—this text develops an alternative genealogy of the projective—linked to the diagrammatic, the atmospheric and cool performance."[15]

Perhaps not surprisingly, this schema leads them in turn to propose, as an alternative to the precedent offered by Eisenman, one they ascribe to Rem Koolhaas. In doing so, they contrast: "two orientations toward disciplinarity: that is, disciplinarity as autonomy and process, as in the case of Eisenman's reading of the Dom-ino, and disciplinarity as force and effect, as in Koolhaas's staging of the Downtown Athletic Club." And they conclude: "Rather than looking back or criticizing the status quo, the Doppler projects forward alternative (not necessarily oppositional) arrangements or scenarios."[16] So even though they eschew the extreme polemical stance taken up by Speaks, they do not, in the end, differ all that fundamentally from the position he espoused. For his part, in his contribution to the *Harvard Design Magazine*'s "Stocktaking," Stan Allen offered up a commentary broadly parallel to the two just cited. Like Speaks, Allen identified a need to go "beyond the traditional avant-garde models" and to make use of "popular culture and the creativity of the marketplace." Indeed, he explicitly endorsed both Speaks's and Somol and Whiting's arguments, citing both texts in his own.

Most recently, in parallel presentations at Princeton, Harvard, and Toronto, Sylvia Lavin has entered into the debate and has made a distinctive contribution to it, calling for a new appreciation of and consideration for "the provisional" and the "ephemeral" in the world of contemporary architecture and design. Characterizing Modernism as excessively preoccupied with the "fixed" and the "durable" in the world, she argues that reconsideration of such qualities in the environment could be both liberating and productive of new design possibilities.[17]

What should we make of this unfolding divergence of opinion between two important generations of thinkers on the scene of American architectural theory? Let me conclude by offering a few observations of my own. First, let us step back a little from the front lines of this battle and take a closer look at figures that lie in the background. From my comments thus far, I think it is clear that Manfredo Tafuri looms large behind American formulations of a "critical architecture" and that, having long exhibited discomfort in regard to its implications, Rem Koolhaas has served as a model for some of the orientations to practice that have been proposed as alternatives to it. But there is an additional éminence grise looming in back of a number of the members of the camp who have criticized the influence of "criticality." This is the American art critic and commentator Dave Hickey.

Not yet as well known in architectural circles as Tafuri once was, Hickey is a recently selected MacArthur Fellow who has written on a wide range of social and cultural issues in the United States and elsewhere. A keen observer of a wide range of popular culture and an art critic with a decidedly skeptical view of the continuing pertinence of the artistic tradition of minimalism—this alone places him far from Eisenman—Hickey is cited by Somol and Whiting as the author of an interpretation that opposes the performing styles of two American film actors, Robert Mitchum and Robert De Niro. Interpreting Hickey on the two American actors, Somol and Whiting contrast the styles as, respectively, "cool" and "hot." While cooling suggests a process of mixing (and thus the Doppler Effect would be one form of cool), the hot resists through distinction and connotes the overly difficult, belabored, worked, complicated. Cool is "relaxed, easy." Thus, it is clear that Somol and Whiting are eager to employ Hickey as part of their effort to dispel the American legacy of Tafuri in our field.

For me—and let me say that I share the two authors' fascination with Hickey—this possibility is not so clear. I shall return to this in a moment, but first I want to review a few interesting paradoxes that arise within the overall spectrum of opinion I have outlined above.

To start with, let us take the matter of the design avant-garde (as Allen calls it) or vanguard (as Speaks does). Both commentators dismiss it as obsolete and irrelevant. This is clearly a rebuff to Eisenman, who has always seen a certain American cultural avant-garde as being the embodiment of resistance. Yet, interestingly enough, Tafuri himself declared the avant-garde in architecture obsolete and irrelevant long before the new critics of criticality did. So strong is the tendency of American theorists to see Tafuri through an Eisenmanian lens that they fail to take note of the fact that the American architects and planners he most admired were not avant-gardists at all but rather such figures as Eliel Saarinen, Clarence Stein, and Henry Wright—not to mention the New Deal creators of the Tennessee Valley Authority. So preoccupied are Tafuri's American readers with "architecture in the boudoir," that they fail to pay comparable attention to "socialpolitik and the city in Weimar, Germany," where Tafuri's impatience with avant-gardism and his strong commitment to professional "engagement" indisputably lie. So, in the first of our paradoxes we may observe that were he still alive, Tafuri would align himself with the disenchantment of the younger Americans with their own avant-garde and would support their desire for "a form of practice committed to public legibility, to the active engagement of new technologies, and to creative means of implementation" (Allen).[18]

Then there is the matter of "instrumentality." At one point in their text, Somol and Whiting present "instrumentality" as the definitive opposite to "autonomy." And in doing so, as we saw above, they summarize under this term three of the key features of the new approach they are recommending: projection, performativity, and pragmatics. But, of course, Tafuri was also deeply committed to the idea of projection; indeed, as I noted earlier in this text, his highly activist conception of the architectural "project" lay at the heart of his theoretical position. Similarly, to the extent that we can read "pragmatics" as having at least partly to do with architectural programs, Tafuri was clearly as interested in program as a medium of design innovation as Koolhaas has ever been. But like *Socialpolitik,* Tafuri's powerful commitments to projective efficacy and to programmatic innovation are hard to see through an Eisenmanian lens. (I concede that I do not find a comparable commitment to "performativity" in Tafuri's writings, but I do note that the political stance with which he was associated in the days of his journal *Contropiano* strategically distinguished itself from that of the Italian Communist party on account of its commitment to active participation by workers in the ongoing formulation of party positions, as opposed to the top-down party-line control advocated by the party leaders—and for this reason was labeled an *operaista* political tendency.)

Let me return now to Hickey and to the possibility of his being enlisted for the polemical purposes of the younger generation disillusioned with criticality. To be sure, there is in his heteroclite sensibility a startling and engaging openness to distinctiveness that has attracted Somol, Whiting, and Lavin, and to which they in turn all seem to be committed. Hickey is even willing to engage the "decorative" in ways that would seem to lend support to some of the speculative comments Lavin has made in recent academic discussions. His characterization of Mitchum's acting style and his interests in jazz reinforce further still his association with cultural stances that can be called "relaxed" or "easy."

But, of course, it also remains the case that when all is said and done, Hickey himself continues to be engaged by an obdurate—if implicit—quest for "authenticity." At the first lecture I ever heard him give, he delivered an extended descriptive comparison of two southwestern American cities he knows well, Santa Fe (where his 2002 exhibition Beau Monde was held) and Las Vegas (where he lives). Summing up his critical assessment of the two cities, he made the dazzling observation that he prefers Las Vegas to Santa Fe because he prefers "the real fake to the fake real."[19]

Indeed, to the extent that the protagonists of any version of a postcritical project want to enlist him to challenge the legacy of Eisenman, a comment from his introduction to the Beau Monde show will give them pause. Discussing his selection of artists and works to be included in the show, he observed, "Rather than asking the post-minimalist question: 'How rough can it get and still remain meaningful?' I found myself asking the cosmopolitan question: 'How smooth can it get and still resist rationalization?'"[20] So, we can now see, even the "cool" and speculative Hickey continues to be engaged by a form of "resistance." It seems to me that the provocative question he suggested he had asked himself about his Santa Fe show is one that one could easily imagine being asked in regard to a work of Diller + Scofidio, such as their Soft Sell Forty-second Street installation of 1993.[21]

And speaking of Forty-second Street, is it not interesting also to recall that the very figure with whom I began my account of the erosion of the dominant discourse of criticality was Rem Koolhaas? For Koolhaas himself, notwithstanding his interests in "creative means of implementation" and in other key parts of the postcritical agenda, has nonetheless participated in more than a few recent episodes of vigorous critical engagement. I could start by recounting the fascinating episode during which, having been brought to Harvard to attack Andres Duany and the New Urbanism, he declined to do so, waiting only for an appropriate moment to chastise Duany severely for his failure "as a prominent American architect" to speak out against the destruction of the distinctive street culture of Manhattan's Forty-second Street as a result of its sweeping Disneyfication. And I would probably end with his recent attack on the Chinese authorities for their lamentable and all-too-pragmatic approval of the destruction of extensive historic residential districts of the city of Beijing.

Thus, it seems to me that the political alignments and the theoretical complexities that this interesting divergence of opinions has brought to the surface to date do not so much constitute the conclusion of a story but rather only the beginning. A number of important questions remain to be asked, it seems to me, before a truly robust and durable new professional stance will be able to be achieved. For example, while it is probably true that "relaxed" and "easy" cannot be reconciled with "difficult," it is not so clear to me that they cannot be reconciled with "resistant." And it is equally clear to me that a much more developed pursuit of social and political parallels between architecture and cinema would be one potent way of articulating such subtle distinctions further.

Then, too, I am very curious to see to what extent the putatively "projective" forms of practice being advocated by the new critics of criticality will develop parallel models of critical assessment with which to be able to measure the ambition and the capacity for significant social transformation of such forms. Without such models, architecture could all too easily again find itself conceptually and ethically adrift. For example, while it is clear from a multitude of cultural perspectives that the "decorative" as a formal category can be integrated within new forms of practice, it is also clear that those forms run some risk of reducing to the "merely" decorative. Enough architectural episodes of the "merely" decorative have occurred to serve as a warning.

Most fundamentally, in my view, it is clear that a new projective architecture will not be able to be developed in the absence of a supporting body of projective theory. Without it, I predict that this new architecture will devolve to the "merely" pragmatic, and to the "merely" decorative, with astonishing speed.

May I conclude, then, by calling for much more careful reflection from us all, before the respective roles of critique, innovation, authenticity, and expanded cultural possibility can be integrated in an "operative" new theory of praxis for our times?

2005

Notes

1. See Robert Somol and Sarah Whiting, "Notes around the Doppler Effect and Other Moods of Modernism," *Perspecta* 33 (2002): 73; reprinted in this volume, see chapter 2.

2. Rem Koolhaas, quoted by Beth Kapusta, *Canadian Architect Magazine* 39 (August 1994): 10.

3. Michael Speaks, "Design Intelligence and the New Economy," *Architectural Record*, January 2002, 72–79.

4. Upon hearing me present this text at a June 2004 conference at the Technical University of Delft, Stan Allen suggested that the Joan Ockman and Terry Riley pragmatism symposium held at MoMA in November 2000 might be an earlier challenge to criticality than Speaks's polemic of early 2002. This may be so, but since I did not attend the conference and since it was devoted to pragmatism per se rather than to criticality, there is some question in my mind as to whether this challenge can appropriately be described as "frontal."

5. Somol and Whiting, "Notes around the Doppler Effect," 72–77.

6. Michael Speaks, "Design Intelligence: Part 1, Introduction," *A+U*, December 2002, 10–18.

7. "Stocktaking 2004: Nine Questions about the Present and Future of Design," *Harvard Design Magazine* 20 (Spring/Summer 2004): 5–52.

8. A number of forms of a post-utopian and postcritical European (and mainly Dutch) practice are described in the essay by Roemer van Toorn, "No More Dreams?" chapter 5, this volume.

9. Kapusta, *Canadian Architect Magazine*.

10. Speaks, "Design Intelligence," 12.

11. Ibid., 16.

12. Ibid.

13. Somol and Whiting, "Notes around the Doppler Effect," 73.

14. Ibid., 74.

15. Ibid.

16. Ibid., 75.

17. Sylvia Lavin, in lectures delivered during spring 2004 at Harvard, Princeton, and the University of Toronto.

18. It is interesting to note at this juncture in my argument that in his contribution to *Harvard Design Magazine*'s "Stocktaking," Stan Allen himself observed that such forms of practice as he is endorsing here can be found in a number of locations in Europe but have "so far resisted translation to the United States." So perhaps the collectivist European legacy of Tafuri may remain stronger than has been acknowledged?

19. Dave Hickey, "Dialectical Utopias," *Harvard Design Magazine* 4 (Winter/Spring 1998): 8–13.

20. Dave Hickey, *Beau Monde: Toward a Redeemed Cosmopolitanism* (Santa Fe, N.Mex.: SITE Santa Fe, 2001), 76.

21. *Soft Sell* is documented in Elizabeth Diller and Ricardo Scofidio, *Flesh: Architectural Probes: The Mutant Body of Architecture* (New York: Princeton Architectural Press, 1994), 250–53.

11

Critical of What?
Toward a Utopian Realism

Reinhold Martin

There has long been a tendency in architecture to erect straw figures only to knock them down. In his essay "'Criticality' and Its Discontents," George Baird admirably—and, I think, accurately—summarizes recent efforts to do just that.[1] These entail the identification of and subsequent assault on something called "the critical" or "critical architecture," usually accompanied by a collateral assault on something called "theory." At the risk of erecting yet another straw figure that tramples on the subtleties of Baird's analysis, it might be fair to characterize such practices, variously named "postcritical" or "projective," as sharing a commitment to an affect-driven, nonoppositional, nonresistant, nondissenting, and therefore non-utopian form of architectural production. But as Baird notes, these efforts have thus far failed to deliver an actual, affirmative project, settling instead for vague adjectives like "easy," "relaxed," and—perish the thought—"cool." Baird therefore concludes his essay by asking (with critical overtones?) what they expect to yield in the form of discourse or what he calls "critical assessment." In other words, by what criteria is the "postcritical" asking to be judged, beyond mere acceptance and accommodation of existing societal, economic, or cultural norms?

This question seems worth pursuing but also, perhaps, rephrasing, since as with all the other "posts" that preceded it, the "postcritical"

(or "relaxed" or "projective") assumes the existence of what it de-
nounces or, in any event, criticizes. Here Baird offers a useful, fair
summary of the official history of "critical architecture." To this, we
might append another question: critical of what? since it must also
be noted that this history actually collapses two opposing positions
into one, largely through generational iteration. In the first instance,
the "critical" in architecture is assumed to have been defined by a
Frankfurt School–style negative dialectics associated with historians
and theorists such as Manfredo Tafuri and his American readers, such
as Michael Hays. This position usually winds up testifying not to the
existence of a critical *architecture,* but to its impossibility, or at most,
its irreducible negativity in the face of the insurmountable violence
perpetrated by what the economist Ernest Mandel called, some time
ago, "late capitalism." Meanwhile—as the story goes—architects
like Peter Eisenman have explicitly professed their disinterest in
either resisting or affirming such violence at the level of academic
and professional practice, preferring instead to dedicate themselves
to a vigorous negation and revision of the *internal* assumptions of
the discipline, in the form of the so-called autonomy project. Thus
Eisenman's provocative turn to Giuseppe Terragni's work for the
Italian fascists as a model, under the argument that its formal syntax
could be separated definitively from its political semantics. (This example is dutifully replicated—minus the theory—by postcritics such
as Michael Speaks, in their championing of jargon and techniques
associated with right-wing think tanks and the CIA.) Whereas, the
traditional ground on which the two "critical" approaches have met
is that of a dialectic, in which aesthetic autonomy acts as a kind of
temporary stand-in for the autonomy of the Enlightenment subject
pending the arrival of concrete social transformation, or as Theodor
Adorno would have it, a negative mirror that reflects that subject's
ineluctable demise.

Baird observes that most of the proponents of a "postcritical" position whom he names have passed through academic or professional
circles associated with these other, older names. But more importantly, we might add, they seem to have accepted rather obediently
a central proposition implied by Eisenman's use of the word *critical*
with respect to his own work: that the stakes of an internal critique of
a supposedly autonomous architecture, and the attendant pursuit of
a "new" architecture that continually reinvents its own autonomy are
somehow equivalent to—rather than dialectically engaged with—a

critique of architecture's tragic, a priori collaboration with the external forces it appears to resist, as elaborated by Tafuri with respect to
the Modernist avant-gardes. In other words, the assumption hidden
in naming Eisenman the father of a "critical architecture," which a
subsequent generation now chooses to kill off, is that there is somehow an equivalence between a *political* critique (as adumbrated by
historians and theorists like Tafuri) and an *aesthetic* critique (as adumbrated by architects like Eisenman).

On the other hand, it is somewhat surprising to find the "paranoid-
critical" Rem Koolhaas taken up as a more positive role model by
the postcritics, despite the time he may or may not have spent surfing
on the late capitalist beach. But either way, whether the name of the
father is Peter or Rem, the postcritical project is deeply Oedipal. This
is a point worth making less on the grounds of institutional history
(however substantial the evidence may be) than on the theoretical-
philosophical grounds that continue to haunt even the most resolute
of antitheorists. Since a number of those named by Baird, as well as
their immediate ideological colleagues, have at one time or another
also invoked the name of the philosopher Gilles Deleuze as a comrade in arms—at least before this became too embarrassing, since it
was pointed out time and again that in doing so they were distorting
the Deleuzian politico-philosophical project so as to render it unrecognizable. And yet, folds and rhizomes aside, one source of such
embarrassment persists, in the form of another, "difficult" book that
Deleuze coauthored with Félix Guattari, the *Anti-Oedipus* (1972),
which is nothing less than a frontal assault—epistemological, philosophical, psychoanalytical, historical, political—on the parochial
family trees and "generations" so dear to those who compulsively
fetishize "criticality" in order to kill it off for good.

It has been said many times that the *Anti-Oedipus* is a book of
the 1960s. And, given that Baird explicitly situates the front lines
of the "postcritical" debate in the United States, it is worth noting
that contemporary American electoral politics—down to the most
recent, bloody skirmish in the culture wars—has often been said to
amount to a referendum on the countercultural radicalism associated
with that decade. So, is it possible that the "postcritical" polemic is,
like the more general rightward swing in American politics, actually
a rather thinly disguised effort to bury the utopian politics of the
1960s once and for all? In other words, is it possible that all of the relaxed, "postcritical" oedipality is—in direct opposition to the anti-

authoritarian *Anti-Oedipus*—actually an authoritarian call to order that wants once and for all to kill off the ghost of radical politics by converting political critique into aesthetic critique and then slowly draining *even that* of any dialectical force it may have inadvertently retained?

I ask this question with some regret, since it is addressed mainly to those who rush to denounce serious critique (whether political or aesthetic) as an inconvenient obstacle to professional advancement at the very moment that the very possibility of *any* critique of the status quo must be defended more vigorously than ever. But as an architect, I am also well aware of the very real difficulties of actually practicing architecture (and getting paid for it) while voicing even the most mild of objections. Thus, the usual response is this: architecture is in any case so thoroughly disempowered, so culturally marginal, as to render any critique emanating from within its walls, so to speak, ineffectual if not entirely irrelevant. What must be sought is a more "robust," more "effective" architecture. This is said to apply in extra measure to academic theory, to say nothing of history, which together are judged to be doubly irrelevant by virtue of their supposed obscurity. So why bother?

But these assertions amount to a category error, since the problem is not that architectural discourse is too academic to have any political relevance, but that it is not academic enough. There is nothing "irrelevant" about the very real politics of the universities that post-critics still depend on for their livelihood, where very real professors are regularly denounced by very real cultural conservatives, often prompting anguished symposia on academic freedom (a relevant political concept if there ever was one) in response. The heroic efforts of the late Edward Said and many other such intellectuals are testimony to the significance of academic practice in the international arena of realpolitik. Likewise Jacques Derrida, whose recent passing drew a shameful, defensive "obituary" from the *New York Times* that specifically projected academic discourse onto politics. But perhaps the most telling of such episodes recently was the roundtable of distinguished academics convened in 2003 by the editors of the aptly named journal *Critical Inquiry* to assess the "future of theory." That meeting also drew the attention of the *New York Times,* which concluded that "The Latest Theory Is That Theory Doesn't Matter."[2] While for its part, *Critical Inquiry* published the results of all the fractiousness—coming mainly from the political *left*—while concluding editorially that "theory" does matter after all, just not in the way we might have thought.

But perhaps of greater interest to architecture here are two longer articles not directly associated with the conference that appeared in the same issue. The first, by the philosopher of science Bruno Latour, was titled "Why Has Critique Run Out of Steam? From Matters of Fact to Matters of Concern."[3] It summarized Latour's recent efforts to replace an epistemology infused by the spirit of revolt and radical politics with a new realism founded on ever-contestable "matters of concern" rather than indisputable "facts." For Latour, "critique" is basically code for Marxism, which, along with other modernisms and their denunciatory tendencies, he is at pains to denounce and replace with a vaguely Postmodern version of American pragmatism oriented toward renovating the institutions of parliamentary democracy. Thus, if architecture's self-proclaimed "postcritical" party still resides in the so-called blue states, those of its members still willing to be identified as liberals might find some solace in Latour's method of resolving what used to be called capitalism's "contradictions"— that is, doing "critical" architecture and still getting paid for it.

For those of firmer constitution, that particular issue of *Critical Inquiry* also offered a text by the theorist Slavoj Žižek, titled "The Ongoing 'Soft Revolution.'"[4] There Žižek, an unapologetic (if unorthodox) Marxist, conjures the particularly poignant image of "a yuppie reading Deleuze," through which he provocatively claims certain affinities between the apparatus of desire exemplified by advertising and affect-producing Deleuzian "desiring machines." Žižek is well aware of the reductivism of this claim, and he goes on here and elsewhere to give Deleuze and Guattari their full due as philosophers of radical social transformation. Still, the image of a "yuppie reading Deleuze" stays with us, and it is with this image that I want to offer a brief, concrete response to Baird's call for a critical assessment of an avowedly "postcritical" architecture.

Perhaps the most obvious demonstration of contemporary, theoretically informed architecture's all-too-relevant political efficacy has been in the ongoing debate over the future of the former World Trade Center site in lower Manhattan. From the myriad dimensions in which this has unfolded, I want to excerpt one specific example: the proposal designed by the group of "postcritical" fellow travelers (some of whom represent that tendency's European version) that called itself the United Architects.[5]

The story really begins with the exhibition organized in New York by the gallerist Max Protetch titled "A New World Trade Center" that ran from January 17 through February 16, 2002. There, a mere four months after the attacks, the public was presented with fifty-eight proposals by architects, designers, and artists that, according to the gallery, together represented "a landmark opportunity both for architects and the general public to explore the possibilities for the World Trade Center site."[6] On the one hand (and running parallel with the increased swagger of American foreign policy), this was a raw, unvarnished effort to exploit the "landmark opportunity" offered by 9/11's presumptive clearing of the decks—a chance to fulfill a heroic vision (post-Saddam and post-Postmodern?) already prepared in think tanks and universities but theretofore preempted by the exigencies of professional realism. While on the other hand, the Protetch exhibition was also the first real evidence of the capacities of a neomodern aesthetics to channel the will to power in directions inaccessible to the more literal conformisms of architecture's corporate, contextualist mainstream.

Symptomatic of things to come on this front was the project submitted by Foreign Office Architects (FOA) for an undulating tower of bundled tubes, accompanied by these remarks: "Let's not even consider remembering. . . . What for? We have a great site in a great city and the opportunity to have the world's tallest building back in New York. Ground Zero used to host 1.3M m² of workspace, and that is a good size to attempt to return to NY what it deserves."[7]

Though it remains unclear what New York "deserves" to forget, it is abundantly clear that such willful amnesia refers not only to a salutary rejection of the often sanctimonious imperatives of memorialization but also to an active blindness to the historical conditions of which 9/11 was only one component. Hardly disguised, this "end of history" argument for a new historical type—a new type of skyscraper—exploits its own contradictions to monumentalize, in exemplary "postcritical" fashion, the neoliberal consensus regarding new "opportunities" opened up by techno-corporate globalization. Accordingly, the responsibility of professionals in the new world order is confined to facilitating the arrival of the "new," while washing their hands of the overdetermined historical narratives—and the dead bodies—through which this new is named.

Comparable in posture here was the project submitted by Greg Lynn FORM for a prototypical defensible skyscraper insightfully premised on "the collapse of boundaries between global military conflict and everyday life."[8] Rather than dissent, however, the prototype and its author naturalize this state of affairs—which was long ago given the name "total war"—in a collapse of even the most rudimentary critique into an excited monotone. The resulting hymn to total war only makes sense when seen against the backdrop of Lynn's ongoing commitment to the supposed inner, digital logic of the instruments of production and consumption associated with Hollywood's military-entertainment complex, with overtones of the German military aesthete Ernst Jünger. Thus, Lynn asserts, with a lucid cynicism, "The transfer of military thinking into daily life is inevitable."[9]

In September 2002 the United Architects, an international collection of relatively young designers including Lynn and FOA, were among the six teams chosen by the Lower Manhattan Development Corporation (LMDC) to produce what the LMDC called "innovative" designs for the site. In support of their selection, the LMDC press release referred to the team as "visionaries" in possession of an expertise in, among other things, "theory," an official characterization that uncannily reproduces Žižek's hilarious image of a "yuppie reading Deleuze."

Also included in the team of young professionals that called itself the United Architects was the Hollywood-based entertainment, design, and marketing firm Imaginary Forces. And, indeed, at Ground Zero the public relations message emanating from the team began with their name, which resourcefully morphed the United States into the United Nations, a hybrid that itself dissolved into a transnational becoming-Benetton in the team's group portrait—assembled multiracial faces in a field of colored squares. In support of the implied theme of resolute unity-within-diversity (in the face of a "faceless" enemy?), the project statement offered rhetoric about solemnly moving forward, while images of the scheme proclaimed the result—the crystalline "United Towers"—a "bold vision of the future" dedicated to "returning pride to the site."[10]

And the Deleuzianism? Difference within continuity: a "single continuous building" that differentiated itself into five linked towers built in five phases. A monument to corporate "diversity," the project internalized the naturalized growth fantasies of global capitalism in the form of a relentless, evolutionary development of the site. Affective, nationalist unity ("pride") was shown not to preclude "difference"—a basic premise of the kinder, gentler imperialism recently ratified by the American electorate. An architectural avant-garde thus switches sides in the ongoing culture wars that brought (critical, poststructuralist) "theory" into the discipline with a vengeance in the 1980s. By responding obediently to the call for architectural "vision" while remaining utterly blind to the violence of the package they served up, these architects and others put themselves in a position of docile compliance with the imperatives of a nation at war.

Likewise for the proposal's symbolism, which in many ways crossed nationalism with theological pathos more systematically than did Daniel Libeskind's expressionist winning entry. It required only a little "imaginary force" to see the corporate, crypto-Gothic "cathedral" (their term) designed by United Architects as a baldly symbolic response to an act associated with militant Islam. The skyscraper—Cass Gilbert's "cathedral of commerce"—meets Philip Johnson's Crystal Cathedral. But by melting such ruthlessly "meaningful" religious symbolisms into a dynamic series of visual effects that had the buildings dissolving into a majestic forest in an accompanying video while simultaneously allowing the more unconscious impression of a family of skyscrapers holding hands in the absence of the missing "twins," the project also set in motion a fluid dynamics comparable to that which organized subsequent militarization, as American political fantasies morphed Osama into Saddam. In the architecture of becoming that mixed spirituality with marketing offered up by the United Architects, the particular, violent irony of the United States claiming to act morally on behalf of the United Nations (to *become*, in effect, the United Nations) in invading Iraq was prefigured, affectively and aesthetically.

Though their project was apparently not his favorite, then–*New York Times* architecture critic Herbert Muschamp proposed renaming the United Architects (using rhetoric reminiscent of Dave Hickey, a favorite "postcritical" aesthetic theorist) "The International House of Voluptuous Beauty" in recognition of their apparent efforts to realize "form for form's sake,"[11] while elsewhere in the *Times*, theologian and erstwhile architecture theorist Mark C. Taylor was enlisted into the cause. Surprisingly, Taylor complied by offering the extraordinary exhortation to avoid "becoming obsessed with a past we will never understand" and instead turn optimistically toward the future. Though aimed primarily at the memory industry, such collateral (if unintentional) dismissals of any effort to *articulate* the historical

dimensions of 9/11 as so much backward-looking nostalgia continued to confuse images of "progress" with positive historical change,
and mystification with critical reflection. Chillingly, as if to under-
line the elision, Taylor approvingly concluded his summary with the
message he heard coming from the United Architects: *"e pluribus
unum."*[12] Again, what looks progressive fades into its opposite.

The subsequent chapters in the story are well known, down to the
made-for-television struggle between Libeskind and David Childs
for control of the project's architectural image, which Childs eventually won. Like the distorted smatterings of "theory" in the discourse
of those who would eventually become the United Architects, it is
possible that Libeskind's emotionalism simply became redundant,
as images of "progressive" architecture—including Libeskind's—
circulating in the winter of 2002–3 were replaced on American television screens that spring with images of the "shock and awe" bomb-
ing campaign in Baghdad. Total war had been waged in the aesthetic
training camp called Ground Zero, only to be projected back out-
ward, in near-perfect symmetry.

This, then, was not merely a sordid rerun of what Walter Benjamin
once famously called the aestheticization of politics. It was aesthetics
as politics. By enthusiastically accepting the protocols of cultural (and
architectural) "progress" for its own sake, "postcritical" architects
showed themselves all too willing to assist politically in the prosecu-
tion of a virtual war that was soon to go live. Even today, many prefer
to misrecognize the demand for "vision" as an "opportunity" that
was later betrayed by the back-room deals of developers and politi-
cians rather than as the overexposed intensification of neoimperial
desires that it represented from the beginning. Thus, the global city
prepared itself to market an image of supposedly enlightened rationality symbolized in a "visionary" architecture. The dilemma, simply
put, was that this gesture was *made in the service of* an emboldened
sense of empire and war on all fronts, and not against it.

To be sure, for more sober practitioners of the "postcritical," the
liberal-humanist idea of the "project" supplants theological vision as
a guide. Hence, architecture and/or architects who are merely critical
(or "merely" antiwar?) are judged to have insufficiently fulfilled the
old, Modernist mission of being "projective" and of thereby affirming an enlightened alternative. But just as we can justifiably ask of the
straw figure called critical architecture, "critical of what?" we might
ask the affirmative, projective practitioners of the "postcritical" just

what sort of world they are projecting and affirming in their architecture and in their discourse.

If the answer is anything close to that offered by the United Architects, then I vote "No"—despite its many legitimate claims to an authentic, technologically enabled urbanity.[13] Still, those who lament the relentless negativity of much critique (such as, perhaps, that offered above) are at least partly right, since the problem is not that critical discourse is too difficult and therefore ineffectual. The problem is that it is often too easy. Bruised by the complicities of what Tafuri called "operative criticism," much critical work does not risk intervening in the future in the systematic manner for which, I think, many architects rightly yearn. Similarly, the need to engage directly with messy realities called for by some postcritics is indeed urgent. The question is which realities you choose to engage with and to what end. In other words: what's your project? This also means avoiding the elementary mistake of assuming that reality is entirely real—that is, pre-existent, fixed, and therefore exempt from critical reimagination. For this, alliances are necessary.

So, what is to be done? To begin with, rather than lapse into the post-utopian pragmatism of that grandfather of the "postcritical" Colin Rowe, the question of utopia must be put back on the architectural table. But it must not be misread as a call for a perfect world, a world apart, an impossible totality that inevitably fades into totalitarianism. Instead, utopia must be read literally, as the "non-place" written into its etymological origins that is "nowhere" not because it is ideal and inaccessible, but because, in perfect mirrored symmetry, it is also "everywhere." Utopia is both glamorous and boring, exceptional and prosaic. Among its heralds is another, earlier denizen of lower Manhattan, Herman Melville's Bartleby the Scrivener, an anonymous, modest clerk who, when asked literally to reproduce what the 1960s would later call "the system," simply and politely refused, declaring, "I would prefer not to."

Utopia, then, is what Derrida called a "specter," a ghost that infuses everyday reality with other, possible worlds, rather than some otherworldly dream. And if another name for the so-called postcritical is "realism," we have already seen at Ground Zero how architecture's realist fantasies of twisting, dancing skyscrapers have worked systematically to exorcise utopia's ghost with crystal cathedrals dedicated to a fundamentalist oligarchy. But like all ghosts, that specter is never quite dead, returning to haunt architectural projects already quietly among us and others coming soon. We can call these projects the first evidence of a "utopian realism" (details to follow). Meanwhile, utopian realism must be thought of as a movement that may or may not exist, all of whose practitioners are double agents. Naming them, or their work, would blow their cover. (They may or may not all be architects.) Those who could voted for Kerry. (So you, too, could be a utopian realist.) Utopian realism is critical. It is real. It is enchantingly secular. It thinks differently. It is a style with no form. It moves sideways, instead of up and down the family tree. It is (other) worldly. It occupies the global city rather than the global village. It violates disciplinary codes even as it secures them. It is utopian not because it dreams impossible dreams, but because it recognizes "reality" itself as—precisely—an all-too-real dream enforced by those who prefer to accept a destructive and oppressive status quo. Utopia's ghost floats within this dream, conjured time and again by those who would prefer not to.

2005

Notes

1. George Baird, "'Criticality' and Its Discontents," chapter 10, this volume.

2. Emily Eakin, "The Latest Theory Is That Theory Doesn't Matter," *New York Times,* April 19, 2003, D9.

3. Bruno Latour, "Why Has Critique Run Out of Steam? From Matters of Fact to Matters of Concern," *Critical Inquiry* (Winter 2004): 225–48.

4. Slavoj Žižek, "The Ongoing 'Soft Revolution,'" *Critical Inquiry* (Winter 2004): 292–323.

5. For a more detailed analysis of the architectural discourse surrounding the World Trade Center projects, see Reinhold Martin, "Architecture at War: A Report from Ground Zero," in *Angelaki* (August 2004): 217–25. My account here of the United Architects project is adapted from that article.

6. Max Protetch, "A New World Trade Center: Exhibition Overview," www.maxprotetch.com/SITE/PREVIOUS/ANEWWTC/index.html.

7. Foreign Office Architects, "A New World Trade Center: Foreign Office Architects Bunch Tower," www.maxprotetch.com/SITE/PREVIOUS/ANEWWTC/FOA/index.html.

8. Greg Lynn FORM, "A New World Trade Center: Greg Lynn FORM, A New World Trade Center," www.maxprotetch.com/SITE/PREVIOUS/ANEWWTC/FORM/index.html.

9. Ibid.

10. Lower Manhattan Development Corporation, "Introduction," www .renewnyc.com/plan_des_dev/wtc_site/new_design_plans/firm_f/default .asp.htm.

11. Herbert Muschamp, "The Latest Round of Designs Rediscover and Celebrate Vertical Life," *New York Times,* December 19, 2002, B10.

12. Mark C. Taylor, "Beyond Mourning, Building Hope on Ground Zero," *New York Times,* December 29, 2002, Arts & Leisure, 40.

13. It must be noted that two other projects in the LMDC study, associated with other figures in the current debate over criticality, played out somewhat more convincing endgames: the mute, negative symbol of architecture-as-such (a grid turning a corner) produced by Eisenman, Charles Gwathmey, Steven Holl, and Richard Meier; and the equally mute field of leaning towers (Hilberseimer with a twist?) produced by Stan Allen and James Corner in collaboration with Skidmore, Owings and Merrill, and others. Neither project, however, offered a systematic alternative to the politically charged demand for symbolism in which the LMDC study was framed.

12

Design Will Save the World! On Bruce Mau's *Massive Change* and the Mediatization of Culture

Robert Levit and Evonne Levy

Massive Change (MC), a noisy exhibition (with catalog, radio program, and Web site), offers an opportunity to study some of the recent effects of new visual media on our culture and its mental life. *MC*, which originated at the Vancouver Art Gallery, went to the Art Gallery of Ontario, and will go to the Museum of Contemporary Art in Chicago, was conceived by graphic designer Bruce Mau and student assistants. It announces off the bat that it's not what we might expect from the ubiquitous graphic designer: It "is not about the world of design but the design of the world."[1] With its emphasis on technology, its ebullient optimism, and boundless claims for design's responsibility and power, *MC* is a cross between a world's fair, a futurama, and a technology expo. Although it was mostly lambasted in the press, its central claims about design warrant further diagnosis, for as problematic as *MC* is—in the all-encompassing role it accords to design, its sole authorship, and its abdication of institutional expertise—it is symptomatic of the contemporary tryst of design and business and of a crisis of purpose facing our museums.

The catalog opens with catastrophe: earthquakes, floods, and human-made disasters that reveal the previously hidden—the "design" of infrastructure. Design, Mau argues, aspires to ubiquity, and with ubiquity comes invisibility. Disasters disrupt invisible systems and

Massive Change, interior of exhibit, Art Gallery of Ontario, Toronto, 2005. Photograph by Robert Levit.

thereby reveal them and design's ubiquity. For Mau, what is designed is nearly every made thing.

The designed world is mapped out in the rooms of the exhibition and sections of the catalog organized according to varying "economies" (rather than disciplines) with emphatic goals, posed by the curators, guiding the viewers. Interspersed as yellow pages in the catalog and in a variety of formats in the exhibition are interviews with scientists and urban designers, researchers and futurists. Using manifesto-like assertions, *MC* pictures our present world, describes solvable global problems and their alleged solutions (to be provided by a nebulous collective) in the following sequence: *Urban Economies,* accompanied by images of cities and their edges ("We will create urban shelter for the entire world population"[2]); *Movement Economies,* loosely related to Urban Economies, with bicycles, electric cars, wheelchairs, and computer simulations that improve safety testing ("We will enable sustainable mobility"); *Energy Economies,* science-fair-like in presenting green energy sources—solar and other simple technologies deployed especially in developing countries ("We will bring energy to the entire world"); *Information Economies,* about collective problem-solving and world culture resulting from digital communication ("We will build a global mind"); *Image Economies,* about rendering the universe visible through digital technologies and the unbounded embrace of the image in contemporary culture ("We will make the invisible visible"); *Market Economies,* about the positive aspects of globalized markets and massive industry ("We will seamlessly integrate all supply and demand around the world"); *Material Economies,* about smart materials ("We will build intelligence into materials and liberate form from matter"); *Military Economies,* about the mutual influence of military and civilian technologies and a plea to choose peace ("Will we shift from the service of war to the service of life?"—this the only question in the sequence); *Manufacturing Economies,* about waste ("We will eliminate the need for raw material and banish all waste"); *Living Economies,* about the redesign of nature (man, animals, food) through genetic engineering ("We will design evolution"); *Wealth and Politics,* about the empowerment of the poor ("We will eradicate poverty").

Though *MC*'s technology-heavy content is conventional for expos, Mau articulates a distinct perspective on design. Unlike a recent exhibition comparable in its subject, *Expo 2000* in Hanover, which was generated by powerful conglomerates presenting cutting-edge research, *MC* was the product of a single personality, a designer whose expertise lies outside of any disciplines represented here. It is both in the singular authorship of Mau and its use of design as the organizing principle that *MC* must be evaluated. What was its purpose? What does the redesignation of separate disciplines under "design" add to our understanding or capacities? What does the collection of so much diverse and complex information into one show accomplish? What does it mean for an art museum to cede its curators' expertise to a graphic designer, and what is the museum-going public supposed to find now in its art museums? And, of key importance, what is the effect on our understanding of the contemporary world of the design of the show's information?

Design is a key term in the exhibition, although its scope and practitioners are thoroughly redefined. The prelude to the redefinition appeared in *Life Style,* in which Mau made "no claims for our own advances in these redefinitions," while calling attention to the fact that the "role of the navigator—the one who gives pattern, shape, and direction to the noise" is "more powerful than ever."[3] In *MC* design is offered as a master term to describe forms of "creative" activity that ordinarily go by other names: biology, materials engineering, urban design, graphic design, mechanical and civil engineering, economic and urban planning, and so on. In using the term for such a broad range of activities, Mau voices a pervasive rendering these days of various activities of "making" and planning as "design." Because design is given as the new episteme, there could be no section on "Design Economies," for all of the economies described in the exhibition spring from this invisible base, what Hal Foster has tentatively called the "political economy of design."[4]

Between Foster's Baudrillardian take on the ascendancy of design and Naomi Klein's critique of the global branding phenomenon,[5] some terms of a critique of *MC* are already in place. One way of understanding the organizing role claimed for the designer (and this explains part of the museum's interest in the project) is in the branding effect of Mau himself, one of the few well-known authors in the design world, quite apart from his role in branding others. But more to the point, design's ascendancy is not owing to the designer's expertise in the technologies whose conception, development, and production *MC* posits as design's responsibility. Nor, of course, does design as a discipline replace or achieve the expertise of the disciplines represented. Rather, design's preeminence arises because of the utter ubiquity of the economy's "mediation." Again this is Foster. By mediation of the economy, he means more than the "culture of marketing" and "marketing of culture." Mediation gains preeminence through digitizing and computing, the effect of which is to gather the production of all objects under the sovereignty of design in the virtuality of the digital. Design is not so much the active agent that produces as the framework of mediation, which is to say the presentation that organizes the will to produce.

In *MC* design is given a central role in the making of the present, but Mau leaves open the question, "What kind of making?" He does not want design merely to decorate, but we wonder if worrying about merely decorating isn't a cover for worrying about what it really does, which is much more than decorating but much less than making the world (at least in the way Mau suggests). We would like to come at this question from several angles. The first traces the drawing together of the terms *creativity* and *design* in an emblematic episode of advertising's history, one that begins to track the ascendance of these two terms in business.

In the *Conquest of Cool,* Thomas Frank describes the dramatic transformations of advertising culture in the 1960s. Creativity and design replaced the purported communicative clarity of 1950s market research–driven advertising.[6] One particular episode stands out in Frank's account: the story of the "Pepsi Generation." Pepsi undertook no marketing study for consumer demand and discovered no latent and built-up desire. Rather it fabricated a consumer constituency—a "generation"—that in terms of consuming patterns had no bearing on any actual age-based generation or any other group other than its (proposed) consumption of Pepsi. Frank is relating an early episode of lifestyle advertising. Now, branding and lifestyle advertising have become so much the norm that, as Mau might say, its ubiquity makes it invisible—so much so that Mau himself never brings it up as the possible explanation for design's ascendancy.

Frank's account of the emergence of creative types from the back rooms to overtake conventional forms of business management in advertising made evident what had not yet become an absolute of business wisdom: Creativity, through its mediation of goods, produced the real good that people sought. The power to mediate goods and thus consumer desire is the story behind design's ascendancy, not its ability to better coordinate social goals or technical or social production.

Mau is situated where he is not because design is a new episteme, but because design and "creativity" are the engine of our mediatized economy. Spurred by Richard Florida's *Rise of the Creative Class,* a flurry of business writing has design and creativity paired as key to successful new enterprises. The words *creativity* and *design* are cropping up everywhere. Roger Martin, the University of Toronto's Rotman School of Business Management's dean, argues for bringing the "creative" qualities associated with the design professions into business to break free of constraining hierarchies and traditions.[7] *BusinessWeek* recently ran a special report called "Get Creative!" describing the overtaking of the Knowledge Economy by the Creativity Economy. In this "commoditization of knowledge," in which understanding consumer desire is key, design occupies a very prominent place.[8] The business schools are exposing their students to high-end practitioners of the traditional design disciplines (the addition of design to business schools—"Tomorrow's B-School? It might be a D-School"—was one of the topics of the special report),[9] but they also mean by *design* simply product development, which amounts to, it seems, business itself. Martin's plan for the School of Management is to start a master's in business design—but *design* here substitutes for *administration*. Has design become synonymous with business? The foregrounding of creativity and the equating of design and business management point in several directions. Along the lines of Frank's narrative, the elevation in status of design and creativity simply recognizes the growing, if hierarchical, union between production and the apparatus of advertising/marketing, which is to say the secondary status of products relative to the medium through which their importance is created. At the same time, the increasing degree to which advanced economies are administrative/service economies entails an increase in the degree to which they are primarily dedicated to mediating economic activity.

The idea that *design* may be a synonym for *business management* speaks to another point. Design is now openly recognized as holding a key to, among other things, the kind of change that must take place for success in the marketplace. The market-driven necessity for the appearance of constant change affects not just production but all of our institutions (universities, museums, even governments) that previously banked on the value of tradition but that now, to retain their viability, must constantly refashion themselves. Instead of *progress* we now speak of *creativity*. This explains in part the appeal of *MC* as an exhibition to at least one of its venues, the Art Gallery of Ontario (AGO), which is engaged in a reinvention of itself through a Frank Gehry renovation. That the message of the exhibition so closely matched the museum's major message (what it calls its "word mark") to its constituents ("Transformation AGO"—"New Art, New Building, New Ideas, New Future") could not have been made more evident than when the title of the show was painted billboard style over the museum's brick facade, which was soon to meet a wrecking ball.

But *MC*'s claims for design extend far beyond naming it as the creative principle, for, positioned here as the new master discourse, design not only poses creative solutions; it also does nothing less than order the world. This is especially apparent in the exhibition's section on images of the world, in which the closely related processes of imaging and design provide our understanding of the world from the microscopic (nanotechnology) to the macroscopic ("global portraits"). In being posited as an epistemological project, design now takes its place in a historic chain of master discourses: Design replaces rhetoric, which had replaced philosophy, which had replaced theology. What is more, one of *MC*'s premises is to "make the invisible visible," that is to say, to reveal the hidden role of design. That the exhibition should place at its center a phrase as portentous as this Christian one seems in keeping with the grandiosity of the project.

One of the powers attributed to design (and imaging technologies) is its ability to order a complex world—and thereby (somehow) save us. The exhibition catalog remarks upon the "poignant message" that the first data image of the ozone hole over Antarctica "delivered to the general public" and how "it was because of the image that we became aware of the significant impact our actions have on the global environment." In the exhibition an image of enhanced dots of light surrounding the earth accompanies frightening observations about threats to our communications and future space travelers posed by proliferating satellite debris.

In the spirit of the exhibit's futurist tenor, something threatens, and invention—technological invention—helps. Design is capable, Mau reminds us, of among other things, reducing complexity, which threatens to overwhelm our ability to understand. Legibility has become a legitimate concern of design. The communication theorist Edward R. Tufte has become a cult figure through his championing of clarity in the presentation of information.[10] It was he who made the claim (echoed in the potential of design failure disasters with which the *MC* catalog opens) that the space shuttle explosion occurred as a result of a confusing display of data in a PowerPoint presentation to NASA engineers. Who can object to the need for clarity when the presentation of life-saving information is concerned?

While *MC* affirms "legibility," its affirmation of legibility is curiously at odds with the exhibition's own presentation. Because *MC* is first and foremost an exhibition, the question of its visual qualities, its design, and the role attributed to it are paramount. Rarely sober, more often giddy in its graphics and material displays, the exhibit itself reveals another less mentionable ambition of design, which is not to clarify information but to revel in a purely visual excess. It does so in the room in which statistics are figured as Warhol-like silver balloons in various sizes (to visualize percentages that one can only understand after intense translation of a wall text). It does so in the room dedicated to military and other technologies presented as silkscreened images on superhero-sized banners hung randomly from a high ceiling in a fun house–like room lined with reflective acrylic surfaces. In a display about the ubiquity of images, images are literally ubiquitous: floor to ceiling, on the floors, on the furniture. For each room, a new mode of presentation was invented (or redeployed, for *MC* draws upon some of Mau's previous projects), and in most cases the rule was "saturate and immerse."

Here we get to one of the great shibboleths of Modernist design (and architecture): utility. Design is there to make buildings more useful, and books, posters, and other forms of visual information more legible. On the other hand, one of the essences of design is that it violates such logic—that it reveals a formal insistence that is visual potlatch, an excess for nothing. Alan Liu describes the most striking characteristic of "cool web sites" as their virtuosic excesses of graphic design.[11] Oblique about content, they reveal a dedication to pure formal experiment. Technology's purposeful activity—its roots as tool—is turned on its head. Design becomes a mode of liberation from communicative purpose.

Contrary to *MC*'s overt dedications, its overall mood or tone—its technique—is cool, in Liu's sense of the word. Liu writes of how virtuosic display of graphic/technical skill and sensibility in cool design relates to a more general characteristic of cool, combining a businesslike coolness of emotional affect—ordinarily associated with efficient instrumental purposes—with a contrarian's dedication to apparently purposeless activity. Liu uses examples drawn from the 1950s hot-rod culture in which customization of cars and motorcycles rededicated technical expertise to the development of "unnecessary" personal aesthetic elaboration in the direction of appearance and noise. Here, we wish to emphasize Liu's observation that within the heart of an increasingly technologized society a style emerged based upon the bending of technical skills toward purposeless activity.

Our point here is that *MC*'s overt dedication to purposes is at odds with itself. The project's purpose is to create an ethical world, to present design's ability as engineering and urbanism to make better tools for movement, habitation, and eating, and to increase the world's legibility. And yet the show is full of graphic elaboration—stylings of information that cannot be reduced to their content. It borrows from the effects of graphical excess. It is cool not only for its participation in specifically current fashions (which Mau himself has done much to establish) but for its excess of means, of display techniques.

As in the exhibition design, so in some of the designed objects on display. Thus, for example, in the section on transportation it is not clear which is more important to the exhibition—the cool designs of some of the vehicles or their eco-friendly engineering. The show may be largely about overcoming bare subsistence—a condition that suggests careful tending of means—but it luxuriates in a utopian excess of design.

An aristocratic "waste" of graphical energies and modes of presentation creates a central effect of the exhibit. Solutions to world poverty, housing the homeless, feeding the starving, and saving nature will arise from appealingly styled information and products. Good deeds are served up as a prospect of, a result of a natural allegiance with, taste for design. The question here is whether this allegiance is an incentive to make a union of what history shows to have no natural allegiance—culture and ethics. Is the consuming audience drawn toward ethical action or, as we believe, toward the comforting illusion that a taste for current modes of representation, an excitement about new technologies and their appearance, is tantamount to a good deed? This point is made most pithily in the tableware products developed by Mau for Umbra that "visually explore the core themes of *Massive Change* through colorful and detailed information graphics. Illustrated through statistics, concepts such as biodiversity, energy optimization, international travel and NGOs, land protection, information flow, and urbanization patterns are conveyed." On *MC*'s Web site, Mau figures that the move from decorated souvenir plate to engagement goes like this: "Since eating is commonly a social activity, tableware was created with the intent of spurring heated conversation over the diverse topics presented."[12] This in spite of the warning in Mau's *Life Style* that "unless we can come to terms with the global image economy and the way it permeates the things we make and see, we are doomed to a life of decorating and redecorating."[13]

We are less convinced about *MC*'s virtuous idealism and more convinced that something the show does not say it sets out to do it does quite effectively. In aesthetic practice, the desire to make visible the invisible is a grand vocation. But this practice does not communicate in scientific fashion, and it does not purport to explain anything or help anyone. It may produce language of forms through which one may have an intuition of the unrepresentable. The network drawing on the cover of the *MC* catalog, in its alluring, complex interconnectivity, provides an example. The network drawing, regardless of how it may derive from some automated metric, provides an aesthetically rather than instrumentally compelling representation of the network of the Internet. The diagram does not really explain anything; it does not help any network programmer to do his or her work better. It does, though, give us an intuition of the incommensurable world of the Net. But we insist that it takes something that starts out as information and does not play it back to us as information but rather as an aesthetic artifact that presents something that is not data but an intuition of an order that has no real appearance or form. One of the virtues of the formal aspects of the presentation itself is as a form of liberation from the underlying purposefulness that dedication to data can imply.

Mau's team has emphasized the world-shaping aspect of design while downplaying design as a mode of presentation. Where presentation is discussed, it seems to be largely in relationship to design's ability to make for more transparent communication. And yet the profusion of the show's forms produces something more complex than the communication of information—more complex and more opaque. Its graphic elaborations are a kind of ornament. In seeming to draw upon the installations of Andy Warhol and Yayoi Kusama rather than the diagrammatic clarity of Tufte, *MC* comes closer to the art museum's dedications than its organizers would like to admit. We would like to think that had *MC* articulated its angling toward treating information as symbolic ornament, the museum would have been quite prescient in capturing an attitude toward aesthetic practice. One of the most important points or contemporary conditions that *MC* gives concrete form to is what we might call the ornament of information. In our time communication can have an impact disconnected from its content. If we consider Times Square, an early example of this phenomenon, we can better grasp the spectacular nature of communication as ornament.

In spite of its actual exuberance of design and the effects that arise from it, *MC* is primarily trying to communicate information that will lead to action to solve worldwide problems.[14] It belongs in a genealogy of futurist projects like those of Buckminster Fuller and Alvin Toffler that cajole through portentous observations about the present while promoting faith in technology to solve millennial human dilemmas. Part of the futurists' creative spark resides in imagining that problems, regardless of origin, are solvable through some essentially technical feat.[15] Our own opinion is that such views have the effect of suggesting, erroneously, that preeminently political challenges are technical problems susceptible to technical solutions.

Many of the technologies presented in *MC* do contribute to solving particular problems, but we wonder whether the exhibit clarifies the issues related to the urgent dilemmas—climate change, hunger, and shelter—that it seeks to solve. For example, the exhibition's assertion that dense, compact development patterns establish more sound resource management sets a tone of gravitas but also suggests that simply choosing the right urban model is enough, without any reference to the nexus of self-interests that can make urban planning close to impossible. For example, it was not insufficient technical know-how or accessibility of relevant information but the influence on political decision making of real estate developers that led to the endless consumption of agricultural land outside Los Angeles.

The futurist thought in *MC* appeals to audiences precisely because it leapfrogs over the labyrinth of politics by lending a phantasmal empowerment to technical experts.[16] The way *MC* puts it ("What will we do now that we can do *anything?*"), the mind's power to conceive becomes tantamount to actually achieving in this fantasy of effortless (i.e., politics-free) agency. By contrast, the most recent international expo, *Hanover 2000*, the goals of which were quite similar to those of *MC*, made substantive efforts to link its optimism to actual political organization by engineering a consensus of government, nongovernment, industry, and the exhibition-attending public through programming and participation, and through the creation of the nonprofit Global Partnership Hanover.[17] Did *MC*'s point of origin in the art museum suggest its imaginary (as opposed to imaginative) project? Should we consider *MC* a conservative riff on the *Gesamtweltkunstwerk,* whose message is that the world can stand outside of politics, that it can be fixed by art?

When the Vancouver Art Gallery originally approached Mau, it had in mind a show about the history of design. What Mau came back with is a stretch of any art museum's typical mandate and a stretch for Mau's own expertise. Along with the faith placed by the museum in Mau comes a real shift in the use of expertise, not all good. Experts are quite present—in the exhibition there is an installation of talking heads in video kiosks, and the "yellow pages" in the catalog are dedicated to interviews with experts. Unlike at Hanover, where, for instance, the Fraunhofer Institute for Material Flow and

Logistics organized the section on mobility,[18] in *MC* the role of the designer/curator is as a compiler of expertise, akin to the *Time* magazine editor whose mandate is to bring readers up to date on ideas and trends. In sponsoring this exhibition, the museum has effectively mediatized the museum, abandoning its own claims to expertise in favor of its constituency's comfort with familiar forms of information delivery.

For all of the powers attributed to design, practitioners like Mau are assuming their new roles primarily because we live in a media-driven world. Actors become president and governor because they are effective communicators; analogously, designers like Mau are being asked to conceptualize much more than packaging because it is their visual effects that seize our attention. With the designer tail wagging the museum dog, the actual subject of the exhibition became of less consequence. One is reminded of advertisements that no longer show their product but seek the viewer's positive identification with an image then metonymically transferred to the product.

We imagine that the people attracted to the exhibition come away either impressed by the museum's agility or dismayed by its confusion in presenting something beyond its mandate. The museums showing *MC* are associated with progress, and design now seems hipper and more mainstream than art itself. With exhibitions becoming effects rather than substantive and original contributions, it is obvious, as Michael Kimmelman recently put it, that "money rules. It always has, of course. But at cultural institutions today, it seems increasingly to corrupt ethics and undermine bedrock goals like preserving collections and upholding the public interest. Curators are no longer making decisions."[19] The museum's abdication of its own claim to expertise in *MC* is part of a larger loss of confidence in having a particular knowledge to offer to its audience. In devaluing its own claims to knowledge, the museum falls in with Richard Florida's rejection of the "knowledge economy" as elitist for what by contrast is, in his definition, the open, tolerant, and inclusive "creative class."

In the end, we would like to propose that *Massive Change* can be understood as an artful representation by a talented graphic designer of the organization of much of the contemporary world. This will save us from the agony of what is probably more to the point: that *MC* confuses organizing the world with selling the world.

2006

Notes

1. Bruce Mau, Jennifer Leonard, and the Institute without Boundaries, et al., *Massive Change: A Manifesto for the Future of Global Design* (New York: Phaidon Press, 2004), 11.

2. This and the following quotations appeared in the exhibition and in the catalog.

3. Bruce Mau, *Life Style* (New York: Phaidon Press 2000), 579–81.

4. Hal Foster, "Design and Crime," *Praxis 5* (2003): 13. Versions of this essay appeared first as "Hey, That's Me," a review of Bruce Mau's, *Life Style* in *London Review of Books*, April 5, 2001, and in *Design and Crime (and Other Diatribes)* (London: Verso, 2002).

5. Naomi Klein, *No Logo: No Space, No Choice, No Jobs* (New York: Picador, 2000).

6. Thomas Frank, *The Conquest of Cool: Business Culture, Counterculture, and the Rise of Hip Consumerism* (Chicago: University of Chicago Press, 1997).

7. Bill Breen, "The Business of Design," *Fast Company* 93 (April 2005): 68. Our thanks to Charles Waldheim for this and other references and fruitful debate.

8. Bruce Nussbaum, "Get Creative! How to Build Innovative Companies," *BusinessWeek*, August 1, 2005, 62.

9. Jennifer Merritt and Louis Lavelle, "Tomorrow's B-School? It Might Be a D-School," *BusinessWeek*, August 1, 2005, 80–81. For example, the Rotman School of Management has launched joint courses with the Ontario College of Art and Design, the Illinois Institute of Technology's Institute of Design now has an executive master's degree in design methods (for managers without design experience), and the Stanford Institute for Design is geared for businesspeople to learn "design thinking." See also Bill Breen, "The Business of Design," *Fast Company* 93 (April 2005): 69.

10. Edward R. Tufte, *Visual Explanations: Images and Quantities, Evidence and Narrative* (Cheshire, Conn.: Graphics Press, 1997); Edward R. Tufte, *Envisioning Information* (Cheshire, Conn.: Graphics Press, 1990); Edward R. Tufte, *The Visual Display of Quantitative Information* (Cheshire, Conn.: Graphics Press, 1983).

11. Alan Liu, *The Laws of Cool: Knowledge, Work, and the Culture of Information* (Chicago: University of Chicago Press, 2004).

12. www.massivechange.com/projProduct_01.html.

13. Mau, *Life Style,* 13.

14. "*Massive Change* online is moving into a new phase, from communication to action. Join the project and connect with people around the world to share your ideas, discuss the critical issues, and collaborate on changing the world"; www.massivechange.com.

15. It is true that the Toynbee quote with which they open the exhibit's accompanying book elevates thought over technical and political invention as the central agent moving us toward the "practical objective" of resolving "the welfare of the whole human race." However, the exhibit for the most part showcases technical invention.

16. Here we do not mean to say that members of the public imagine themselves to be experts, but rather that the notion that an expert has solutions to big problems is deeply appealing. The figure of the expert provides an empowering prospect for the individual imagination—particularly when the nomenclature describing different activities is absorbed into an all-inclusive category that designates the human creativity. See Adam Philips, *Terrors and Experts* (Cambridge, Mass.: Harvard University Press, 1996).

17. Five thousand experts worldwide came to ten discussion forums organized by agencies already engaged in the kind of issues being discussed. Birgit Breuel, *Visions of the Future: Projects around the World, Global Dialogue and the Thematic Area at Expo 2000 Hanover* (Berlin: Jovis, 2001).

18. Ibid., 185.

19. Michael Kimmelman, "What Price Love? Museums Sell Out," *New York Times,* July 17, 2005.

13

The Muses Are Not Amused: Pandemonium in the House of Architecture

Jorge Silvetti

This essay was first presented as the Gropius Lecture at the Harvard University Graduate School of Design in April 2002, on the occasion of the honoring Professor Silvetti for his seven years as chairman of the Department of Architecture. The lecture was propelled by almost two hundred images, only a fraction of which can be reproduced here; the text therefore required appropriate modification. In the spring of 2003, Professor Silvetti added a postscript outlining possible implications of his talk.[1]

If there is one consistent trait that propels my intellectual and artistic pursuits, it is a desire to explore, explain, and experiment with all the forces that converge in the conception, imagination, and proposition of architectural form, ultimately to produce it and have it perform. The fundamental and specific thing that we architects do is imagine and produce architectural form. The "form" I am talking about is not just concerned with a priori elaborated aesthetic stances or received vocabularies. Rather, it is architectural form that involves all the forces that converge in the final result, be they cultural, social, economic, or ideological as well as technical or methodological. Thus, language, buildings, topography, art, fashion, TV and movies, new and old materials—just to name some of all that is form and begets form—have been and still are the flora and fauna that inhabit and nourish the topography of my intellectual path. Moreover, in the cases that interest me, this effort of producing form happens because the architect has a will to produce this form, to author it, be it by necessity, interest, or irrepressible desire.

This introductory self-profile is necessary because it helps explain why I am distraught about what I perceive to be a progressive dissipation of the centrality of our mission as educators to teach and learn rigorously and vigorously about form making and its consequences, a process that is slowly becoming secondary and peripheral. I consider this ever-increasing neglect, which I see in design school reviews, in writings, and in discussions, as nothing less than suicidal for a profession whose creativity and standing depend ultimately on its absolute command of this unique and difficult task. The conditions under which this progressive loss takes place are doubly unfortunate because they occur under the deceiving euphoria of a proliferation of different modes, approaches, and techniques of form production that purport to have eased and multiplied our abilities to generate form. Yet, as I see it, they instead are turning the architect into a dazed observer of seductive wonders.

Nevertheless, during this past decade that serves as the somewhat arbitrary period that provides my cases, we have had evidence that architecture matters and that it is through its forms that it impresses us. Such evidence is the result of an accumulation of events that have been moving and enlightening both in joyful and painful ways for architecture and in particular architecture's physical presence in the city. And since I want to focus not on specific buildings and architects but instead on design strategies and techniques that produce architectural form, and the ideas and ideologies behind them, suffice it to say that the period and corpus I am looking at could be bracketed by the exultant irruption in the world and in our imagination of the Guggenheim Museum Bilbao and by the wound to our affects left by the physical consequences of the September 11 attack, the disappearance of two buildings we did not know we would miss so much.

Today, I will focus mainly on the issues involved in the production of form and the designer's will to produce it within academia. In this context, the theoretical underpinnings reflect my continuing preoccupation with understanding how ideas are represented or embedded in architecture and how to teach this aspect of the process of design. I have chosen four cases that I believe present a wide spectrum of that aspect of the creative process. Of course, there have been many other things of importance going on in this past decade that affect this process and that would certainly be worth discussing, mostly in technology and building construction, and in sustainability and the environment. But in my view these are ultimately dependent for their success on the ability with which architects transcend their purely technical achievements and give them intentional and adequate form.

My victims today are, first, a much discussed trend (or method?) for which we have no official name and meager literature but that one of my colleagues has called "Programism";[2] second, a widespread mode of production of architecture that has hit schools at a high intellectual level, mostly as a topic for analysis, and that the architectural and general media has called "Thematization"; third, "Blobs"; and fourth, "Literalism" in architectural representation. This is an odd grouping of heterogeneous "architectures" that nevertheless share common traits. Ultimately they will help me open up the discussion to the larger issue of what the task of architectural theory could be in the coming years.

Programism

First, Programism, the current trend that derives from an overenthusiastic embrace of the otherwise healthy revisitation of the idea of "program" (as opposed to "function") as the generator of architecture, program understood as a protocol of complex nonlinear conglomerates of information that animates, inspires, impacts, grounds, influences, and colors a design, a building, or any physical condition for habitation. The vagueness in trying to define it is part of its attraction and peril.

Programism is the extreme development of a tendency to accumulate and manipulate information that by the sheer power of its quantity, uncritical method of being gathered, apparent authority as "neutral data," and compelling graphic representation becomes, with little transformation, the very form of the architecture proposed or its figurative inspiration. This bizarre development belongs more to the realm of primitive magic than of design, since it relies on sympathies between diverse media that seem to act interchangeably as cause-and-effects agents—the "form" of the data matrices or charts

Program   Structure

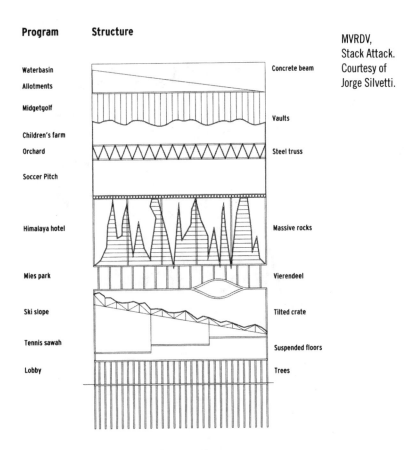

Waterbasin
Allotments

Midgetgolf

Children's farm
Orchard

Soccer Pitch

Himalaya hotel

Mies park

Ski slope

Tennis sawah

Lobby

Concrete beam

Vaults

Steel truss

Massive rocks

Vierendeel

Tilted crate

Suspended floors

Trees

MVRDV,
Stack Attack.
Courtesy of
Jorge Silvetti.

producing the form of the architecture, and in turn, the "form" of such architecture supposedly inducing the "actions" promoted by the program.

We can take this as a first example of a process that potentially exonerates the architect from his or her creative role. But behind this surrender also lies a suspect methodological operation that assumes that an arbitrary graphic rearrangement of data, coordination of figures, and composition of data in charts automatically provide the solution to the very problems they contain. Crass empiricism, tautological doctrine of inference, this poverty of imagination is not too far from the ideological structure of well-established, worn-out, and discredited methodological doctrines of the recent past, such as those of the Pattern Language or General Systems theories. In all this we relive the 1960s naïveté about the creative process, and it is not surprising that "the program" was also first elevated to primacy then.

MVRDV,
Stack Attack.
Courtesy of
Jorge Silvetti.

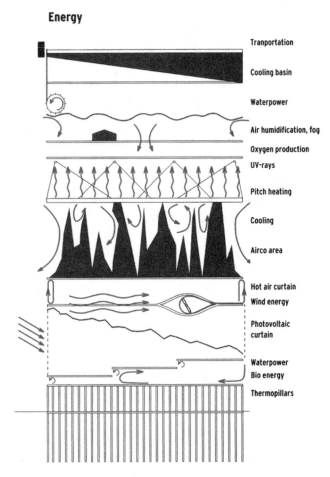

Energy

Tranportation

Cooling basin

Waterpower

Air humidification, fog

Oxygen production

UV-rays

Pitch heating

Cooling

Airco area

Hot air curtain
Wind energy

Photovoltaic
curtain

Waterpower
Bio energy

Thermopillars

I am not ready to discard entirely what is still an in-progress development based on an unimpeachable initial consideration of program, but as one witnesses the steady spread of this idea as a mindless method of design based on graphic mimesis, one's uneasiness over the resulting undermining of our abilities grows.

To be convincing and useful, Programism would have to be intellectually more serious about how to assess the quality of the data it uses and how to articulate intelligently the passage from data to form, which is not more or less than the quintessential and minimum ability that an architect ought to display, but which would require, as always, hard work, knowledge about architecture's own history, rigor, imagination, and the cultivation of the creative talents, rather than the automatisms that so far typify its moves.

Circulation

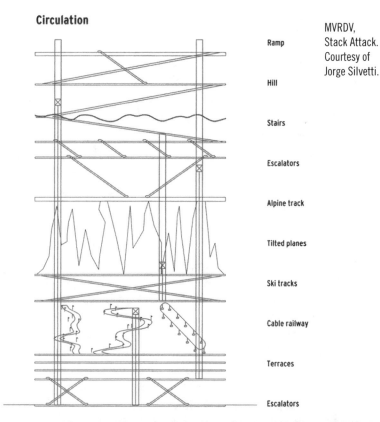

Ramp	
Hill	MVRDV, Stack Attack. Courtesy of Jorge Silvetti.
Stairs	
Escalators	
Alpine track	
Tilted planes	
Ski tracks	
Cable railway	
Terraces	
Escalators	

Elevation

Street view

MVRDV, Stack Attack. Courtesy of Jorge Silvetti.

Thematization

Thematization is, surprisingly as we will see, a mirror image of Programism, operating as the latter's simile or analogue.[3] *Thematization* was not coined specifically to define this mode of operation in architecture and planning, but rather (and significantly) it was borrowed from marketing and advertising, which coined it to identify very particular developments called "theme parks." The reasons are clear.

The idea is simple but powerful and implies that architectural design is guided by the goal of exerting total control on the forms of an environment, not only on its physical vocabulary and its syntax but also on its messages themselves, which means that an appropriate rhetoric is required within well-defined physical precincts. Importantly, whether its general sources of referents come from either historical precedents or popular culture, its vehicle is always architecture itself. Its aim is to conjure up something that cannot be present, either because it exists only in the past, in memory, or in literary fiction or because, while contemporaneous, it exists in some exotic, far-off, or inaccessible place.

With these goals as guides, Thematization's formal operations are kept to a minimum, since it seeks to shorten the distance between the model used as referent and the architecture produced to invoke it, and aims to elicit in the beholder either the pleasure of a momentary, playful, and contrived enactment or the delusion of the restitution of a whole way of life and its values. The difference between these two effects is fundamental enough to warrant an attempt to define them as distinct modes of Thematization. And for that, good old rhetoric serves us best to sort it out, since it provides us with the figures of *parody* and *mimesis* to circumscribe with some precision a typology of this rather complex set of phenomena and their correspondent ideological consequences.

Here a bit of history would help. Alluding to a preexisting or contiguous architecture is not new in architecture. We could go back to Imperial Rome and interpret some of Hadrian's efforts at Tivoli intended to evoke his favorite spots in his Mediterranean domains, but indeed Hadrian's is too sophisticated, erudite, and subtle an operation for my current purposes. Marie Antoinette's *hammeau* at Versailles is the classic example, and it is more directly related to Thematization. It was the outpost retreat of the queen, where she and her guests could relieve their boredom and indulge in the silly game of acting like peasants.

It has come all the way to us reincarnated in the modern theme park, of which the supreme example is Las Vegas—not just a theme park but a whole city whose success relies on the extravagant idea of creating a heterogeneous conglomerate of adjacent "theme" experiences. Unlike Marie Antoinette's, which was private entertainment by means of mimesis, we have now mass entertainment by means of parody.

On the other side of these two examples driven by the forces of "Thematization for entertainment" is a more troubling instance that I would call "Thematization for living," and that, with humorlessness, pomposity, and unbearable earnestness, attempts to occupy, by right, the title of architecture. Although it has been around for some time, it has only recently been catapulted to the fore because of its sudden, uneasy double fame of being both the most contemporary example of Thematization and successful real estate development.

Now on the one hand, in the two previous cases of Las Vegas and Versailles, the fakery of thematic architecture is not only overt but also actually underlined by the way in which it is deployed, always within well-confined boundaries that provide the necessary thresholds to promote and effectively induce the suspension of disbelief that makes them palatable.

Thematization for living, on the other hand, implies a double fakery: the formal operation of mimicking a well-known architecture and the promise that such architecture will deliver a predetermined, good way of life. Or to put it in another way, the attempt at mimesis is total—not just of forms but also of actions and contents. Thematization for living not only suppresses disbelief but also posits amnesia as the necessary condition to permit moralistic prescription of the way of life it wants to enforce.

The two best examples, which have been gestating for at least two decades but which have come into full being in the past few years, are the extreme contextualism that has acquired legal status in many cities and the most recalcitrant excesses of New Urbanism.

And it is both amusing and disturbing to verify, briefly, how much Programism shares with Thematization, in spite of their radically divergent aesthetic and stylistic proclivities. While on the one hand Programism attempts to avoid associations with any preestablished referent by spreading in front of us overwhelming arrays of apparently exhaustive, neutral information that conveys a sense of coolness, indifference, and objectivity about "reality out there" and, contrarily, on the other hand, thematized projects, like some promoted by New Urbanism, prescribe only one solution based on one precedent, in both cases their uncritical reliance on carefully selected empirical evidence of the world "as is" serves to validate their formulation. The two ideological positions are wrapped by different rhetorical ploys, in the former one of indifferent inclusiveness, in the latter one of exclusive moral example. Aesthetically they are archenemies, but at the more profound philosophical and ideological levels they are siblings in their passive ratification of the status quo.

But now on to an entirely different story of formal production, which swept the academic scene, magazines, exhibitions, and biennials in the past few years, although few exemplary actual buildings yet exist.

Blobs

For some of us involved directly with working for the progress of architecture, the sudden outburst appeared strange, a few years ago, of shapeless creatures, seemingly from outer space or some bad intestinal condition. On the other hand, for those more involved with technical developments in digital technology and its applications, particularly in academia, this outburst could be seen as the logical result of the fast development of that technology in three-dimensional representation. What happened in this past decade was an exhilarating and exciting evolution of a technology that not only sped up the process of describing and representing complex form, enhanced the accuracy of its representation, and multiplied the architect's ability to manipulate it as if it were actually plastic matter, but also allowed production of actual 3-D prototypes directly from the screen at the push of a button.

What a feast this offered! What tremendous repercussions these developments had and are still having in the transformation of architectural processes, from design to construction to the profession itself, without an end in sight!

And what a sudden, frightening abyss it opened up in front of us as the computer certainly intimated that it could produce forms that not only do not have precedent but, more perplexing, may not even have referents! Freedom from semantics, history, and culture was perhaps made possible for the first time in civilization.

My reaction upon this realization was then, as it is today, "So what?" Who wants that? My only interest in producing architecture is because it is a practice within cultural practices (in the anthropological sense), which is to say that the play with referents is not only of interest to me but also inherent in the very idea of architecture. To be sure, I do not want to reproduce such referents but instead appropriate and use them in some fashion in order to engage people, to criticize ideas, to transform them into other things, to debunk or to enhance, to undermine or to sanction, to produce beauty and pleasure.

However, that does not seem to have been the reaction of many who could not resist the temptation of generating certain *forms just because they could*—because of the sheer fascination of this seemingly God-like power bestowed suddenly on the ever power-deprived profession of architecture.

We make Blobs because we can, and that was for a while sufficient reason. Both their proliferation and quick fall into benign indifference today (by 2002 the whole thing had subsided in both magazines and schools) speak clearly about their fascinating but somewhat misguided pursuit. Yet I would like to emphasize their valid promise of more substantial achievements, which must be pursued, since the technology has become a natural part of our doings.

Blobs have also exposed an important element of our current Zeitgeist: a nostalgia for the future, a position almost predetermined as the inevitable swing of the pendulum of trends reversed itself in the 1990s from the nostalgia for the past that dominated the 1970s and 1980s, as it finally became asphyxiating and we ran out of decades to revive. It is only a matter of time before our nostalgia for the future will become just as ridiculous and debilitating.

But I am not done with Blobs yet, since they afford a unique opportunity to explore our architectural culture. Why did the emergence of the possibility of producing form without a referent elicit such an enthusiastic response, and how did architecture proceed to attempt this? The "why" is clear. Highly sought after by maverick thinkers, envisioned as a chimerical possibility in literary fiction, the idea of producing form without meaning seemed irresistible and has always deserved a Promethean try.

But what did we actually do with this "thing" that appeared on our computer screen? Very quickly, we stuffed it with meaning. Since as creatures that may wish to produce a form without meaning also harbor the even more compelling and contrary impulse to be repulsed by that which we cannot name or understand, we began to invest Blobs with the meaning of whatever we could associate with them. We proceeded to see Blobs as representative of many conditions, as vehicles of more esoteric referents, so there was resurgence of organic, biological analogues to architecture, followed by processes, informational flows, then more abstract manifestations such as statistical data, in short, all those "formless" things that perhaps, given our sudden acquired power to produce them, could supplant other more traditional, simpler, historical, some would say, conservative generative forces of architecture.

Thus, the deliberate assigning of meaning to Blobs has produced a new generation of more evolved creatures that, while having the same source in digital representation, have acquired both a higher architectural status and an identity of their own, which I would like to describe, conceptually, as the phenomenon of literal representation, our fourth category of cases.

Literalism

Literalism is the defining attribute of a more evolved and difficult-to-name species of creatures, more purposeful and meaningful, since it interprets and invests formlessness with concrete physical attributes. For example: a meaningless blob, when seen as liquid, suggests a flow; when seen as viscose, suggests adaptability; and when seen as a malleable solid, suggests flexibility. And more: indeterminacy (they have no center), process (they seem to "evolve," to be alive), parasitism (they seem to stick), and so on—all physical properties that may suggest architectural properties, if what these forms, with their continuity and smoothness, evoke can be used to illustrate an architectural idea. All we need to do is label them. And since adaptability, flexibility, flow, indeterminacy, process, malleability, and so on are general descriptive terms favored today (some for very good reasons) to describe certain conditions of either the contemporary city or contemporary life in general, they have become useful metaphors for speaking about those conditions in architectural design.

What has been tremendously disappointing, however, is the mindless embracing of such tempting liquid-viscous-plastic formal intimations as the actual formal architectural solutions to those urban or social conditions considered as problems to be resolved. Such an attempt can only be the result of an impoverished imagination reenacting the worst nightmares of Postmodernism. And that is because if an aspect of a complex activity can be described, insightfully, as "a flow," it does not follow that architecture and urbanism can address it by making it look like, well, a flow. Yet, even though we thought by now we knew better, we are still being subjected to the same insufferable process of illustration of ideas that gave us, a decade earlier, deconstructed, folded, and historicist projects and buildings. To no avail do we know that buildings are not really organic things, even though we can use organic metaphors to describe them. Yet there is continuous insistence in making them look as if they were. Nor has there ever been any good real reason to build a building that looks broken simply because its creator adheres to deconstruction as a philosophy, nor, of course, buildings that flow, fold, or are old if they really do not or are not. Buildings cannot be "flexible" or "indeterminate" either. They are hard and immobile no matter what (although they may, with some effort, alter and adapt their forms to particular purposes).

Perhaps it is time to accept that metaphor in architecture is useful as a sparkle, as a starter, as a guide, or as a shadow, but that it

UN Studio,
Yokohama Port
Terminal, Japan,
1994. Courtesy
of Jorge Silvetti.

becomes a dangerous game every time it leaves its comfortable abode in language and poetry for excursions into other media, a fact that we know well at least since baroque times, when it was widely used, under control, but always treading on dangerous borderlines between the sublime and the ridiculous.

Just to make sure the point I am trying to make is not missed, what I suggest is that the use of metaphor in architecture, as in any practice, should be looked at as an enrichment of meaning and not as a replacement for the thing itself.[4] Metaphor is most useful when either we find no words to explain something on its own terms and we need an analogy to draw an insight, or as an inspiration for properties that cannot be described better than with an analogy. As such, metaphor will always be indispensable for the advancement of knowledge.

By and large, Literalism is the most weakening formal development of the last twenty years of architecture. Yet, not surprisingly, it is the one with widespread acceptance because of its easy consumption, since it is the domain par excellence of the one-liner.

And as if closing a circle, I am one thought away from connecting Literalism with Programism, which would allow me to make Literalism the general condition of architectural representation today in all the cases we have covered and the real target of this essay as the dominant design strategy and method in the academy. I leave such sweeping speculation aside for the time being, since I would like to advance the argument in another direction.

Temporary Conclusion

What perhaps is evident by now is the fact that, disparate as these four strategies for the generation of form may seem, they all share a weakening of the designer's indispensable volition to create it. Perhaps seduced by the possibility of minimizing efforts and costs with the help of preexisting models and machines, the architect is inadvertently minimizing also the quality of the intellectual work that the architectural imagination requires, as he or she steps aside from the role of the knowing, willing, acting agent in the creation of architectural form.

Let there be no mistake: these developments are all honest and well-intentioned attempts to produce form, in some cases born from genuine and positive criticism of existing conditions, to be sure, since they want to generate good architecture and address issues and problems.[5] But nobody involved in these attempts seems to want to be responsible for the outcome and its authorship insofar as *form* is concerned. Interestingly, for all their superficial ideological differences, they all relegate the architect to the role of intermediary—the midwife, as Colin Rowe would have said—in the delivery of form that somehow is understood as the product of the marriage of other agents, external and independent of the architect. The architect, a lonely, aseptic figure, then remains chaste and pure.

It will not be useful to belabor further the sterile consequences of Thematization, contextualism, and new urbanisms, in short all those literal resorts to architectural precedents, since they have been evident to all of us for a while. Yet, on the other side of this landscape, as we see these examples of Literalism (Blobs, flows, flexibility, etc.) and Programism marching together as the bearers of the torch that illuminates the heroic path toward an architecture presumably without representation, without historical precedent, without shadows of itself, unbeknownst to them we also notice that such a path leads to an inevitable cul-de-sac where the representation of all the things *other than architecture* reign free, available, and predatory. And since, from any serious cultural perspective, we know that representation is unavoidable, in this trapped condition architecture would be condemned to wear costumes that do not suit it.

Baroque

I would like first to bring in a historical analogy that would permit the advancement of the argument to a point where we may see where all this comes from, and then to conclude.

Let me affirm, as an apparent paradox, that most of the salient conditions under which this contemporary condition of form-giving denials operate resonate as analogues with the operations that controlled the exuberant formal production during the baroque period— a paradox indeed, since the baroque is associated with an excess of consciously controlled form production based on a precedent, namely, the classical language of architecture. And yet just about all the characteristics that we described in the contemporary scene can be found in the aesthetics of baroque architecture.

From the perspective of our discussion today, there has never been a period so similar to ours in which the art of rhetoric was so close to the art of architecture; the roles of entertainment and popular art were so dominant; the boundaries among the traditional art forms were so much probed and violated, challenged, eroded, and transgressed; the role of metaphor was so active; and within the latter, the widespread use of the literal representation of movement in architecture was so prevalent. Indeed, preferred among the metaphors of the baroque is that of movement.

And let's start with that. One could say that architecture, being such a physically heavy and inert art, has an innate longing for movement, that the baroque period was the time when such predisposition was the dominant formal impulse, and that today we reencounter such longing expressed in many an undulating surface. There is nothing wrong with the "formal desires" of an epoch. Anybody walking around Rome or any major Italian city from the end of the seventeenth century to the middle of the eighteenth would have felt a bit dizzy about the undulating walls, about alternatively imploding and exploding facades. Anybody walking around the studios of architecture schools in the past few years would have felt that such forms were about to return to our streets. But to understand the fundamental difference between the baroque metaphor of movement and that of current explorations that represent movement in architecture beyond what is undoubtedly a similar formal proposition is to grasp that there is a sense of "performance," theatricality, and self-consciousness about such conceit in baroque architecture that we do not find in the literal, naive representations of these principles of flow and dynamism today.

On the one hand, the support provided by the classical language of architecture, by then two thousand years old and still thriving in myriad incarnations, gave both a recognizable vocabulary and a resounding proof of its very artificiality. Metaphor was just a poetic maneuver in search of an effect. On the other hand, there is the baroque effect itself, which has the concrete aim of producing *wonder*. Wonder is baroque's effect, clear and simple. In all of it, the suspension of disbelief that the baroque work of art expects from the beholder is no more than a generalized complicit strategy about the role and possibilities of the arts and of the gentile and entertaining game that they proposed. While awed by the dexterity, virtuosity (but we architects know about the hard work and intellectual rigor that this smoothness required), and seemingly magic power of these representations, nobody ever really believed that buildings moved, facades undulated, basilicas could embrace, or domes could eat you alive.

Of course, I am not bringing this up because I think this baroque operation is what we need to revive. History does not repeat itself (this is the only "lesson" of history), and a look at the baroque for similarities now could only help us distinguish better the differences with our times and possibilities. So here there are two other seemingly similar characteristics that the baroque could share with the current moment, whose true nature and understanding would help us push this discussion to its tentative conclusion.

In baroque visual arts, the first one is the recourse to a "conceit," usually a literary theme, as the operative force, and the second is the dissolution of the traditional boundaries among the arts. The conceit, usually a climatic moment in narrative, most often involved the representation of an instant in which movement was frozen. As for the dissolution of boundaries, it was found mostly in the seemingly indifferent and highly effective transgression of boundaries among architecture, sculpture, painting, through the subtle and ambiguous manipulation of color, materials, and natural light. These two constitutive characteristics of the baroque correspond directly, in my view, to two defining conditions of contemporary Art, namely, the primacy of the Concept and its logical sequel, the loss of medium specificity of works of art.

I would argue that in the passage from a world where "the arts" reigned, each one easily associated and defined by aspects of a medium (sound, color, flatness, matter, actions, stories, etc.), into another, our own world, where more and more the arts have collapsed into a single idea of "Art," where the specificity of the medium no longer has validity, somehow architecture got confused by being defined by two clear but incompatible conditions.

It is either *Architecture as Art* or remains the *art of architecture.*[6]

Just to make sure that we can ground this, let me bring in one of architecture's favorite art critics, Rosalind Krauss, who throughout her writing confirms the advent of the termination of the individual arts as medium specific and the supreme reign of Conceptual Art.[7] She has convincingly asserted that art has finally freed itself from attachments to specific media, which is to say, conversely, that any medium can serve as the vehicle for Art. But, of course, this is now Art with a capital A, the one and only one, not any "specific" art like those that were once associated with specific media, such as painting, sculpture, music, drama, and architecture, each one with its own Muse. In this contemporary condition, which I believe exists, Conceptual Art occupies the triumphant center—Conceptual Art with its privileging of the Big Idea and its necessary indifference to medium.

This, in retrospect, seemingly inevitable denouement of the history of Western art is the undeniable achievement of the modern art's avant-garde, whose successful and brilliant debunking of the notion of medium specificity commenced almost at the moment when art theory was founded by Gotthold Lessing in 1766 by the very act of identifying the artistic medium as the indispensable condition to define the specificity of each art, an effort that, by the way, could be seen as the Enlightenment's critique of the baroque.[8] Of course, the latter's demise was prematurely celebrated then.

It is fairly obvious to me that the relatively recently acquired possibility of architecture to maneuver so freely outside its traditional formal and material boundaries, opting instead for unconventional referents for its forms as well as media for its expression, has a direct, perhaps even sole, source in this atmosphere of debunking the specificity of the medium in the arts.[9] It is also clear to me that such ease has been facilitated directly by Architectural Theory's equal softening and drifting away from a core of conventional architectural substances during the same period to become exclusively dependent on, if not subservient to, the overall discourse of Art Theory, of which it is today, in fact, a chapter.

It is actually spectacularly good for Art that Architecture has become a medium readily available to it, the vehicle for some of its Big Ideas, and that, as such, it can have a protagonist's role in performing many of its different manifestations, such as earth art installations, happenings, and other forms in which it is either content or container. In fact, some truly remarkable moments in contemporary art have architecture as their vehicle, and I relish them as much as I relish good buildings.

Yet to the extent that the real contents of all these media-unspecific instances of Art are concepts and ideas, sometimes quite honestly represented by words themselves, the processes by which they are generated are not necessarily reversible so as to warrant an inversion of the equation that would claim *that any medium can be architecture,* which is, I am afraid the basis of many of our confusions today.

Architecture as Art is an instance of the most advanced condition of Art today. Art as Architecture is a travesty.

We have heard in writings, symposia, reviews, and courses that "architecture" can now be many things, even words, and perhaps

Mark Wigley at Columbia University would still disagree with me in the friendly feud we started eight years ago in New Orleans as to whether he is an architect simply because he writes and thinks about architecture. If so, I would continue to say he is not, even as he continues to write about architecture so intelligently and lucidly. And for me, this is not a play of words or definitions. The difference is real and vital and almost a matter of survival.

What we have now is a phenomenal confusion, mostly prevalent in academia, journalism, and museums, between two conditions in which architecture finds itself performing absolutely legitimate but absolutely different roles, one as the support of artistic ideas and another as the inspiration for buildings, but most of the time without realizing on what stage it is actually standing.

Let's just spell it out clearly, because it is simpler than it seems: on the one hand, as the vehicle of the Big Idea, architecture is standing in the grand proscenium of Art. On the other, as the proper vehicle for human actions, it is standing, naked as a building, in the social arena where real life takes place. Both are legitimate and inspiring. However, they are different and not interchangeable and very rarely concurrent. The way we maneuver, sort through, and get out of this confusion is at the heart of the future of architectural education and ultimately of architecture itself. This is the challenge that I would like Architectural Theory to take earnestly in order to reenergize what I perceive is its languid state as an appendage of Art Theory.

Epilogue: The Music Analogy

To conclude, let me turn to a totally different field, music, where visuality is not dominant, and the interaction (and confusion) between creator and performer place it in an entirely different conceptual and material realm from architecture and the visual arts. As an amateur pianist, I marvel at music's staunch resistance to dissolve itself into Art; it is one of the last traditional arts that is incorruptible and able to hold its own in terms of specificity of medium—not without attempts to the contrary. In the past year or so, I became more interested in the work of the contemporary composer György Ligeti. Recently, at a New York shop, I grabbed the only Ligeti score they could find for keyboard, a single piece called *Continuum,* which at first sight seemed easy enough for me to perform.

But when I actually sat at the piano at home and tried to articulate the first bars, it was another story. To my surprise, the two notes that repeat themselves in sequence for the first few bars are exactly the same for both hands but are played alternatively. So as the middle right finger depressed B-flat in conjunction with the middle left finger depressing G, the following move requires a reversal, as the right thumb depresses G while the left one does the same with B-flat—a difficult and uncomfortable proposition. If to such an inconvenient physical state we add the particular dynamics that the author prescribes for the piece—"prestissimo," extremely fast, with absolute continuity of sound—the result is that the movements cancel each other out and (surprise, surprise) no sound is produced.

What a bummer if you really wanted to play and hear some music! But this is not all. As I became more familiar with the score and unfolded its pages, I began to realize that perhaps really this piece is not about the sound, melody, or any of those old-fashioned things that we found in music—perhaps it is about pattern-making, about graphic design, about a visual narrative, a pictorial metamorphosis, a visual form that by the way would also produce some sound. Perhaps.

I was both fascinated and troubled by this frustrating smart trick.[10] As it turned out, I was wrong in my initial reading of the score: I found out later that it is intended for a two keyboard instrument (harpsichord), and its first bars can be played and will produce sound. So why do I use this wrong example? In a funny way, my misguided disappointment is nonetheless historically validated by a condition under which my own artistic judgment operates. For one, the very idea that I could accept as possible the fact that Ligeti wanted to produce, through the act of performance, a piece of music that denied its very nature by producing silence describes the state of mind in which we all now think about art. But more importantly, such instances have already been produced, as with John Cage's famous piece 4'33" of 1952, in which the musicians, on stage and ready to play, remained silent, and the concert was in effect whatever were the sounds in the environment where the "concert" took place, or less radically as with his *Music of Changes,* in which musical decisions are made by "chance operations" decided by coin-tossing procedures (hence the typical "language" pun of Conceptual Art), and in general as with all the avant-garde music of the second half of the twentieth century that starts with an idea outside music itself, with a "concept" if you wish, and then applies it to the medium of sound, such as Stockhausen's *Refrain* of 1959 for piano, celesta, and percussion, in which the "refrain" is printed on a transparent strip that can be rotated to different positions for different performances. Not surprisingly, these attempts to align music with Conceptual Art's ideas have resulted in these pieces surviving only in textbooks, rather than in concert halls, where they have rarely returned after their first "performances." The point was some Big Idea, somewhere. This is Music as Art. OK. It is smart. It is intelligent. It is interesting, isn't it?

But next to this score on my piano was the score of Bach's *French Suites*, with its well-established form, a sequence of dances rendered totally anew. And suddenly I could not contain the flow of thinking that this juxtaposition produced. Because here in Bach's creation I had an undisputed work of art that aimed at something fairly precise yet humble. *No Big Idea here.* It tried only to exist within the confines of "the art of music." As such, this particular genre of suites was intended for home playing and dancing. But as one hears it even today, it is possible to experience its exuberant richness and power to evoke or suggest to our imagination all the things it represented and engaged: the petit bourgeoisie interior decor of a German house; its gentle, imperfect acoustics; the discoveries by the adolescent dancers of their bodies with their rhythms, their temperatures, their contacts and incipient eroticism; the melodies alluding to a foreign land; the sound of garments touching furniture, shoes scratching the floor; and a great sense of pleasure, of intimate fun. All the while the art of music is being well served and advanced as probably never before.

Today, of course, we would pay a lot of money to hear some of the greatest keyboard soloists play Bach's *French Suites* at a large concert hall, even though Bach never conceived them to be played that way. He was just a composer and player, a music maker who made money as best as he could, publishing dances and keyboard exercises, and playing and composing for the local church.

Well, too bad if music today were not able to look at the life of people and nourish itself directly from it, to get inspiration, to transform itself and advance its own traditions. Yet as a music lover, I do not despair, since the world of sound seems to find other venues outside Art that continue to make us happy.

Music, whatever realm it is relegated to, never stops.

Postscript: A Year after the Gropius Lecture

For those familiar with the developments of Architectural Theory in the past decades, it would appear that the whole line of reasoning I presented is full of traps, some potentially fatal. But I feel nonetheless prepared to confront and avoid these traps, since I am too aware that accepting such warnings and changing directions would play into the arms of those mutually exclusive extremes that result from that pervasive yet silent and lethal pendulum that regulates so much of the Zeitgeist, the pendulum that swings between conservative and avant-garde, reactionary and progressive, classic and modern, past and future.

One thing I learned after the pendulum had already swung from extreme to extreme a few times during my professional life (and in doing so deprived both theory and architecture itself of any richness and accumulated wisdom) was to ignore the opposites as such and work with what I think is good from both. That is why I have identified a few topics that are currently repressed by Theory, topics that insinuate themselves throughout all my arguments and that appear to me, for all their dangers, necessary to bring back to the fore without throwing out what we have gained in the recent past, even if Theory has cast each as anathema to the other.

A threat of creative paralysis might be inferred from my assertion that once we accept representation in architecture as inevitable, its referents must come only from architecture itself. This could be read as reopening the door to stifling historicism. Yet we are now at a stage, thanks to theory and history, in which we understand "architecture itself" not to mean exclusively its received figurative repository. Today it means, rather, that architecture *as the sole source of architecture* could look at anything as formal inspiration, *but from its inside out,* keeping its footings in its building core, anchoring its imagination in a programmatic research beyond literal formal translations, and continuing in the flow of its own cultural trajectory, both responsive to and critical of its conventions, which does not imply the literal figurative use of referents. Thus, the most promising developments of Blobs are not those resulting from a metaphorical reading of their formal properties but from the logical integration of advanced computer technologies with tectonic consciousness and an historical/ anthropological knowledge of the discipline.[11]

As a corollary of this, it seems inevitable that a reconsideration and reformulation of the heated issue of disciplinary "autonomy" must be undertaken without denying the "intertextuality" and cultural "contamination" that we so much appreciate now in architecture. It seems to me that, for instance, a judicious, unbiased reading of Rossi's most important writing and ideas always reveals such rich understanding of architecture and the city, understanding that is not irreconcilable with some of the most advanced aesthetic and formal notions of, for example, Herzog and de Meuron.

It also seems urgent, even imperative, to renew and promote a discussion seriously focused on popular culture, not as a figurative source for architecture but as the operative cultural mechanism with which architecture cannot avoid interaction. It seems that carefully selected ideas from Venturi and Scott Brown's iconographic theory of architecture, some of Gehry's artful yet seductive and persuasive tricks to manipulate emotions, and Koolhaas's understanding of cultural phenomena (reformulated after a serious critique of his suspect silence with respect to the political implications of some of his stands) should be able to propel and circumscribe the territory of architecture in novel and more fruitful ways.

And I also believe that we must overcome definitively the avant-garde clichés of inflated and unrealistic portrayals of the power of architecture to "criticize" and subvert society.

Which brings me back to the polemic about "Architecture as Art" and "Art as Architecture."

The Muses may very well be unamused by the current state of architecture. But frankly, who cares? Erato, Clio, Euterpe, Melpomene, and the rest are old ladies who long ago lost their credibility as art changed and they were left playing, idle or irrelevant, with the worn attributes of dead art forms. And, of course, we could not think of reestablishing the orderly world of Bach.

But the pandemonium in the house of architecture is real, in my view, and an effort to understand what the Muses represent, namely, that there is a territory and a certain specificity that a métier such as architecture could claim as its own, is worthy of exploration, particularly in good schools of architecture, where we are concerned, above all, with education and the advancement of knowledge.

2003

Notes

I would like to thank Scott Cohen, professor at Harvard University Graduate School of Design; Gary Rohrbacher, assistant professor at the School of Architecture, University of Texas, Austin; and Mark Pasnik, associate, Machado and Silvetti Associates, for their comments and encouragement as I worked on this version of the Gropius Lecture.

1. A CD recording of the Gropius Lecture with all the images and the

original wording delivered on April 25, 2002, together with the written versions of other public interventions by Professor Silvetti during his tenure as chair of the Department of Architecture, was published by the Harvard University Graduate School of Design during fall 2003.

2. The culprit is Preston Scott Cohen, who coined the term during the Harvard University Graduate School of Design's thesis reviews season of 2000.

3. This symmetry is already noticeable in the fact that while Programism is prevalent and even rampant in schools, Thematization is much more "triumphant" in the fields of design practice and the real estate industries.

4. When Frank Lloyd Wright's architecture was referred to as "organic," it was not because it looked like an organism, but because its characteristics suggested the attributes, the analogue characteristics of an organic phenomenon: it was neither confused with a natural living organism nor dressed up to look like one.

5. I am alluding to many good and encouraging examples that experiment with and use the technology and principles of these recent developments, such as the work of Foreign Office Architects in Japan.

6. I owe much of the thinking implied in this dichotomy to the writings of Spanish writer and philosopher Félix de Azúa, particularly his *Diccionario de las Artes* (Barcelona: Editorial Planeta, S.A., 1999).

7. See Rosalind E. Krauss, *A Voyage on the North Sea: Art in the Age of the Post-Medium Condition* (London: Thames & Hudson, 2000).

8. Gotthold Ephraim Lessing, *Laocoön: An Essay on the Limits of Painting and Poetry* (Baltimore: Johns Hopkins University Press, 1962; originally published in 1766).

9. Unlike the formally analogous, intermittent, and intrinsically different "expressionist" outbursts during the twentieth century, such as Mendelsohn's, Scharoun's, Utzon's, and even Gehry's, all highly individualistic and still rooted in an idea of the architect as an artist that is alien to the phenomena I am addressing. Yet despite the fundamental changes that separate "expressionism" from the developments I am addressing, such lineage is often alluded to and invoked as a legitimizing provenance by the promoters of the latter.

10. This paragraph was added after the original Gropius Lecture as a necessary clarification and correction to a wrong assumption I made regarding Ligeti's *Continuum*. In turn, as the mistake reinforces rather than changes or modifies the argument presented in the "Epilogue," it was important to keep it within the original text.

11. This is a line of thinking and research that I am proud to see flourishing at the Graduate School of Design at all levels: see, for instance, *Inmaterial/Ultramaterial: Architecture, Design and Materials,* ed. Toshiko Mori (Cambridge, Mass.: Harvard Design School in association with George Braziller, 2002).

Contributors

Stan Allen is dean of the School of Architecture at Princeton University and principal of Stan Allen Architect. His books include *Points and Lines: Diagrams and Projects for the City* and *Practice: Architecture, Technique and Representation*.

George Baird is dean of the Faculty of Architecture, Landscape, and Design at the University of Toronto and a partner in the firm Baird Sampson Neuert Architects, Inc. He is the author of many books, including *The Space of Appearance*.

Lucy Bullivant is an architectural critic and curator in London. She writes for *Domus, Blueprint, Architectural Record, I.D.*, and *AD*. She is the author of *All Systems Go: UK Architecture's Rising Generation*.

James Corner is chair of the Department of Landscape Architecture at the University of Pennsylvania and founder and director of Field Operations in New York. He is coauthor of *Taking Measures across the American Landscape* and editor of *Recovering Landscape: Essays in Contemporary Landscape Theory*.

Hal Foster is Townsend Martin Professor of Art and Archaelogy at Princeton University and an editor of *October* magazine. He is the author of many books, including *Design and Crime*.

Kenneth Frampton is Ware Professor of Architecture at Columbia University and the author of many books, including *Labour, Work, and Architecture: Collected Essays on Architecture and Design.*

K. Michael Hays is Elliot Noyes Professor of Architectural Theory at the Harvard University Graduate School of Design. His books include *Modernism and the Posthumanist Subject: The Architecture of Hannes Meyer and Ludwig Hilberseimer.*

Dave Hickey is a freelance writer of fiction and cultural criticism working out of Las Vegas. His books include *Air Guitar: Essays on Art and Democracy.*

Robert Levit is a practicing architect and associate professor and director of the Masters of Urban Design Program in the Department of Architecture, Landscape, and Design at the University of Toronto.

Evonne Levy is associate professor in art history at the University of Toronto and the author of *Propaganda and the Jesuit Baroque.*

Reinhold Martin is associate professor of architecture in the Graduate School of Architecture, Planning, and Preservation at Columbia University. He is coeditor of *Grey Room* and author of *The Organizational Complex.*

William S. Saunders is editor of *Harvard Design Magazine* and author and editor of many books, including *Modern Architecture: Photography by Ezra Stoller.*

Jorge Silvetti is Nelson Robinson Jr. Professor of Architecture at the Graduate School of Design at Harvard University and principal in Machado and Silvetti Associates Architects in Boston. He is author of *The Getty Villa* and *Introductions.*

Robert Somol is director, School of Architecture, University of Illinois at Chicago. He is author of the forthcoming *Nothing to Declare.*

Philippe Starck is a French designer of everything from spoons to hotels. He is author of *Philippe Starck.*

Roemer van Toorn is head of the Projective Theory program at Berlage Institute in Rotterdam. He is the author of the forthcoming *In Search of Freedom in Contemporary Architecture: From Fresh Conservatism to Radical Democracy.*

Sarah Whiting is assistant professor of history and theory in the School of Architecture at Princeton University and design principal in the architectural firm WW. She is editor of *Differences: Topographies of Contemporary Architecture.*

Alejandro Zaera-Polo was dean of Berlage Institute in Amsterdam and is Berlage chair at TU Delft. He is a partner in Foreign Office Architects in London.